Philosophical Writings

Philosophical Writings

P. F. Strawson

EDITED BY

Galen Strawson and Michelle Montague

UNIVERSITY PRESS

Great Clarendon Street, Oxford, OX2 6DP,
United Kingdom

Oxford University Press is a department of the University of Oxford.
It furthers the University's objective of excellence in research, scholarship,
and education by publishing worldwide.

Oxford is a registered trade mark of Oxford University Press
in the UK and in certain other countries

© in this volume the Estate of P. F. Strawson 2011

The moral rights of the author have been asserted

First Edition published in 2011
First published in paperback 2014

All rights reserved. No part of this publication may be reproduced, stored in
a retrieval system, or transmitted, in any form or by any means, without the
prior permission in writing of Oxford University Press, or as expressly permitted
by law, by licence or under terms agreed with the appropriate reprographics
rights organization. Enquiries concerning reproduction outside the scope of the
above should be sent to the Rights Department, Oxford University Press, at the
address above

You must not circulate this work in any other form
and you must impose this same condition on any acquirer

Published in the United States of America by Oxford University Press
198 Madison Avenue, New York, NY 10016, United States of America

British Library Cataloguing in Publication Data
Data available

Library of Congress Cataloging in Publication Data
Data available

ISBN 978–0–19–958729–2 (Hbk)
ISBN 978–0–19–870791–2 (Pbk)

Preface

Galen Strawson

During his life my father P. F. Strawson published three collections of papers. *Logico-Linguistic Papers* appeared in 1971, *Freedom and Resentment* in 1974, and *Entity and Identity* in 1997. They contained all the papers he wished to republish up until that time. They omitted one famous piece, 'In Defence of a Dogma', co-authored or rather co-thought with Paul Grice (Strawson did the writing), and a considerable number of other papers on which, for one reason or another, Strawson did not wish to confer the double *imprimatur* of republication in a volume of which he was sole author.

In the case of some of the papers, no doubt, this was because he felt that the subjects they treated of had been sufficiently covered, or better covered, in other work by himself. He may, for example, have felt that 'Proper Names' (1957) was superseded by what he had to say on that subject in his book *Individuals: An Essay in Descriptive Metaphysics* (1959); I found the offprint of 'Proper Names' in an envelope marked 'papers not worth reprinting'. In the case of others, it was because he thought they were too slight, or not sufficiently self-standing, too geared to the particular occasion for which they were written. There were also some he thought inadequate, in one way or another. I believe that 'Ethical Intuitionism' (*Philosophy*, 1949) falls into this category. He thought his early paper 'Necessary Propositions and Entailment Statements' (*Mind*, 1948) plain wrong, and it is not reprinted here. Nor was he fully satisfied with his last published paper, 'A Category of Particulars'.

In making the present selection I have followed the extremely helpful advice of the three anonymous Oxford University Press advisers, and Peter Momtchiloff, philosophy editor at the Press. I have included all those papers whose republication they recommended, including some that I was at first doubtful about. I am confident that this is the right thing to do. A sufficient reason to reprint 'Ethical Intuitionism', apart from its intrinsic interest, is that it had a considerable influence in its day, and this volume is, among other things, a resource for future research. When I consulted

Tony Kenny on the matter, he replied that 'anything Peter published will undoubtedly be worth republishing even if he did not collect it himself'.

The papers are presented in chronological order of their publication, with two pieces of intellectual autobiography reserved to the end. They were not written to be read one after another, and there is some overlap in content and wording, especially among the most recent. Two of them have not been previously published. The first is an intellectual memoir of Paul Grice given to a graduate seminar on 'Oxford Philosophers of the Twentieth Century' held by Peter Hacker and David Wiggins in Trinity Term 1997. The second is a short talk that Strawson gave to the University College Undergraduate PPE group in 2003.

I would like to thank Javier Kalhat and Thomas Strawson for their help with proof reading; Thomas Strawson again, for preparing the index; my co-editor Michelle Montague for working through the whole book with me in preparing it for publication; and Elmandi du Toit and Sarah Parker of Oxford University Press for their expert guidance through the production process.

Contents

Acknowledgements	viii
1. Ethical Intuitionism	1
2. In Defence of a Dogma (with H. P. Grice)	13
3. Construction and Analysis	30
4. Proper Names	39
5. 'The Post-Linguistic Thaw'	71
6. Analysis, Science, and Metaphysics	78
7. Bennett on Kant's Analytic	91
8. Does Knowledge Have Foundations?	100
9. Knowledge and Truth	109
10. Scruton and Wright on Anti-Realism	118
11. Perception and its Objects	125
12. Liberty and Necessity	146
13. Sensibility, Understanding, and the Doctrine of Synthesis	157
14. Two Conceptions of Philosophy	166
15. Review of Paul Grice, *Studies in the Way of Words*	178
16. Knowing From Words	186
17. What Have We Learned from Philosophy in the Twentieth Century?	191
18. A Category of Particulars	196
19. Paul Grice	206
20. Why Philosophy?	222
21. Intellectual Autobiography	227
22. A Bit of Intellectual Autobiography	248
Index of Names	257

Acknowledgements

The essays were originally published as follows:

'Ethical Intuitionism' (1949), *Philosophy* 24, pp. 23–33.

'In Defense of a Dogma' (1956), with H. P. Grice, *Philosophical Review* 65, pp. 141–58.

'Construction and Analysis' (1956), in A. J. Ayer et al., *The Revolution in Philosophy* (London: Macmillan), pp. 97–110.

'Proper Names' (1957), *Proceedings of the Aristotelian Society*, suppl. vol. 31, pp. 191–228.

'The Post-Linguistic Thaw' (1960), *The Times Literary Supplement*, 9 Sept., p. lx.

'Analysis, Science and Metaphysics' (1967), in R. Rorty (ed.), *The Linguistic Turn* (Chicago: University of Chicago Press), pp. 312–20.

'Bennett on Kant's Analytic' (1968), *Philosophical Review* 77, pp. 332–9.

'Does Knowledge Have Foundations?' (1974), in *Conocimiento y Creencia* (Valencia), pp. 99–110.

'Knowledge and Truth' (1975), *Indian Philosophical Quarterly* 3, pp. 273–82.

'Scruton and Wright on Anti-realism' (1976), *Proceedings of the Aristotelian Society* 77, pp. 15–22.

'Perception and its Objects' (1979), in G. Macdonald (ed.), *Perception and Identity: Essays presented to A. J. Ayer* (London: Macmillan), pp. 41–58.

'Liberty and Necessity' (1983), in N. Rotenstreich and N. Schneider (eds), *Spinoza, His Thought & Work* (Jerusalem: Israel Academy of Sciences and Humanities), pp. 120–9.

'Sensibility, Understanding and the Doctrine of Synthesis: Comments on D. Henrich and P. Guyer' (1989), in E. Forster (ed.), *Kant's Transcendental Deductions* (Stanford: Stanford University Press), pp. 69–74.

'Two Conceptions of Philosophy' (1990), in R. B. Barrett and R. F. Gibson (eds), *Perspectives on Quine* (Oxford: Blackwell), pp. 310–20.

Review of Paul Grice, *Studies in the Way of Words* (1990), *Synthese* 84, pp. 153–61.

'Knowing From Words' (1992), in B. K. Matilal and A. Chakrabati (eds), *Knowing From Words* (Dordrecht: Kluwer Academic Publishers), pp. 23–7.

'What Have We Learned from Philosophy in the Twentieth Century?' (2000), in *Contemporary Philosophy, Proceedings of the Twentieth World Congress of Philosophy*, vol. 8 (Bowling Green, OH: Philosophy Documentation Center, Bowling Green State University), pp. 269–74.

'A Category of Particulars' (2006), in P. F. Strawson and A. Chakrabarti (eds), *Universals, Concepts and Qualities* (Farnham: Ashgate), pp. 301–8.

'Intellectual Autobiography' (1998), in E. Hahn (ed.), *The Philosophy of P. F. Strawson*, (Chicago: Open Court), pp. 3–31.

'A Bit of Intellectual Autobiography' (2003), in H.-J. Glock (ed.), *Strawson and Kant* (Oxford: Oxford University Press), pp. 7–14.

Previously unpublished:

'Paul Grice', paper given to a seminar ('Oxford Philosophers of the Twentieth Century') held by Peter Hacker and David Wiggins at Oxford University in Trinity Term 1997.

'Why Philosophy?', paper read to the University College Undergraduate PPE Society, Oxford University, in 2003.

1
Ethical Intuitionism

North.—What is the trouble about moral facts? When someone denies that there is an objective moral order, or asserts that ethical propositions are pseudo-propositions, cannot I refute him (rather as Moore refuted those who denied the existence of the external world) by saying: 'You know very well that Brown did wrong in beating his wife. You know very well that you ought to keep promises. You know very well that human affection is good and cruelty bad, that many actions are wrong and some are right'?

West.—Isn't the trouble about moral facts another case of trouble about knowing, about learning? We find out facts about the external world by looking and listening; about ourselves, by feeling; about other people, by looking and listening *and* feeling. When this is noticed, there arises a wish to say that the facts *are* what is seen, what is heard, what is felt; and, consequently, that moral facts fall into one of these classes. So those who have denied that there are 'objective moral characteristics' have not wanted to deny that Brown's action was wrong or that keeping promises is right. They have wanted to point out that rightness and wrongness are a matter of what is felt in the heart, not of what is seen with the eyes or heard with the ears. They have wanted to emphasize the way in which 'Promise-keeping is right' resembles 'Going abroad is exciting', 'Stories about mothers-in-law are comic', 'Bombs are terrifying'; and differs from 'Roses are red' and 'Sea-water is salt'. This does not prevent you from talking about the moral order, or the moral world, if you want to; but it warns you not to forget that the only access to the moral world is through remorse and approval and so on; just as the only access to the world of comedy is through laughter; and the only access to the coward's world is through fear.

North.—I agree, of course, that we cannot see the goodness of something as we see its colour, or identify rightness by the sense of touch;

though I think you should add that the senses are indispensable as a means of our becoming aware of those characteristics upon which moral characteristics depend. You may be partly right, too, in saying that access to the moral world is obtained through experience of the moral emotions; for it may be that only when our moral feelings have been strongly stirred do we first become clearly aware of the characteristics which evoke these feelings. But these feelings are not identical with that awareness. 'Goodness' does not stand to 'feeling approval', 'guilt' to 'feeling guilty', 'obligation' to 'feeling bound', as 'excitingness' stands to 'being excited' and 'humorousness' to 'feeling amused'. To use the jargon for a moment: moral characteristics and relations are non-empirical, and awareness of them is neither sensory nor introspectual. It is a different kind of awareness, which the specialists call 'intuition': and it is only empiricist prejudice which prevents your acknowledging its existence. Once acknowledged, it solves our problems: and we see that while 'Promise-keeping is right' differs from 'The sea is salt', this is not because it resembles 'Detective-stories are exciting'; it differs from *both* in being the report neither of a sensible nor an introspectible experience, but of an intuition. We may, perhaps, know some moral characteristics mediately, through others. ('Obligation' is, perhaps, definable in terms of 'goodness'.) But at least one such characteristic—rightness or goodness—is unanalysable, and known by intuition alone. The fundamental cognitive situation in morals is that in which we intuit the rightness of a particular action or the goodness of a particular state of affairs. We see this moral characteristic as present in virtue of some other characteristics, themselves capable of being described in empirical terms, which the action or state of affairs possesses. (This is why I said that sense perception is a necessary, though not a sufficient, condition of obtaining information about the moral order.) Our intuition, then, is not a bare intuition of the moral characteristic, but also the intuition of its dependence on some others: so that this fundamental situation yields us, by intuitive induction, knowledge of moral rules, generalizations regarding the right and the good, which we can apply in other cases, even when an actual intuition is lacking. So much do these rules become taken for granted, a part of our habitual moral life, that most of our everyday moral judgements involve merely an implicit reference to them:[1] a reference

---

[1] Cf. D. Daiches Raphael, *The Moral Sense*, chs V and VI.

which becomes explicit only if the judgement is challenged or queried. Moral emotions, too, assume the character of habitual reactions. But emotions and judgements alike are grounded upon intuitions. Emotion may be the gatekeeper to the moral world; but intuition is the gate.

West.—Not so fast. I understand you to say that at least one fundamental moral characteristic—rightness or goodness—is unanalysable. Perhaps both are. The experts are divided. In any case, the fundamental characteristic (or characteristics) can be known only by intuitive awareness of its (their) presence in some particular contemplated action or state of affairs. There is, then, a kind of analogy between the word 'right' (or 'good') and the name of some simple sensible characteristic such as 'red'.[2] Just as everybody who understands the word 'red' has seen some red things, so everybody who understands the word 'right' or the word 'good' has intuited the character, rightness, in some actions, or the character, goodness, in some states of affairs; and nobody who has not intuited these characters understands the words 'right' or 'good'. But this is not quite enough, is it? In order for me to know *now* the meaning of an indefinable word, it is not enough that a certain perceptual or intuitional event should have occurred at some particular point in my history; for I might not only have forgotten the details of that event; I might have forgotten what *kind* of an event it was; I might not know *now* what it would be like for such an event to occur. If the word 'red' expresses an indefinable visual concept, then it is self-contradictory to say: 'I know what the word "red" means, but I can't remember ever *seeing* red and I don't know what it would be *like* to see red.' Similarly, if the word 'right', or the word 'good', expresses an indefinable intuitive concept, then it is self-contradictory to say: 'I know what the word "right" or the word "good" means, but I can't remember ever *intuiting* rightness or goodness, and I don't know what it would be *like* to intuit rightness or goodness.' If your theory is true, then this statement is a contradiction.

But it is not at all obvious to me that it is a contradiction. I should be quite prepared to assert that I understood the words 'right' and 'good', but that I couldn't remember ever intuiting rightness or goodness and that I couldn't imagine what it would be like to do so. And I think it is quite certain that I am not alone in this, but that there are a large number of

---

[2] Cf. G. E. Moore, *Principia Ethica* (Cambridge: Cambridge University Press, 1903), pp. 7 et seq.

people who are to be presumed capable of accurate reporting of their own cognitive experience, and who would find nothing self-contradictory in saying what I say. And if this is so, you are presented with a choice of two possibilities. The first is that the words 'right' and 'good' have quite a different meaning for one set of people from the meaning which they have for another set. But neither of us believes this. The second is that the intuitionist theory is a mistake; that the phrase 'intuitional event having a moral characteristic as its object (or a part of its object)' is a phrase which describes nothing at all; or describes misleadingly the kind of emotional experience we both admit. There is no third possibility. It is no good saying: 'All people who succeed in learning the meaning of moral words do as a matter of fact have moral intuitions, but unfortunately many people are inclined to forget them, to be quite unable to remember what they are like.' True, there would be nothing self-contradictory in saying this: but it would simply be a variant of the first possibility; for I cannot be said to know *now* the meaning of a word expressing an intuitive concept unless I know now what it would be like to intuit the characteristic of which it is a concept. The trouble with your intuitionist theory is that, if true, it should be a truism. There should be no doubt about the occurrence of the distinctive experience of intuiting rightness (or goodness), and about its being the only way to learn the meaning of the primary moral words; just as there is no doubt about the occurrence of seeing red (or blue), and about this being the only way to learn the meaning of the primary colour words. But there *is* doubt; and over against this doubt there rises a certainty: the certainty that we all know what it is to *feel* guilty, to *feel* bound, to *feel* approving.

North.—What I have said *is* a truism; and that is its strength. It is not I who am inventing a mythical faculty, but you, irritated, perhaps, by the language of intuitionism, who are denying the obvious. When you said that you couldn't *imagine* what it would be like to have moral intuitions, isn't it clear that you wanted 'intuiting a moral characteristic' to be like seeing a colour or hearing a sound? Naturally you couldn't *imagine* anything of the sort. But I have already pointed out that moral characteristics are dependent on others of which the presence *is* ascertainable by looking and listening. You do not intuit rightness or goodness independently of the other features of the situation. You intuit *that* an action is (or would be) right, a state of affairs good, *because* it has (or would have) certain other empirically ascertainable qualities. The total content of your intuition includes the 'because' clause. Of course, our ordinary moral judgements register unreflective reactions. Nevertheless 'This act is right (or this state of affairs is good) because it has P, Q, R'—where 'P, Q, R' stand for such empirically ascertainable qualities—expresses the type of fundamental cognitive situation in ethics, of which our normal judgements are copies, mediated by habit, but ready, if challenged, to become explicit as their original. Consider what happens when someone dissents from your opinion. You produce reasons. And this is not a matter of accounting for an emotional condition; but of bringing evidence in support of a verdict.

West.—When the jury brings in a verdict of guilty on a charge of murder, they do so because the facts adduced in evidence are of the kind covered by the definition of 'murder'. When the chemical analyst concludes that the material submitted for analysis is a salt, he does so because it exhibits the defining properties of a salt. The evidence is the sort of thing that is *meant* by 'murder', by 'salt'. But the fundamental moral word, or words, you say, cannot be defined; their concepts are unanalysable. So it cannot be in this way that the 'because' clause of your ethical sentence functions as evidence. 'X is a right action because it is a case of promise-keeping' does not work like 'X is a salt because it is a compound of basic and acid radicals'; for, if 'right' is indefinable, 'X is right' does not *mean* 'X is an act of promise-keeping or of relieving distress or of telling the truth or . . .'.

When I say 'It will be fine in the morning; for the evening sky is red', the evidence is of a different sort. For I might observe the fine morning without having noticed the state of the evening sky. But you have rightly stressed the point that there is no *independent* awareness of *moral* qualities: that they are always 'seen' as dependent on those other features mentioned in the 'because' clause. So it is not in this way, either, that the 'because' clause of your ethical sentence functions as evidence. And there is no other way. Generally, we may say that whenever q is evidence for p, *either q* is the sort of thing we mean by 'p' ('p' is definable in terms of 'q') *or* we can have knowledge of the state of affairs described by 'p' independently of knowledge of the state of affairs described by 'q'. But neither of these conditions is satisfied by the q, the 'because' clause, of your ethical sentence.

The 'because' clause, then, does not, as you said it did, constitute evidence for the ethical judgement. And this, it seems to me, should be a serious matter for you. For where is such evidence to be found? It is no good saying that, after all, the ethical judgements of other people (or your own at other times) may corroborate your own present judgement. They may agree with it: but their agreement strengthens the probability of your judgement only on the assumption that their moral intuitions tend on the whole to be correct. But the only possible evidence for the existence of a *tendency* to have correct intuitions is the correctness of *actual* intuitions. And it is precisely the correctness of actual intuitions for which we are seeking evidence, and failing to find it.

And evidence you must have, if your account of the matter is correct. You will scarcely say that ethical intuitions are infallible; for ethical disagreements may survive the resolution of factual disagreements. (You might, of course, say that *genuine* intuitions were infallible: then the problem becomes one of finding a criterion for distinguishing between the genuine ones and those false claimants that carry the same inner conviction.) So your use of the language of 'unanalysable predicates ascribed in moral judgement to particular actions and states of affairs' leads to contradiction. For to call such a judgement 'non-infallible' would be meaningless unless there were some way of checking it; of confirming or confuting it, by producing evidence for or against it. But I have just shown that your account of these judgements is incompatible with the possibility of producing evidence for or against them. So, if your account is true, these judgements are both corrigible and incorrigible; and this is absurd.

But the absurdity points to the solution. Of course these judgements are corrigible: but not in the way in which the diagnosis of a doctor is corrigible; rather in the way in which the musical taste of a child is corrigible. Correcting them is not a matter of *producing evidence* for them or their contraries, though it is (partly) a matter of *giving reasons* for them or their contraries. We say, warningly, that ethical judgements are corrigible, because ethical disagreement sometimes survives the resolution of factual disagreement. We say, encouragingly, that ethical judgements are corrigible, because the resolution of factual disagreement sometimes leads to the resolution of ethical disagreement. But the one kind of agreement leads (when it *does* lead) to the other, not in the way in which agreed evidence leads to an agreed conclusion, but in the way in which common experience leads to sympathy. The two kinds of agreement, the two kinds of judgement, are as different as chalk from cheese. Ordinary language can accommodate the difference without strain: it is the pseudo-precise philosophical use of 'judgement' which slurs over the difference and raises the difficulty. Is it not clear, then, what people have meant when they said that ethical disagreements were like disagreements in taste, in choice, in practical attitude?[3] Of course, as you said, when we produce our reasons, we are not often simply giving the causes of our emotional condition. But neither are we producing evidence for a verdict, for a moral diagnosis. We are using the facts to back our attitudes, to appeal to the capacity of others to feel as we feel, to respond as we respond.

North.—I think I see now what you have been leaving out all the time. First, you accused me of inventing a mythical faculty to give us ethical knowledge. Then, when I pointed out that ethical qualities are not intuited out of all relation to other empirically ascertainable features of actions and states of affairs, but are intuited as dependent upon these, you twisted this dependence out of all recognition. You wanted to make it like the causal dependence of a psychological disposition upon some empirical feature of its object: as a child's fondness for strawberries depends upon their sweetness. But the connection between wrongness and giving pain to others is not an accident of our constitution; nor does its perception require any special faculty—but *simply that which we use in all our reasoning.* From the fact that an action involves inflicting needless pain upon others, *it follows* necessarily that the action is wrong, just as, from the fact that a triangle is equilateral, it follows necessarily that its angles are equal. This is the kind of dependence that we intuit; not an analytic dependence, but a synthetic entailment; and this is why the 'because' clause of my ethical sentence does, after all, constitute evidence for the ascription of the moral characteristic.

I can anticipate the obvious objection. No moral rule, you will say, no moral generalization concerning the rightness of acts or the goodness of conditions, holds without exception. It is always possible to envisage circumstances in which the generalization breaks down. Or, if the generalization is so wide that no counterexample can be found, if it can be so interpreted as to cover every case, then it has become too wide: it has become tautologous, like 'It is always right to do that which will have the best results on the whole', or intolerably vague, like 'It is always right to treat people as ends in themselves' or 'The greatest good is the greatest general welfare'. It is plainly not with the help of such recipes as these that we find out what is right, what is good, in a particular case. There are no

[3] Cf. Charles Stevenson, *Ethics and Language*, ch. 1.

criteria for the meaning of 'treating a man as an end', for 'the greatest general welfare', which do not presuppose the narrower criteria of rightness and goodness of which I spoke and which seem always to have exceptions. All this is true. But it calls only for a trifling amendment to those narrower criteria. We cannot, for example, assert, as a necessary synthetic proposition, 'All acts of promise-keeping are right' or 'All states of aesthetic enjoyment are good'. But we *can* assert, as a necessary synthetic proposition, 'All acts of promise-keeping *tend as such* to be right (or have *prima facie* rightness)'[4] or 'All states of aesthetic enjoyment *tend as such* to be good'. And we derive our knowledge of such general necessary connections from seeing, in particular cases, that the rightness of an action, the goodness of a state, *follows from* its being an action or state of a certain kind.

West.—Your 'trifling amendment' is a destructive one. When we say of swans that they tend to be white, we are not ascribing a certain quality, namely 'tending to be white', to each individual swan. We are saying that the number of swans which are white exceeds the number of those which are not, that if anything is a swan, the chances are that it will be white. When we say 'Welshmen tend to be good singers', we mean that most Welshmen sing well; and when we say, of an *individual* Welshman, that *he* tends to sing well, we mean that he sings well more often than not. In all such cases, we are talking of a *class* of things or occasions or events; and saying, not that *all* members of the class have the property of *tending-to-have* a certain characteristic, but that *most* members of the class do in fact have that characteristic. Nobody would accept the claim that a sentence of the form '*Most* As are Bs' expresses a necessary proposition. Is the claim made more plausible by rewriting the proposition in the form '*All* As *tend to be* Bs'?

But, waiving this point, there remains the difficulty that the need for such an amendment to our moral generalizations is incompatible with the account you gave of the way in which we come to know both the moral characteristics of individual actions and states, and the moral generalizations themselves. You said that we intuited the moral characteristic as *following from* some empirically ascertainable features of the action or state. True, if we did so, we should have implicitly learnt a moral generalization: but it would be one asserting *without qualification* the entailment of the

---

[4] Ross, *Foundations of Ethics* (Oxford: Oxford University Press, 1939), pp. 83–6; Broad, 'Some of the Main Problems of Ethics', *Philosophy*, 1946, p. 117.

moral characteristic by these other features of the case. In other words, and to take your instance, if it *ever* follows, from the fact that an act has the empirically ascertainable features described by the phrase 'being an act of promise-keeping', that the act is right, then it *always* follows, from the fact that an act is of this kind, that it has this moral quality. If, then, it is true that we intuit moral characteristics as thus 'following from' others, it is false that the implied generalizations require the 'trifling amendment'; and if it is true that they require the amendment, it is false that we so intuit moral characteristics.[5]

And this is all that need be said of that rationalist superstition according to which a quasi-logical necessity binds moral predicates to others. 'Le coeur a ses raisons, que la raison ne connaît pas': this is the whole truth of the matter, but your attention was so riveted to the first half of it that you forgot the second.

Looking for a logical nexus where there was none to be found, you overlooked the logical relations of the ethical words among themselves. And so you forgot what has often enough been pointed out: that for every expression containing the words 'right' or 'good', used in their ethical senses, it is always possible to find an expression with the same meaning, but containing, instead of these, the word 'ought'. The equivalences are various, and the variations subtle; but they are always to be found. For one to say, for example, 'I know where the good lies, I know what the right course is; but I don't know the end I *ought* to aim at, the course I *ought* to follow' would be self-contradictory. 'Right'-sentences, 'good'-sentences are shorthand for 'ought'-sentences. And this is enough in itself to explode the myth of unanalysable characteristics designated by the indefinable predicates, 'right' and 'good'. For 'ought' is a *relational* word; whereas 'right' and 'good' are *predicative*. The simplest sentences containing

---

[5] One desperate expedient might occur to North. He might say that it is not the bare presence of the promise-keeping feature that entails the rightness of the act, but the presence of this feature, coupled with the absence of any features which would entail its wrongness. His general rules would then be, not of the form '"χ has ϕ" entails "χ is right"', but of the form '"χ has ϕ and χ has no ψ such that 'χ has ψ' entails 'χ is wrong'" entails "χ is right"'. But the suggestion is inadmissible, since (i) the establishment of the general proposition 'χ has no ψ, etc.' would require the enumeration of all those features which would make it wrong to keep a promise, and (ii) any rule of the form '"χ has ψ" entails "χ is wrong"' would require expansion in exactly the same way as the 'right-making' rule, which would involve an infinite regress of such expansions. Besides having this *theoretical* defect, the suggested model is, of course, *practically* absurd.

'ought' are syntactically more complicated than the simplest sentences containing 'right' or 'good'. And hence, since the equivalences of meaning hold, the various ethical usages of 'right' and 'good' *are all definable*: variously definable in terms of 'ought'.

Of course this last consideration alone is not decisive against intuitionism. If this were all, you could still re-form the ranks: taking your stand on an intuited unanalysable non-natural *relation* of obligation, and admitting the definability of the ethical predicates in terms of this relation. But the objections I have already raised apply with equal force against this modified position; and, in other ways, its weakness is more obvious.[6]

North.—Well, then, suppose we agree to bury intuitionism. What have you to offer in its place? Has any analysis of moral judgements in terms of feeling ever been suggested which was not monstrously paradoxical or artificial? Even the simplest ethical sentence obstinately resists translation: and not in the way in which 'Life, like a dome of many-coloured glass, stains the white radiance of eternity' resists translation. For the ethical language is not the language of the poets, but the language of all the world. Somehow justice must be done both to this irreducible element of significance in ethical sentences, and to the community of knowledge of their correct, their appropriate, use. Intuitionism, at any rate, was a way of attempting to do this.

West.—Yes, intuitionism was a way of attempting to do this. It started from the fact that thousands and thousands of people can say, with perfect propriety: 'I know that this is right, that is good'; and ended, as we have

---

[6] e.g. there was a certain plausibility in saying 'My feeling morally obliged to pursue such a course (or end) presupposes my believing that it is right (or good)', and thence concluding that this belief cannot be 'reduced to' the feeling which it arouses. (For examples of this sort of argument, see Ross, pp. 261–2, and Broad, p. 115.) But the weakness of the reasoning is more clearly exposed when the sentence is rewritten as 'My feeling morally obliged to pursue such a course presupposes my believing that I *am* morally obliged to pursue it.' The point is that 'presupposes' and 'believing' are both ambiguous. If 'presupposes' means 'causally requires' and 'believing' is used in its ordinary sense, then it is obviously false that the beliefs which *occasion* such a feeling invariably include some belief which would be correctly described in these terms. (Compare: 'My feeling frightened presupposes my believing that I am frightened.') But the argument begins to have weight against the 'analysability' of beliefs correctly so described only if they are invariably present as occasioning factors. If, on the other hand, 'presupposes' means 'logically requires', then 'believing' might be used in a queer sense such that the sentence is *tautologically* true. But this result is secured only by defining 'believing' (used in this sense) in terms of feeling (compare the sense in which 'thinking χ funny' means 'being amused by χ'): and this was precisely the result which North sought to avoid.

seen, by making it inexplicable how anybody could ever say such a thing. This was because of a failure to notice that the whole sentence, including the 'I know', and not just the last word in the subordinate clause, is a unit of the ethical language; and, following upon this failure, a feverish ransacking of the drawers of a Theory of Knowledge for an 'I know' which would fit. (Do I, perhaps, work it out like the answer to a sum?)

The man who attempts to provide a translation sees more than this. He sees, at any rate, that the sentence must be treated as a unit. His error is to think that he can find a substitute, in a different language, which will serve the same purpose. So long as he confines himself to describing how, in what sort of circumstances, the sentence is used, he does valuable work. He errs when he talks as if to say how a sentence is used is the same as to use it. The man who says he can translate ethical sentences into feeling sentences makes the same sort of mistake as some who said they could (if they had time) translate material-object sentences into sentences about actual and possible sense-experiences. What they *mean*—the commentary they are making on the use of the ethical language or the material-object language—is correct. And it is precisely because the commentary would be incorrect as a translation that it is useful as a commentary. For it brings out the fact that the irreducibility of these languages arises from the systematic vagueness of the notation they use in comparison with that of the commentary-languages, and not from their being used to talk of, to describe, different things from those of which the commentary-languages talk. This descriptive vagueness is no defect: it is what makes these languages useful for the kinds of communication (and persuasion) for which they are severally required. But by being mistaken for something more than it is, it leads to one kind of metaphysics: the metaphysics of substance (the thing-in-itself), or of intuited unanalysable ethical characteristics. And by being ignored altogether, it leads to another kind of metaphysics: the tough metaphysics of translation, the brutal suggestion that we could get along just as well without the ethical language. Neither metaphysics—neither the tender metaphysics of ultimacy, nor the tough metaphysics of reduction[7]—does justice to the facts: but the latter does them less injustice; for it doesn't seek to supplement them with a fairy tale.

[7] Cf. Wisdom, 'Metaphysics and Verification', *Mind*, 1938.

And so the alternative to intuitionism is not the provision of translations. For the communication and sharing of our moral experience, we must use the tools, the ethical language, we have. No sentences provided by the philosopher will take their place. His task is not to supply a new set of tools, but to describe what it is that is communicated and shared, and how the tools are used to do the work. And though the experience he describes is emotional experience, his descriptions are not like those of the psychologist. The psychologist is concerned with the relation of these experiences to others of a different sort; the philosopher is concerned with their relation to the ordinary use of ethical language. Of course, then, it would be absurd for the philosopher to deny that some actions are right (fair, legitimate, etc.) and others wrong (unfair, illegitimate, etc.), and that we know this; and absurd to claim that we can say what such sentences say without using such words. For this *is* the language we use in sharing and shaping our moral experience; and the occurrence of experience so shared, so shaped, is not brought into question.

We are in the position of the careful phenomenalist, who, for all his emphasis on sense-experience, neither denies that there is a table in the dining room, nor claims to be able to assert this without using such words as 'dining room' and 'table'. A phenomenalism as careful as this has been said to forfeit the right to be called a 'philosophical doctrine'.[8] Then let the title be reserved for the productions of those who rest in myth or paradox, and fail to complete that journey, from the familiar to the familiar,[9] which is philosophical analysis.

---

[8] Hardie, 'The Paradox of Phenomenalism', *Proceedings of the Aristotelian Society*, 1945–6, p. 150.
[9] Wisdom, 'Metaphysics and Verification'.

2

In Defence of a Dogma

With H. P. Grice

In his article 'Two Dogmas of Empiricism',[1] Professor Quine advances a number of criticisms of the supposed distinction between analytic and synthetic statements, and of other associated notions. It is, he says, a distinction which he rejects.[2] We wish to show that his criticisms of the distinction do not justify his rejection of it.

There are many ways in which a distinction can be criticized, and more than one in which it can be rejected. It can be criticized for not being a sharp distinction (for admitting of cases which do not fall clearly on either side of it); or on the ground that the terms in which it is customarily drawn are ambiguous (have more than one meaning); or on the ground that it is confused (the different meanings being habitually conflated). Such criticisms alone would scarcely amount to a rejection of the distinction. They would, rather, be a prelude to clarification. It is not this sort of criticism which Quine makes.

Again, a distinction can be criticized on the ground that it is not useful. It can be said to be useless for certain purposes, or useless altogether, and, perhaps, pedantic. One who criticizes in this way may indeed be said to reject a distinction, but in a sense which also requires him to acknowledge its existence. He simply declares he can get on without it. But Quine's rejection of the analytic–synthetic distinction appears to be more radical than this. He would certainly say he could get on without the distinction, but not in a sense which would commit him to acknowledging its existence.

---

[1] W. V. O. Quine, *From a Logical Point of View* (Cambridge, MA, 1953), pp. 20–46. All references are to page numbers in this book.
[2] Page 46.

Or again, one could criticize the way or ways in which a distinction is customarily expounded or explained on the ground that these explanations did not make it really clear. And Quine certainly makes such criticisms in the case of the analytic–synthetic distinction.

But he does, or seems to do, a great deal more. He declares, or seems to declare, not merely that the distinction is useless or inadequately clarified, but also that it is altogether illusory, that the belief in its existence is a philosophical mistake. 'That there is such a distinction to be drawn at all', he says, 'is an unempirical dogma of empiricists, a metaphysical article of faith.'[3] It is the existence of the distinction that he here calls in question; so his rejection of it would seem to amount to a denial of its existence.

Evidently such a position of extreme scepticism about a distinction is not in general justified merely by criticisms, however just in themselves, of philosophical attempts to clarify it. There are doubtless plenty of distinctions, drawn in philosophy and outside it, which still await adequate philosophical elucidation, but which few would want on this account to declare illusory. Quine's article, however, does not consist wholly, though it does consist largely, in criticizing attempts at elucidation. He does try also to diagnose the causes of the belief in the distinction, and he offers some positive doctrine, acceptance of which he represents as incompatible with this belief. If there is any general prior presumption in favour of the existence of the distinction, it seems that Quine's radical rejection of it must rest quite heavily on this part of his article, since the force of any such presumption is not even impaired by philosophical failures to clarify a distinction so supported.

Is there such a presumption in favour of the distinction's existence? Prima facie, it must be admitted that there is. An appeal to philosophical tradition is perhaps unimpressive and is certainly unnecessary. But it is worth pointing out that Quine's objection is not simply to the words 'analytic' and 'synthetic', but to a distinction which they are supposed to express, and which at different times philosophers have supposed themselves to be expressing by means of such pairs of words or phrases as 'necessary' and 'contingent', 'a priori' and 'empirical', 'truth of reason' and 'truth of fact'; so Quine is certainly at odds with a philosophical tradition which is long and not wholly disreputable. But there is no

---

[3] Page 37.

need to appeal only to tradition; for there is also present practice. We can appeal, that is, to the fact that those who use the terms 'analytic' and 'synthetic' do to a very considerable extent agree in the applications they make of them. They apply the term 'analytic' to more or less the same cases, withhold it from more or less the same cases, and hesitate over more or less the same cases. This agreement extends not only to cases which they have been *taught* so to characterize, but to new cases. In short, 'analytic' and 'synthetic' have a more or less established philosophical *use*; and this seems to suggest that it is absurd, even senseless, to say that there is no such distinction. For, in general, if a pair of contrasting expressions are habitually and generally used in application to the same cases, *where these cases do not form a closed list*, this is a sufficient condition for saying that there are *kinds* of cases to which the expressions apply; and nothing more is needed for them to mark a distinction.

In view of the possibility of this kind of argument, one may begin to doubt whether Quine really holds the extreme thesis which his words encourage one to attribute to him. It is for this reason that we made the attribution tentative. For on at least one natural interpretation of this extreme thesis, when we say of something true that it is analytic and of another true thing that it is synthetic, it simply never is the case that we thereby mark a distinction between them. And this view seems terribly difficult to reconcile with the fact of an established philosophical usage (i.e. of general agreement in application in an open class). For this reason, Quine's thesis might be better represented not as the thesis that there is *no difference at all* marked by the use of these expressions, but as the thesis that the nature of, and reasons for, the difference or differences are totally misunderstood by those who use the expressions, that the stories they tell themselves *about* the difference are full of illusion.

We think Quine might be prepared to accept this amendment. If so, it could, in the following way, be made the basis of something like an answer to the argument which prompted it. Philosophers are notoriously subject to illusion, and to mistaken theories. Suppose there were a particular mistaken theory about language or knowledge, such that, seen in the light of this theory, some statements (or propositions or sentences) appeared to have a characteristic which no statements really have, or even, perhaps, which it does not make sense to suppose that any statement has, and which no one who was not consciously or subconsciously influenced by this theory would ascribe to any statement. And suppose that there were other statements which, seen in this light, did not appear to have this characteristic, and others again which presented an uncertain appearance. Then philosophers who were under the influence of this theory would tend to mark the supposed presence or absence of this characteristic by a pair of contrasting expressions, say 'analytic' and 'synthetic'. Now in these circumstances it still could not be said that there was no distinction at all being marked by the use of these expressions, for there would be at least the distinction we have just described (the distinction, namely, between those statements which appeared to have and those which appeared to lack a certain characteristic), and there might well be other assignable differences too, which would account for the difference in appearance; but it certainly could be said that *the* difference these philosophers supposed themselves to be marking by the use of the expressions simply did not exist, and perhaps also (supposing the characteristic in question to be one which it was absurd to ascribe to any statement) that these expressions, as so used, were senseless or without meaning. We should only have to suppose that such a mistaken theory was very plausible and attractive, in order to reconcile the fact of an established philosophical usage for a pair of contrasting terms with the claim that *the* distinction which the terms purported to mark did not exist at all, though not with the claim that there simply did not exist a difference of any kind between the classes of statements so characterized. We think that the former claim would probably be sufficient for Quine's purposes. But to establish such a claim on the sort of grounds we have indicated evidently requires a great deal more argument than is involved in showing that certain explanations of a term do not measure up to certain requirements of adequacy in philosophical clarification—and not only more argument, but argument of a very different kind. For it would surely be too harsh to maintain that the *general* presumption is that philosophical distinctions embody the kind of illusion we have described. On the whole, it seems that philosophers are prone to make too few distinctions rather than too many. It is their assimilations, rather than their distinctions, which tend to be spurious.

So far we have argued as if the prior presumption in favour of the existence of the distinction which Quine questions rested solely on the fact of an agreed *philosophical* usage for the terms 'analytic' and 'synthetic'. A presumption with only this basis could no doubt be countered by a strategy such as we have just outlined. But, in fact, if we are to accept Quine's account of the matter, the presumption in question is not only so based. For among the notions which belong to the analyticity group is one which Quine calls 'cognitive synonymy', and in terms of which he allows that the notion of analyticity could at any rate be formally explained. Unfortunately, he adds, the notion of cognitive synonymy is just as unclarified as that of analyticity. To say that two expressions x and y are cognitively synonymous seems to correspond, at any rate roughly, to what we should ordinarily express by saying that x and y have the same meaning or that x means the same as y. If Quine is to be consistent in his adherence to the extreme thesis, then it appears that he must maintain not only that the distinction we suppose ourselves to be marking by the use of the terms 'analytic' and 'synthetic' does not exist, but also that the distinction we suppose ourselves to be marking by the use of the expressions 'means the same as', 'does not mean the same as' does not exist either. At least, he must maintain this insofar as the notion of *meaning the same as*, in its application to predicate-expressions, is supposed to differ from and go beyond the notion of *being true of just the same objects as*. (This latter notion—which we might call that of 'co-extensionality'—he is prepared to allow to be intelligible, though, as he rightly says, it is not sufficient for the explanation of analyticity.) Now since he cannot claim this time that the pair of expressions in question (namely 'means the same', 'does not mean the same') is the special property of philosophers, the strategy outlined above of countering the presumption in favour of their marking a genuine distinction is not available here (or is at least enormously less plausible). Yet the denial that the distinction (taken as different from the distinction between the co-extensional and the non-co-extensional) really exists, is extremely paradoxical. It involves saying, for example, that anyone who seriously remarks that 'bachelor' means the same as 'unmarried man' but that 'creature with kidneys' does not mean the same as 'creature with a heart'—supposing the last two expressions to be co-extensional—*either* is not in fact drawing attention to any distinction at all between the relations between the members of each pair of expressions *or* is making a philosophical mistake about the nature of the distinction between them. In either case, what he says, taken as he intends it to be taken, is senseless or absurd. More generally, it involves saying that it is always senseless or absurd to make a statement of the form 'Predicates x and y in fact apply to the same objects, but do not have the same meaning.' But the paradox is more violent than this. For we frequently talk of the presence or absence of relations of synonymy between kinds of expressions—e.g. conjunctions, particles of many kinds, whole sentences—where there does not appear to be any obvious substitute for the ordinary notion of synonymy, in the way in which co-extensionality is said to be a substitute for synonymy of predicates. Is all such talk meaningless? Is all talk of correct or incorrect *translation* of sentences of one language into sentences of another meaningless? It is hard to believe that it is. But if we do successfully make the effort to believe it, we have still harder renunciations before us. If talk of sentence-synonymy is meaningless, then it seems that talk of sentences having a meaning at all must be meaningless too. For if it made sense to talk of a sentence having a meaning, or meaning something, then presumably it would make sense to ask 'What does it mean?' And if it made sense to ask 'What does it mean?' of a sentence, then sentence-synonymy could be roughly defined as follows: Two sentences are synonymous if and only if any true answer to the question 'What does it mean?' asked of one of them, is a true answer to the same question, asked of the other. We do not, of course, claim any clarifying power for this definition. We want only to point out that if we are to give up the notion of sentence-synonymy as senseless, we must give up the notion of sentence-significance (of a sentence having meaning) as senseless too. But then perhaps we might as well give up the notion of sense. It seems clear that we have here a typical example of a philosopher's paradox. Instead of examining the actual use that we make of the notion of *meaning the same*, the philosopher measures it by some perhaps inappropriate standard (in this case some standard of clarifiability), and because it falls short of this standard, or seems to do so, denies its reality, declares it illusory.

We have argued so far that there is a strong presumption in favour of the existence of the distinction, or distinctions, which Quine challenges—a presumption resting both on philosophical and on ordinary usage—and that this presumption is not in the least shaken by the fact, if it is a fact, that the distinctions in question have not been, in some sense, adequately clarified. It is perhaps time to look at what Quine's notion of adequate clarification is.

The main theme of his article can be roughly summarized as follows. There is a certain circle or family of expressions, of which 'analytic' is one, such that if any one member of the circle could be taken to be satisfactorily understood or explained, then other members of the circle could be verbally, and hence satisfactorily, explained in terms of it. Other members of the family are: 'self-contradictory' (in a broad sense), 'necessary', 'synonymous', 'semantical rule', and perhaps (but again in a broad sense) 'definition'. The list could be added to. Unfortunately each member of the family is in as great need of explanation as any other. We give some sample quotations: 'The notion of self-contradictoriness (in the required broad sense of inconsistency) stands in exactly the same need of clarification as does the notion of analyticity itself.'[4] Again, Quine speaks of 'a notion of synonymy which is in no less need of clarification than analyticity itself'.[5] Again, of the adverb 'necessarily', as a candidate for use in the explanation of synonymy, he says, 'Does the adverb *really make sense?* To suppose that it does is to suppose that we have already *made satisfactory sense* of "analytic".'[6] To make 'satisfactory sense' of one of these expressions would seem to involve two things. (1) It would seem to involve providing an explanation which does not incorporate any expression belonging to the family-circle. (2) It would seem that the explanation provided must be of the same general character as those rejected explanations which do incorporate members of the family-circle (i.e. it must specify some feature common and peculiar to all cases to which, for example, the word 'analytic' is to be applied; it must have the same general form as an explanation beginning, 'a statement is analytic if and only if...'). It is true that Quine does not explicitly state the second requirement; but since he does not even consider the question whether any other kind of explanation would be relevant, it seems reasonable to attribute it to him. If we take these two conditions together, and generalize the result, it would seem that Quine requires of a satisfactory explanation of an expression that it should take the form of a pretty strict definition but should not make use of any member of a group of interdefinable terms to which the expression belongs. We may well begin to feel that a satisfactory explanation is hard to come by. The other element in Quine's position is one we have already commented on in general, before enquiring what (according to him) is to count as a satisfactory explanation. It is the step from 'We have not made satisfactory sense (provided a satisfactory explanation) of *x*' to '*x* does not make sense'.

It would seem fairly clearly unreasonable to insist *in general* that the availability of a satisfactory explanation in the sense sketched above is a necessary condition of an expression's making sense. It is perhaps dubious whether *any* such explanations can *ever* be given. (The hope that they can

---

[4] Page 20.   [5] Page 23.   [6] Page 30, our italics.

be is, or was, the hope of reductive analysis in general.) Even if such explanations can be given in some cases, it would be pretty generally agreed that there are other cases in which they cannot. One might think, for example, of the group of expressions which includes 'morally wrong', 'blameworthy', 'breach of moral rules', etc.; or of the group which includes the propositional connectives and the words 'true' and 'false', 'statement', 'fact', 'denial', 'assertion'. Few people would want to say that the expressions belonging to either of these groups were senseless on the ground that they have not been formally defined (or even on the ground that it was impossible formally to define them) except in terms of members of the same group. It might, however, be said that while the unavailability of a satisfactory explanation in the special sense described was not a *generally* sufficient reason for declaring that a given expression was senseless, it was a sufficient reason in the case of the expressions of the analyticity group. But anyone who said this would have to advance a reason for discriminating in this way against the expressions of this group. The only plausible reason for being harder on these expressions than on others is a refinement on a consideration which we have already had before us. It starts from the point that 'analytic' and 'synthetic' themselves are technical philosophical expressions. To the rejoinder that other expressions of the family concerned, such as 'means the same as' or 'is inconsistent with', or 'self-contradictory', are not at all technical expressions, but are common property, the reply would doubtless be that, to qualify for inclusion in the family-circle, these expressions have to be used in specially adjusted and precise senses (or pseudo-senses) which they do not ordinarily possess. It is the fact, then, that all the terms belonging to the circle are *either* technical terms *or* ordinary terms used in specially adjusted senses, that might be held to justify us in being particularly suspicious of the claims of members of the circle to have any sense at all, and hence to justify us in requiring them to pass a test for significance which would admittedly be too stringent if generally applied. This point has some force, though we doubt if the special adjustments spoken of are in every case as considerable as it suggests. (This seems particularly doubtful in the case of the word 'inconsistent'—a perfectly good member of the non-technician's meta-logical vocabulary.) But though the point has some force, it does not have whatever force would be required to justify us in insisting that the expressions concerned should pass exactly that test for significance which is in question. The fact, if it is a fact, that the expressions cannot be explained in precisely the way which Quine seems to require, does not mean that they cannot be explained at all. There is no need to try to pass them off as expressing innate ideas. They can be and are explained, though in other and less formal ways than that which Quine considers. (And the fact that they are so explained fits with the facts, first, that there is a generally agreed philosophical use for them, and second, that this use is technical or specially adjusted.) To illustrate the point briefly for one member of the analyticity family. Let us suppose we are trying to explain to someone the notion of *logical impossibility* (a member of the family which Quine presumably regards as no clearer than any of the others) and we decide to do it by bringing out the contrast between logical and natural (or causal) impossibility. We might take as our examples the logical impossibility of a child of three's being an adult, and the natural impossibility of a child of three's understanding Russell's Theory of Types. We might instruct our pupil to imagine two conversations one of which begins by someone (X) making the claim:

(1) 'My neighbour's three-year-old child understands Russell's Theory of Types',

and the other of which begins by someone (Y) making the claim:

(1') 'My neighbour's three-year-old child is an adult.'

It would not be inappropriate to reply to X, taking the remark as a hyperbole:

(2) 'You mean the child is a particularly bright lad.'

If X were to say:

(3) 'No, I mean what I say—he really does understand it',

one might be inclined to reply:

(4) 'I don't believe you—the thing's impossible.'

But if the child were then produced, and did (as one knows he would not) expound the theory correctly, answer questions on it, criticize it, and so on, one would in the end be forced to acknowledge that the claim was literally true and that the child was a prodigy. Now consider one's reaction to Y's claim. To begin with, it might be somewhat similar to the previous case. One might say:

(2′) 'You mean he's uncommonly sensible or very advanced for his age.'

If Y replies:

(3′) 'No, I mean what I say',

we might reply:

(4′) 'Perhaps you mean that he won't grow any more, or that he's a sort of freak, that he's already fully developed.'

Y replies:

(5) 'No, he's not a freak, he's just an adult.'

At this stage—or possibly if we are patient, a little later—we shall be inclined to say that we just don't understand what Y is saying, and to suspect that he just does not know the meaning of some of the words he is using. For unless he is prepared to admit that he is using words in a figurative or unusual sense, we shall say, not that we don't believe him, but that his words have *no* sense. And whatever kind of creature is ultimately produced for our inspection, it will not lead us to say that what Y said was literally true, but at most to say that we now see what he meant. As a summary of the difference between the two imaginary conversations, we might say that in both cases we would tend to begin by supposing that the other speaker was using words in a figurative or unusual or restricted way; but in the face of his repeated claim to be speaking literally, it would be appropriate in the first case to say that we did not believe him and in the second case to say that we did not understand him. If, like Pascal, we thought it prudent to prepare against very long chances, we should in the first case know what to prepare for; in the second, we should have no idea.

We give this as an example of just one type of informal explanation which we might have recourse to in the case of one notion of the analyticity group. (We do not wish to suggest it is the only type.) Further examples, with different though connected types of treatment, might be necessary to teach our pupil the use of the notion of logical impossibility in its application to more complicated cases—if indeed he did not pick it up from the one case. Now of course this type of explanation does not yield a formal statement of necessary and sufficient conditions for the application of the notion concerned. So it does not fulfil one of the conditions which

Quine seems to require of a satisfactory explanation. On the other hand, it does appear to fulfil the other. It breaks out of the family-circle. The distinction in which we ultimately come to rest is that between not believing something and not understanding something; or between incredulity yielding to conviction, and incomprehension yielding to comprehension. It would be rash to maintain that *this* distinction does not need clarification; but it would be absurd to maintain that it does not exist. In the face of the availability of this informal type of explanation for the notions of the analyticity group, the fact that they have not received another type of explanation (which it is dubious whether *any* expressions *ever* receive) seems a wholly inadequate ground for the conclusion that the notions are pseudo-notions, that the expressions which purport to express them have no sense. To say this is not to deny that it would be philosophically desirable, and a proper object of philosophical endeavour, to find a more illuminating general characterization of the notions of this group than any that has been so far given. But the question of how, if at all, this can be done is quite irrelevant to the question of whether or not the expressions which belong to the circle have an intelligible use and mark genuine distinctions.

So far we have tried to show that Sections 1 to 4 of Quine's article—the burden of which is that the notions of the analyticity group have not been satisfactorily explained—do not establish the extreme thesis for which he appears to be arguing. It remains to be seen whether Sections 5 and 6, in which diagnosis and positive theory are offered, are any more successful. But before we turn to them, there are two further points worth making which arise out of the first two sections.

(1) One concerns what Quine says about *definition* and *synonymy*. He remarks that definition does not, as some have supposed, 'hold the key to synonymy and analyticity', since 'definition—except in the extreme case of the explicitly conventional introduction of new notations—hinges on prior relations of synonymy'.[7] But now consider what he says of these extreme cases. He says: 'Here the definiendum becomes synonymous with the definiens simply because it has been expressly created for the purpose of being synonymous with the definiens. Here we have a really transparent case of synonymy created by definition; would that all species of

---

[7] Page 27.

synonymy were as intelligible.' Now if we are to take these words of Quine seriously, then his position *as a whole* is incoherent. It is like the position of a man to whom we are trying to explain, say, the idea of one thing fitting into another thing, or two things fitting together, and who says: 'I can understand what it means to say that one thing fits into another, or that two things fit together, in the case where one was specially made to fit the other; but I cannot understand what it means to say this in any other case.' Perhaps we should not take Quine's words here too seriously. But if not, then we have the right to ask him exactly what state of affairs he thinks *is* brought about by explicit definition, what relation between expressions *is* established by this procedure, and why he thinks it unintelligible to suggest that the same (or a closely analogous) state of affairs, or relation, should exist in the absence of this procedure. For our part, we should be inclined to take Quine's words (or some of them) seriously, and reverse his conclusions; and maintain that the notion of synonymy by explicit convention would be unintelligible if the notion of synonymy by usage were not presupposed. There cannot be law where there is no custom, or rules where there are not practices (though perhaps we can understand better what a practice is by looking at a rule).

(2) The second point arises out of a paragraph on page 32 of Quine's book. We quote:

> I do not know whether the statement 'Everything green is extended' is analytic. Now does my indecision over this example really betray an incomplete understanding, an incomplete grasp, of the 'meanings' of 'green' and 'extended'? I think not. The trouble is not with 'green' or 'extended,' but with 'analytic.'

If, as Quine says, the trouble is with 'analytic,' then the trouble should doubtless disappear when 'analytic' is removed. So let us remove it, and replace it with a word Quine himself has contrasted favourably with 'analytic' in respect of perspicuity—the word 'true'. Does the indecision at once disappear? We think not. The indecision over 'analytic' (and equally, in this case, the indecision over 'true') arises, of course, from a further indecision: namely, that which we feel when confronted with such questions as 'Should we count a *point* of green light as *extended* or not?' As is frequent enough in such cases, the hesitation arises from the fact that the boundaries of application of words are not determined by usage in all possible directions. But the example Quine has chosen is particularly unfortunate for his thesis, in that it is only too evident that our hesitations are not *here* attributable to obscurities in 'analytic'. It would be possible to choose other examples in which we should hesitate between 'analytic' and 'synthetic' and have few qualms about 'true'. But no more in these cases than in the sample case does the hesitation necessarily imply any obscurity in the notion of analyticity; since the hesitation would be sufficiently accounted for by the same or a similar kind of indeterminacy in the relations between the words occurring within the statement about which the question, whether it is analytic or synthetic, is raised.

Let us now consider briefly Quine's positive theory of the relations between the statements we accept as true or reject as false on the one hand and the 'experiences' in the light of which we do this accepting and rejecting on the other. This theory is boldly sketched rather than precisely stated.[8] We shall merely extract from it two assertions, one of which Quine clearly takes to be incompatible with acceptance of the distinction between analytic and synthetic statements, and the other of which he regards as barring one way to an explanation of that distinction. We shall seek to show that the first assertion is not incompatible with acceptance of the distinction, but is, on the contrary, most intelligibly interpreted in a way quite consistent with it, and that the second assertion leaves the way open to just the kind of explanation which Quine thinks it precludes. The two assertions are the following:

(1) It is an illusion to suppose that there is any class of accepted statements the members of which are in principle 'immune from revision' in the light of experience, i.e. any that we accept as true and must continue to accept as true whatever happens.

(2) It is an illusion to suppose that an individual statement, taken in isolation from its fellows, can admit of confirmation or disconfirmation at all. There is no particular statement such that a particular experience or set of experiences decides once for all whether that statement is true or false, independently of our attitudes to all other statements.

The apparent connection between these two doctrines may be summed up as follows. Whatever our experience may be, it is in principle possible to hold on to, or reject, any particular statement we like, so long as we are prepared to make extensive enough revisions elsewhere in our system of beliefs. In practice our choices are governed largely by considerations of

---

[8] Cf. pp. 37–46.

convenience: we wish our system to be as simple as possible, but we also wish disturbances to it, as it exists, to be as small as possible.

The apparent relevance of these doctrines to the analytic–synthetic distinction is obvious in the first case, less so in the second.

(1) Since it is an illusion to suppose that the characteristic of immunity in principle from revision, come what may, belongs, or could belong, to any statement, it is an illusion to suppose that there is a distinction to be drawn between statements which possess this characteristic and statements which lack it. Yet, Quine suggests, this is precisely the distinction which those who use the terms 'analytic' and 'synthetic' suppose themselves to be drawing. Quine's view would perhaps also be (though he does not explicitly say this in the article under consideration) that those who believe in the distinction are inclined at least sometimes to mistake the characteristic of strongly resisting revision (which belongs to beliefs very centrally situated in the system) for the mythical characteristic of total immunity from revision.

(2) The connection between the second doctrine and the analytic–synthetic distinction runs, according to Quine, through the verification theory of meaning. He says: 'If the verification theory can be accepted as an adequate account of statement synonymy, the notion of analyticity is saved after all.'[9] For, in the first place, two statements might be said to be synonymous if and only if any experiences which contribute to, or detract from, the confirmation of one contribute to, or detract from, the confirmation of the other, to the same degree; and, in the second place, synonymy could be used to explain analyticity. But, Quine seems to argue, acceptance of any such account of synonymy can only rest on the mistaken belief that individual statements, taken in isolation from their fellows, can admit of confirmation or disconfirmation at all. As soon as we give up the idea of a set of experiential truth conditions for each statement taken separately, we must give up the idea of explaining synonymy in terms of identity of such sets.

Now to show that the relations between these doctrines and the analytic–synthetic distinction are not as Quine supposes. Let us take the second doctrine first. It is easy to see that acceptance of the second doctrine would not compel one to abandon, but only to revise, the suggested

---

[9] Page 38.

explanation of synonymy. Quine does not deny that individual statements are regarded as confirmed or disconfirmed, are in fact rejected or accepted, in the light of experience. He denies only that these relations between single statements and experience hold independently of our attitudes to *other* statements. He means that experience can confirm or disconfirm an individual statement, only given certain assumptions about the truth or falsity of other statements. When we are faced with a 'recalcitrant experience', he says, we always have a choice of what statements to amend. What we have to renounce is determined by what we are anxious to keep. This view, however, requires only a slight modification of the definition of statement-synonymy in terms of confirmation and disconfirmation. All we have to say now is that two statements are synonymous if and only if any experiences which, *on certain assumptions about the truth values of other statements*, confirm or disconfirm one of the pair, also, *on the same assumptions*, confirm or disconfirm the other to the same degree. More generally, Quine wishes to substitute for what he conceives to be an over-simple picture of the confirmation-relations between particular statements and particular experiences, the idea of a looser relation which he calls 'germaneness' (p. 43). But however loosely 'germaneness' is to be understood, it would apparently continue to make sense to speak of two statements as standing in the same germaneness-relation to the same particular experiences. So Quine's views are not only consistent with, but even suggest, an amended account of statement-synonymy along these lines. We are not, of course, concerned to defend such an account, or even to state it with any precision. We are only concerned to show that acceptance of Quine's doctrine of empirical confirmation does not, as he says it does, entail giving up the attempt to define statement-synonymy in terms of confirmation.

Now for the doctrine that there is no statement which is in principle immune from revision, no statement which might not be given up in the face of experience. Acceptance of this doctrine is quite consistent with adherence to the distinction between analytic and synthetic statements. Only, the adherent of *this* distinction must also insist on another; on the distinction between that kind of giving up which consists in merely admitting falsity, and that kind of giving up which involves changing or dropping a concept or set of concepts. Any form of words at one time held to express something true may, no doubt, at another time, come to be held to express something false. But it is not only philosophers who would distinguish between the case where this happens as the result of a change of opinion solely as to matters of fact, and the case where this happens at least partly as a result of a shift in the sense of the words. Where such a shift in the sense of the words is a necessary condition of the change in truth value, then the adherent of the distinction will say that the form of words in question changes from expressing an analytic statement to expressing a synthetic statement. We are not now concerned, or called upon, to elaborate an adequate theory of conceptual revision, any more than we were called upon, just now, to elaborate an adequate theory of synonymy. If we can make sense of the idea that the same form of words, taken in one way (or bearing one sense), may express something true, and taken in another way (or bearing another sense), may express something false, then we can make sense of the idea of conceptual revision. And if we can make sense of this idea, then we can perfectly well preserve the distinction between the analytic and the synthetic, while conceding to Quine the revisability-in-principle of everything we say. As for the idea that the same form of words, taken in different ways, may bear different senses and perhaps be used to say things with different truth values, the onus of showing that this is somehow a mistaken or confused idea rests squarely on Quine. The point of substance (or one of them) that Quine is making, by this emphasis on revisability, is that there is no absolute necessity about the adoption or use of any conceptual scheme whatever, or, more narrowly and in terms that he would reject, that there is no analytic proposition such that we *must* have linguistic forms bearing just the sense required to express that proposition. But it is one thing to admit this, and quite another thing to say that there are no necessities within any conceptual scheme we adopt or use, or, more narrowly again, that there are no linguistic forms which do express analytic propositions.

The adherent of the analytic–synthetic distinction may go further and admit that there may be cases (particularly perhaps in the field of science) where it would be pointless to press the question whether a change in the attributed truth value of a statement represented a conceptual revision or not, and correspondingly pointless to press the analytic–synthetic distinction. We cannot quote such cases, but this inability may well be the result of ignorance of the sciences. In any case, the existence, if they do exist, of statements about which it is pointless to press the question whether they are analytic or synthetic, does not entail the non-existence of statements which are clearly classifiable in one or other of these ways and of statements our hesitation over which has different sources, such as the possibility of alternative interpretations of the linguistic forms in which they are expressed.

This concludes our examination of Quine's article. It will be evident that our purpose has been wholly negative. We have aimed to show merely that Quine's case against the existence of the analytic–synthetic distinction is not made out. His article has two parts. In one of them, the notions of the analyticity group are criticized on the ground that they have not been adequately explained. In the other, a positive theory of truth is outlined, purporting to be incompatible with views to which believers in the analytic–synthetic distinction either must be, or are likely to be, committed. In fact, we have contended, no single point is established which those who accept the notions of the analyticity group would feel any strain in accommodating in their own system of beliefs. This is not to deny that many of the points raised are of the first importance in connection with the problem of giving a satisfactory general account of analyticity and related concepts. We are here only criticizing the contention that these points justify the rejection, as illusory, of the analytic–synthetic distinction and the notions which belong to the same family.

3
Construction and Analysis

In earlier lectures in this series, Mr. Pears has described the metaphysics of Logical Atomism; Professor Ayer has set out the programme of Logical Positivism; and Mr. Paul has spoken of the work of Professor Moore in Cambridge from 1900. You will perhaps have noticed that, in spite of their differences, Atomists, Positivists, and Professor Moore all have something in common, even if it is only a word, to be pronounced with approval. The word is 'analysis'. Certainly they did not all have exactly the same conception of analysis. Wittgenstein, in the *Tractatus*, gave no indication of thinking that analysis into the ultimate elements could actually be carried out; nor did he indicate at all clearly what he thought the ultimate elements were. The Positivists, on the other hand, were less non-committal. They had the ultimate elements clearly identified as 'sense-contents'; and they thought that at least the principles of analysis could be laid down, even if the details could not always be filled in. Atomists and Positivists alike accepted the skeleton language of the new mathematical logic as providing the formal structure of the ultimate and penultimate statements. Professor Moore stands rather apart from the members of both these groups. For he was not committed, as they were, to ultimate elements, nor was he tied so closely to the forms of mathematical logic; he was not bound, as they were, by a foreknowledge of the pattern to be revealed. For him, analysis was not the instrument of a wholesale metaphysics, but the method of a piecemeal elucidation. For him, analysis was not a programme, but a practice.

But what exactly did those who prescribed or practised philosophical analysis *mean* by this expression? In particular, what were they claiming to analyse? Was it, for example, *sentences*, of the indicative or assertive kind? Or was it the meanings of those sentences—by some, rather unhappily, called *propositions*? Or was it the *thoughts* or *beliefs* which the sentences expressed? Or the *statements* they were used to make? It does not matter much, now, which we say; though each of these answers may, in its own way, be misleading. Analysis of sentences, for example, suggests the grammarian; analysis of thoughts or beliefs, the psychologist; and analysis of statements, perhaps the policeman or the advocate. Maybe it is best to say, as Moore always said, that the objects of analysis were propositions. This answer, whatever its shortcomings, emphasizes, without over-emphasizing, the linguistic nature of the enterprise, the preoccupation with meaning. For, however we describe the objects of analysis, particular analyses, whether given in detail or sketched in outline, always looked much the same. A sentence, representative of a class of sentences belonging to the same topic, was supposed to be elucidated by the framing of another sentence. This second sentence was to be more or less equivalent in meaning to the first, but was to make explicit at least some of the complexities of meaning concealed by the verbal form of the first. Presumably, for those who held that analysis had a terminus in logical atoms, there would exist, in theory, for every sentence of common speech, a *final analysis*—a sentence in which *all* complexities of meaning would be made *completely* explicit, in terms of the ultimate logical elements. Not that all analyses were thought of as reducing the complex to simpler elements. Some were thought of, rather, as a *recasting* of the verbal form of a sentence in such a way as to reveal the logical affinities of the proposition it expressed, and to dispel the illusion of other logical affinities which it did not really possess. It was as if propositions belonged to logical families, most of the members of each of which wore a certain kind of verbal dress; but some members of some families masqueraded in the verbal clothing characteristic of other families; and had to be re-garbed to prevent confusion. This, too, was the task of analysis.

So, then, the general conception of analysis was that of a kind of translation, or, perhaps better, a kind of paraphrase. For it was to be translation within a language, not from one language to another: a translation from a less explicit to a more explicit form, or from a misleading to an unmisleading form. If your problem was, say, the nature of *truth*, or, say, the nature of *existence*, you hoped to solve it by finding a formula for translating sentences in which the adjective 'true' or the verb 'exists' occurred, into sentences in which these expressions did not occur, and in which no straightforward synonyms of them occurred either. Nor was this, after all, so very revolutionary a conception of philosophy. The search for definitions of problematic ideas was almost as old as philosophy itself.

What was new was rather the substitution of sentences for words, of propositions for concepts, as the unit upon which analysis was to be practised. And for this change, as earlier lectures have shown, there were very good reasons.

Although, in Cambridge, Wittgenstein was already doing something very different, on the whole the method of analysis dominated English philosophy in the thirties. It brought some advances in some fields. But in the main the results were disappointing. The sentences of common speech seemed somehow to resist the simplifying expansions which theory had prepared for them. Even Russell's earlier brilliant glosses on the structure of ordinary sentences, in terms of the syntax of the new formal logic, began in the end to seem a little queer. And those who went to work with fewer preconceptions about their results were apt to find that if they preserved the sense of the original, they achieved no simplification: and that if they gained a simplification, they did so at the cost of losing the sense.

So what was to be done? Philosophers sought understanding of the concepts which were the apparatus of our thinking. They looked—and this seemed natural enough—to the propositions, the sentences, in which these concepts found their employment, the sentences in which we commonly express our thoughts and beliefs. But if these sentences resisted translation into more perspicuous forms, what was to be done? Well, of course, there were many possibilities. But, among them, two have been of dominant importance in post-war philosophizing. One involves turning away from the forms of common speech, while preserving much of the apparatus of the original programme of analysis. The other involves continued close attention to the forms of common speech, together with a vastly altered and extended conception of the nature and techniques of analysis.

Let me say more about these two contrasting courses. The first method, incidentally, is pursued mainly in America, and is associated especially with the names of Carnap and Quine. The second method is pursued mainly in England, and is associated especially with the names of Austin and Ryle. For the sake of convenience, I may speak of the American School and the English School. But I need hardly say that the titles cover quite wide divergences between individuals. The main inspiration of the American School is still, as it was for the Logical Atomists, the new formal logic, due to Frege and Russell. For this logic provides a skeleton language in which the meaning of every element is absolutely precise, and the articulation of the elements absolutely clear. By using this framework, this basic linguistic apparatus, other systems of concepts can be constructed in which the mutual relationships of the parts will have just the same clarity and precision as in formal logic itself. Of course, systems so constructed, and indeed the logical system itself used in their construction, are not natural growths, like the language of daily life, but artificial creations. But just in this very fact, it is claimed, lies the philosophical superiority of system-construction over the attempt to analyse ordinary language. That attempt, it is suggested, is defeated by the looseness, the untidiness, the shifting complexities of common speech. Instead of pursuing it, then, we are to construct clear models of language in which all the essential logical relations of our concepts can be made plain, while the irrelevant tangles of actual usage are cut away. Of course, some preliminary or incidental remark will have to be made, connecting key expressions of the system with expressions we ordinarily use. Otherwise it would not be clear what the system was about, what concepts it was intended to clarify. But once these points of contact are made, the system stands on its own, a precise and rigid structure to which our ordinary conceptual equipment is a rough and confusing approximation. The system of formal logic is itself the greatest of all achievements of this kind, as well as being the prerequisite of others. For it reveals the underlying structure of all our thinking. From those little logical words which are indispensable to all developed discourse—words such as 'the', 'a', 'all', 'some', 'if', 'not, 'or', 'and', 'is'—it distils what is essential and discards the troublesome remainder. Formal logic is the model for other philosophical models, as well as the framework on which the others are to be built.

Very roughly, that is the case, or an important part of the case, for system-construction as a method in philosophy. Evidently, it has its appeal. It offers something clear and orderly, in the place of something apparently confused and imprecise. It is not only attractive, but plausible. For there are many things which can be better understood as a result of the construction of a simplified model of their working; and why should not the concepts which exercise philosophers be among these things?

But the case for the alternative method can also be made to sound very plausible. After all, we are seeking to gain an understanding of the concepts and categories in terms of which we carry on our thinking; not only, or primarily, our advanced and technical thinking, but our common, daily thinking. For it is the most general, most fundamental, and most ordinary ideas which give rise to the major problems of philosophy. Is it, after all, so reasonable to think that our ordinary use of language blurs and distorts these ordinary ideas? For common speech is subjected to the severest of all tests for efficiency, as a medium for the expression and communication of our thoughts—the test of constant use. If we want to understand the habits and way of life of an animal, we must carefully observe his behaviour in his natural surroundings; it is no good turning our backs on his actual behaviour, constructing a clock-work model from an engineer's designs and then studying that. So with our concepts. If we want to know how they work, we must watch them at work. As for the failure of the original programme of analysis, as applied to the sentences of common speech, the fault there lay not in common speech, but in a too rigid and too narrow conception of analysis. Why should it be supposed that the only way to gain understanding of the words which express the philosophically puzzling concepts was to translate sentences in which they occurred into sentences in which they did not occur? The belief in the exclusive efficacy of this method is just the troublesome legacy of discredited theories. It is too rigid a conception of analysis, because it supposes the existence of exact quasi-definitional relations between classes of concepts, which do not in fact obtain. It is too narrow, because it neglects altogether very many quite different features of the functioning of language, which it is of the first importance accurately to note and describe, if our philosophical problems are to be resolved. And the programme of system-construction suffers from just these same limitations. For it, too, confines itself to exhibiting quasi-definitional relations between constructed concepts. Admittedly the relations do really obtain in the constructed system; because they are made to. But even this limited success is purchased at too high a price: the price of divorce from the conceptual realities of common speech. So, for the old, limited and theory-ridden programme of analysis, we are to substitute a different aim: that of coming to understand philosophically puzzling concepts by carefully and accurately noting the ways in which the related linguistic expressions are actually used in discourse. Of course, not all features of the use of these expressions will be relevant to the philosopher's task. It is his special skill to discern *which* are relevant, and *how* they are relevant.

I have presented these two views of philosophical method as if they were in sharp and irreconcilable conflict. And, indeed, the partisans of each frequently enough write and speak as if this were so. But it is in fact not so clear that the philosophical builders of artificial languages, and the philosophical investigators of natural language, must necessarily be each other's enemies. Up to a point, at least, each method may be seen as the complementary of the other. For, on the one hand, the simplicities of a constructed model may cast light, if only by contrast, on the complexities of actual usage; and, on the other hand, some observation of the workings of natural language seems necessary for the successful construction of the simplified model. So it might seem that the situation calls for cooperation rather than competition. And so, up to a point, it does. Yet I am partisan enough to want to upset a little the symmetry of this friendly picture—or perhaps I should say, cautious enough to want to delimit spheres of influence. And, to explain my reasons for this, I shall have to try to fill a notable gap in what I have so far said. I shall have, that is, to say something about the general nature of philosophical problems, and of philosophical understanding. I shall have to say what I think the philosopher's tasks are.

There is one task about which there will be little disagreement. Sometimes, instead of just setting our concepts and speech-forms to work in the ordinary way, we reflect upon them, or with them, at a level of unusual generality; and when we do so, we may find ourselves driven towards conclusions not simply bizarre, not simply shocking to common sense, but somehow intrinsically unacceptable; and intrinsically unacceptable because at variance with the ordinary use, and hence with the ordinary meaning, of the very words in which we are tempted to express them. Yet such conclusions may seem, though unacceptable, inescapable. In this situation, some conceptual distortion has taken place; and, in general, the distortion is the consequence of an undue pressure exercised by *some* only of the features of the language in which we express the concept in question, to the temporary exclusion of others. To correct the distortion, we must clearly expose the full logical workings of the distorted concept, and perhaps of others too; and locate, if we can, the source of the distorting pressure. This is one of the tasks confronting the critical philosopher; and is worthy of a first mention, because so much of philosophy begins with paradox and the resolution of paradox. But it would itself be a paradox to represent the whole task of philosophy as the correction of philosophical mistakes. Even if such mistakes provide the initial impulse to this conceptual anatomy, the enterprise then acquires its own momentum and may be pursued for its own sake. There may be pure research as well as *ad hoc* therapy. So the philosopher may undertake a more detailed examination, a more systematic ordering and description, of speech-forms, of types of discourse, of types of concept, than would be necessary simply to relieve the pressures of paradox.

This is still not all that may be required of the philosopher. So far I have represented him as trying to exhibit the ways in which our concepts and forms of thought actually operate—partly for the sake of doing so, partly for the sake of clearing up conceptual confusions, diagnosing philosophical disorders. But there are other and more imaginative sides to his activity, not strictly separable from these, but distinguishable from them. For fully to understand our conceptual equipment, it is not enough to know, to be able to say, how it works. We want to know also *why* it works as it does. To ask this is to ask to be shown how the nature of our thinking is rooted in the nature of the world and in our own natures. This is not an impossible enquiry; for it is quite possible to imagine our experience being different in fundamental ways, and then to consider how our conceptual apparatus might naturally be adjusted to accommodate these differences. In seeing this, we see also how our concepts, as they are, are rooted in the world, as it is. This kind of thinking might be called the explanatory work of the philosophical imagination. There is another kind of thinking which might be called the creative or constructive work of the philosophical imagination. To engage in this kind of thinking is to consider how, without the nature of the world being fundamentally different, we might nevertheless view it through the medium of a different conceptual apparatus, might conduct our discourse about it in forms different from, though related to, those which we actually use. Evidently, both these kinds of imaginative philosophical thinking are complementary to the analytical kinds I first distinguished. In practice, each kind tends to be so interwoven with the others that there is a certain artificiality in so distinguishing them. But it is not wholly artificial. For one strand or another may be decisively dominant in any one piece of work, or in the work of any one philosopher. Let me, for convenience, give names to these different strands in philosophical thought. In the order in which I first mentioned them, I shall distinguish the analytical strands into the therapeutic and the systematic; and the imaginative strands into the explanatory and the inventive.

And now, I think, we are in a better position to assess the relative claims of the English and American schools in post-war philosophy. For the task of therapeutic analysis, as I have described it, it is obvious that the methods of the English school are of primary importance—while the method of system-construction is, at best, of secondary helpfulness. For the paradoxes and perplexities in question had their root in a vivid, but imperfect, picture of the working of the concepts concerned—in a kind of caricature of their logical features. The only fully rational method of correction here is to replace the caricature with an accurate delineation of those features, which will show how the caricature distorted, what it exaggerated, and what it missed out. And it is in the actual use of the linguistic expressions for the concepts concerned, and nowhere else, that we find the data from which we can draw this accurate picture. A simplified diagram from which the puzzle-generating features are, perhaps, absent, is here no substitute, though it may be a help. What of systematic analysis? This, as I described it, was simply a more generalized and systematic attempt to distinguish and describe the logical features of our concepts and speech-forms. Its data, therefore, and its methods are fundamentally the same as those of therapeutic analysis, though it has not the same anxious concern with possible sources of perplexity and paradox. There may appear to be a slight oddity in speaking of systematic analysis of language and then declaring that the way to pursue it is not by the constructing of linguistic systems. But if this does seem odd, it is only a superficial oddity. For evidently there is a difference between constructing a segment of artificial language and systematically describing the workings of a slice of natural language. One must not exaggerate the difference. The task of tracing patterns in living language is difficult, and would be almost impossible if one were not allowed to do a little regimenting. Still the difference remains a vital one. The living creatures of language, even when mildly regimented, are still seen as performing a range of functions of immense diversity; whereas only a few of these functions can be imitated by the logical machines built by the constructionist.

What of the imaginative side of philosophy? Obviously neither a facility in the techniques of system-construction, nor a keen eye for the linguistic facts is of direct help in the *explanatory* task. But when we turn to the *inventive* or *constructive* side—one might almost say, the metaphysical side— the case is different. The system-builder, guided by certain ideals of quasi-mathematical elegance and exactness, provides us with models of ways in which we might have thought and talked, had we been less complex and many-levelled creatures than we are. In doing so, he may, as I have already said, cast much direct and indirect light on fundamental features of the ways in which we actually do think and talk. And this is not all. A philosopher's systematic reconstruction of concepts and speech-forms may sometimes have an application in other branches of knowledge than philosophy. It may provide useful, and even indispensable, tools for the advance of mathematics and the more mathematical sciences. And here again there is a parallel with the inventive speculations of more traditional metaphysics. What begins as metaphysics may end as science. But this is not its only justification; and it is time to drop the prim pragmatism which pretends that it is.

So, then, the appearance of a deathly struggle between these two methods in contemporary philosophy is, in part at least, a misleading appearance, an illusion. The illusion is not necessarily regrettable: it may act as a spur to effort on both sides. And it is not wholly illusion; for there is here something of a clash, almost of temperament—between the desire to understand what exists, and the desire to make something new and, in some sense, better. Nevertheless, the apparent conflict is largely an illusion, even if a useful one. For the two methods are not rival ways of attaining just the same end—ways of which one must be quite wrong if the other is quite right. They are, partly, complementary methods of achieving one end; and, partly, both of them, appropriate and closely related methods of achieving different, though closely related, ends. For me to say which of these different ends I considered the more important would have no more interest than any other expression of personal preference; but it may not be altogether fanciful to find in the *national* preferences which I mentioned earlier, some indication of a characteristic difference between the New World and the Old.

4
Proper Names

A distinction familiar in logical theory is that between (A) expressions used to make singular identifying references, and (B) predicate-expressions. A-expressions have been variously styled: 'singular terms', '(singular) logical subject expressions', 'definite uniquely referring expressions', even 'proper names'. I shall sometimes abbreviate some of these phrases, and speak, for short, of the distinction between *referring expressions* and *predicate-expressions*, or between *subject-expressions* and *predicate-expressions*. All A-expressions are singular substantival expressions, all B-expressions are sentence-parts containing a singular verb-form. In neither case does the converse hold.

Proper names, ordinarily so-called, are a subclass of A-expressions, and are contrasted with descriptive or demonstrative A-expressions. Some A-expressions are used to refer to particulars, some are used to refer to non-particulars. This division holds also for the proper name subclass: some proper names (Ruskin, the Caspian, France) are names of particulars; others (the Decameron, the Pons Asinorum, the Marseillaise) are not. I shall be mostly, but not exclusively, concerned with reference to particulars. My use of the philosopher's word, 'particular', is not eccentric, so I shall give no general explanation of it. For instance, in mine, as in most familiar philosophical uses, historical occurrences, material objects, people and their shadows are all particulars; whereas qualities, properties, species, numbers, and types (as opposed to tokens) are not. One general way of *indicating* the distinction I have in mind is to say that the principle of the Identity of Indiscernibles is not necessarily true of particulars, whilst it is necessarily true of universals (properties, types, etc.).

There are many interesting questions about proper names, ordinarily so-called: about the demarcation of the class; about the differences between the modes of operation of proper names on the one hand, and of descriptive and demonstrative phrases on the other; about differences within the class. But I shall not discuss these questions, except incidentally. I shall be concerned with the general distinction (or group of associated distinctions) between referring expressions and predicate-expressions, between reference and description, between subjects (things of which things are predicated) and predicates (things which are predicated of things). By way of justification (or excuse) for this extension of the topic, I refer to Frege's extension of the title.

There is a traditional doctrine to the effect that particulars can be referred to, but not predicated; that particulars can appear in propositions as subjects only, never as predicates, whereas universals can appear as both. One way of describing the aim of the ensuing discussion would be to say that it is an attempt to find the rationale of this doctrine. Another would be to say that it is an attempt to arrive at an understanding of the distinction between reference and predication. The course of the discussion will be as follows. I shall begin by developing two apparently independent explanations of the subject–predicate distinction: I shall speak of these as yielding, respectively, the 'grammatical' criterion, and the 'category' criterion, for the distinction. Then I shall point out how these two criteria appear to be harmonized in linguistic practice, even when (so to speak) it costs language an effort to appear to harmonize them. Then I shall discuss, and contrast, the general conditions under which identified particulars and identified universals can respectively be introduced into propositions. Finally, I shall use the results of this last discussion to try to explain the connection between the 'grammatical' and 'categorial' criteria for the subject–predicate distinction, and thereby to explain also the traditional doctrine that particulars cannot be predicated.

Limits of space will compel me to put things *roughly*, to omit much qualification and explanation. But one may sometimes cheerfully sacrifice accuracy and clarity to scope.

Subject and predicate: the 'grammatical' criterion. An assertion made in the words 'John smokes' might, in different contexts, be said to be either an assertion about John (a man) or an assertion about smoking (a habit). An assertion made in the words 'Socrates is wise' might, in different contexts, be said to be either an assertion about Socrates (a man) or an assertion about wisdom (a quality).[1] If we divide the sentences concerned into

---

[1] Cook Wilson made much of this point, and appropriated the expressions 'subject' and 'predicate' accordingly. This was a pity, since the contextual circumstances which make us answer, now in one way, now in another, if asked what an assertion is about, are not, I think,

subject- and predicate-expressions in the standard way, and then ask which of the resulting parts serve, in making the assertions, to introduce the various non-linguistic items (terms) which the assertions might be said to be about, there can be no doubt about the answer. 'John' and 'Socrates' serve to introduce the particular terms, John and Socrates; 'smokes' and 'is wise' serve to introduce the universal terms, smoking and wisdom. The subject- and predicate-expressions, alike, of these sentences may, then, be said to serve to introduce terms.[2] This does not mean, of course, that there is no difference in the style, or the mode, of the introduction. 'John' and 'Socrates' introduce their terms in the referring way, 'smokes' and 'is wise' introduce their terms in the predicative way. But what does this difference amount to?

'John' and 'Socrates' introduce their terms in a grammatical style (the substantival) which would be appropriate to any kind of remark (command, exhortation, undertaking, assertion) or to none. If one merely wanted to make a *list* of terms, without commitment to any introduction into a remark, the substantival style would be the natural one to use. The expressions 'smokes' and 'is wise', on the other hand, introduce their terms in a very distinctive grammatical style, *viz.* the assertive or propositional style. They introduce their terms in a style which overwhelmingly suggests completion into a certain *kind* of remark, *viz.* an assertion. Now it will surely be objected that the fact that the words 'is wise', or even 'Socrates is wise', occur in a remark does not guarantee that the remark is an assertion. For I might pronounce the words 'Socrates is wise' in an interrogative tone of voice, and thereby ask a question instead of making an assertion; or I might use the words 'is wise' in asking a different kind of question, in asking 'Who is wise?' Or again, I might make a remark which begins with the words '*If* Socrates is wise . . .' or '*If* John smokes . . .'; and in these cases I am certainly not asserting that Socrates is wise or that John smokes, and may not be asserting anything at all, but, e.g. giving somebody conditional permission to do something. These points are certainly correct. Yet we must remember that questions invite answers; that questions such as

---

of the first importance for logical theory. But the point is sufficient to show that any attempt to elucidate the subject–predicate distinction rests upon sand in so far as it rests upon the distinguishing powers of the word 'about'. (Cf., for example, Geach, 'Subject and Predicate', *Mind*, 1950, pp. 461–2.)

[2] I use the word 'term' throughout in a non-linguistic way, applying it to any item, of any category, which might be identifyingly introduced, in any style, into any proposition.

'Socrates is wise?' invite us to pronounce on the truth value of *propositions* which the questions themselves supply; that questions such as 'Who is wise?' invite us to complete and assert *propositions* of which the questions themselves supply the propositional form and half the content. And we must remember that it is part of the function of conditional clauses to bring before us *propositions*, though without commitment as to their truth value. So even if we cannot say that the distinctive style in which 'is wise', 'smokes', etc., introduce their terms is the assertive style, we can at least say that it is the propositional style, the style appropriate to the case where the term is introduced into something which has a truth value. And this is why I employed the alternation, 'the assertive or propositional style'. But I think it can be argued that this apparent weakening of the characterization of the style of introduction is really no weakening of it at all. For the standard way of insulating a propositional form of words from that commitment as to its truth value which consists in asserting it, is to add something to it—to add, for example, the conjunction, 'that'. This gives us a reason for saying that the *primary* function of the propositional symbolism of the indicative verb (or verb + adjective, etc.) is assertive. That which is primarily the assertive style of introduction of terms is also the broader thing, the propositional style of introduction. So I shall continue to speak *indifferently* of the 'assertive' or the 'propositional' style of term-introduction. And anyone unconvinced by the last stage of the argument may read 'propositional' for 'assertive' in every relevant case.

These considerations, then, yield one kind of approach to the subject–predicate distinction. Both A-expressions and B-expressions introduce terms; but a B-expression does not merely introduce its term, it introduces it in a distinctive style, the style of the propositional symbolism which shows that what its term is introduced into is a proposition.[3] To borrow a

---

[3] It should be noticed that, in drawing this distinction between A-expressions and B-expressions, I am not merely exploiting the fact that English is a comparatively uninflected language, especially as regards its noun-forms. It is true that in Latin, for example, the name 'Socrates' may appear in a number of grammatical cases; and that the fact that the name appears in a particular grammatical case in a remark tells us something about the way in which the term, Socrates, is introduced into the remark. But it does not tell us whether or not the remark is a proposition. That 'Socrates' is in the vocative does not tell us whether the following remark is assertion or request or undertaking; 'Socrates' is in the nominative case in 'Let Socrates be slain' as well as in 'Socrates is wise', in the accusative case in 'Kill Socrates' as well as in 'Plato loved Socrates', in the ablative case in 'Let the talk be about Socrates' as well as in 'The talk was about Socrates'.

phrase of W. E. Johnson's: the B-expression not only introduces its term, it also carries the assertive tie.

This way of looking at the distinction has the merit of harmonizing well with some of the things which the authorities say about it. To refer only to Frege. He says that a proper name (i.e. an A-expression) can never be a B-expression, though it can be part of one. Now A-expressions do not introduce their terms in the assertive style, B-expressions do. No expression which does not introduce its term in this style can be an expression which does; and vice versa. So no A-expression can be a B-expression, or vice versa. Yet an A-expression can be part of a B-expression. 'John' is an A-expression; and 'is married to John' is a B-expression, for it introduces its term (being married to John) in the assertive style. Again, some of Frege's remarks about concepts and objects are readily intelligible, and even trivially true, on this interpretation. Thus an object may be just the term which an A-expression introduces. But a concept is never just the term which a B-expression introduces. For a B-expression does not *just* introduce a term, but introduces it in the verb-like, propositional style; and a concept, which is thought of as what a B-expression means, and *all* that it means, incorporates in itself just this style of introduction of the term which the B-expression introduces. Hence the apparent paradox that the concept *wise* is an object, not a concept. All this means is that the expression 'the concept *wise*' is an A-expression, not a B-expression, that what it introduces it does *not* introduce in the assertive style. Frege's concept is not what we use a B-expression to ascribe, but rather its use to ascribe what we use it to ascribe. Frege's concept is not a predicated term, but a predicative constituent. Even Frege's metaphors may now command our sympathy. He speaks of predicate-expressions, and of concepts, as 'incomplete' or 'unsaturated'. Ramsey mocked this description, which he found also in Russell, saying that there was no reason why one part of a proposition should be regarded as more incomplete than another: any *part* equally fails to be the whole. But we might now say, in defence of the metaphor, that the expressions 'smokes' and 'is wise' seem more incomplete than the expressions 'Socrates' and 'John', just because they are, in a sense, nearer completion. The name 'Socrates' might be completed into any kind of remark (or clause), not necessarily a proposition, or it might stand by itself as designating an item in a list; but the expression 'is wise' demands a certain kind of completion, namely completion into a proposition or propositional clause. The latter expression looks fragmentary just because it suggests a particular kind of completion; the former expression looks non-fragmentary just because it carries no such suggestion. And what holds for subject-and predicate-expressions holds also for objects and concepts; for the distinction between the latter exactly parallels that between the former.[4]

The present interpretation, then, seems to secure to our distinction some of the characteristics which are authoritatively attributed to it. Yet this interpretation also seems to expose our distinction to the assaults of a scepticism such as Ramsey's. Since both A-expressions and B-expressions introduce terms, and the difference is that B-expressions also carry the assertive indication, the propositional link, could we not undermine the whole distinction by merely making the propositional link something separate in the sentence, not part of a term-introducing expression? Could we not imagine at least simple sentences in which term-introducing expressions *merely* introduced terms, in no particular style, and in which the syntactical functions at present performed by variations in the style of term-introduction were allotted to linguistic devices other than term-introducing expressions? Should we not thereby undercut the subject–predicate distinction completely? So thinking, we echo (and perhaps amplify) Ramsey's remark that one has only to question, in order to doubt, the assumption that 'if a proposition consists of two terms copulated, the two terms must be functioning in different ways, one as subject, the other as predicate'. And when we think further of the grammatical sources of our distinction, we may recall another remark of Ramsey's: 'Let us remind ourselves that the task on which we are engaged is not merely one of English grammar; we are not schoolchildren, analysing sentences into subject, extension of the subject, complement and so on.'[5]

Let us first experiment with the suggestion that the propositional indication should be carried by something extraneous to any term-introducing expression in the sentence. Thus we might represent our sample assertion, 'Socrates is wise', by merely writing down two expressions,

---

[4] I do not claim that this paragraph represents 'what Frege really meant' by the remarks I allude to; only that it presents a way of harmonizing those remarks with a certain interpretation of the subject–predicate distinction.

[5] Ramsey, *The Foundations of Mathematics* [1925], pp. 116–17.

one to introduce each term (say, the expressions 'Socrates' and 'Wisdom'),[6] and then differentiating the result from a simple list, or a command, by means of an extraneous proposition-indicator: say, a bracket round the two expressions, thus:

(Socrates Wisdom).

So far, at least, there seems to be nothing wrong with the notation; the types of the terms safeguard us from any ambiguity. Now, from the vantage point of this suggestion, we can, it seems, regard as a mere alternative convention the ordinary grammatical technique of making one of the term-introducing expressions the carrier of the propositional indication. We could think of ourselves adopting the rule that, instead of representing the fact that we had an assertion (not a list, or a command) by means of a bracket round *both* of the term-introducing expressions, we should represent this fact by bracketing one and not the other. Consistently with the adoption of this rule, we could, by way of stylistic variety, allow ourselves the choice between

(Socrates) Wisdom

and

Socrates (Wisdom)

whereas

Socrates Wisdom

would be simply a list, and

(Socrates) (Wisdom)

would be just ungrammatical. Many doctrines about subjects and predicates could be re-expressed as very evident truths: e.g. the doctrine that bracketed expressions yield assertions when put alongside suitably chosen unbracketed expressions, or the doctrine that no unbracketed expression is bracketed (no subject-expression is a predicate-expression) or conversely.

---

[6] The expressions I here use are, of course, in fact (i.e. in English) nouns; but in a language of sentences such as those here imagined, there would be no basis for the *ordinary* grammatical classification of term-introducing words into nouns, verbs, adjectives, adverbs.

But what of the traditional doctrine that no particular can appear as a predicate? *Prime facie*, this doctrine would look like a proposal to adopt a totally arbitrary convention. It would be as if someone who used both the long-bracket and the short-bracket conventions should say: 'When using the short-bracket convention, always write the assertion

(Socrates Wisdom)

in the form

Socrates (Wisdom)

and never in the form

(Socrates) Wisdom

and observe a similar restriction for all expressions introducing particular terms; i.e. in general, the assertive symbolism is never to be applied to an expression merely introducing a particular.' Now, of course, a convention in itself arbitrary may acquire prestige through being long observed. It may come to seem part of the order of things, even expressive of a profound truth or necessity. So it might come to seem to people utterly senseless to write '(Socrates) Wisdom'; for, it might seem, an expression introducing a particular term just *cannot* have the assertive bracket put around it alone.

So much for the sceptical line of argument. It is important to note its limitations. At most, it shows that *if* we think of the subject–predicate distinction in a certain way, and *if* we confine our attention to a very simple kind of assertion, then—under these two conditions—the distinction between subject and predicate may seem a trivial and easily undermined affair, and, in particular, the doctrine that a particular can never appear as a predicate may seem to lack a rationale and express an arbitrary prejudice. The argument does not show that the doctrine would continue to appear in this light if either one of these two conditions were not fulfilled. Still, the limited point is worth making. For it at least shows that we must look for the rationale of the traditional doctrine, if it has one, outside these limits.[7]

---

[7] It might seem, for a moment, as if the procedure I have followed were exposed to the following objection: that in trying, as it were, to abolish the distinction between the noun-like and the verb-like parts of a simple statement, by separating the assertion-indicating function from the term-introducing function of the verb-like part, I have overlooked another

But where, outside these limits, shall we look? The subject–predicate distinction has so far been represented as essentially a distinction between styles of introduction of terms. It has been presented quite independently of any distinction between *types* or *categories* of terms, between *kinds* of object; and, hence, quite independently of the distinction between particulars and universals. But what if this procedure were fundamentally mistaken? We have to consider the possibility that it might indeed be a mistake, as Ramsey maintained, to try to *found* the particular–universal distinction on the subject–predicate distinction, but only because it was a deeper mistake to think that the subject–predicate distinction could be explained independently of the particular–universal distinction. The latter distinction might be the foundation of the former. So let us now change tack completely, and explore this possibility.

Subject and predicate: the 'category' criterion. Any term, particular or universal, must be capable of being introduced into a proposition, must be capable, that is, of being assertively tied to some other term or terms so as to yield a significant result. A term may be thought of as a principle of collection of those other terms to which it may be assertively tied so as to yield, not only a significant, but also a true, proposition. It is convenient to have, and we do have, names for different kinds of tie, based on differences in the types of the tied terms. Thus we use such forms as '... is characterized by ...', '... has the relation of ... to ...', etc. We must not think of such two- or three-place expressions as these, as themselves the names of terms. Something analogous to Bradley's argument against the reality of relations may be used, not indeed to show that relations are unreal, but to show that such assertible links between terms as these are not to be construed as ordinary relations. Let us speak of them as non-relational ties.[8]

Non-relational ties may bind particulars to universals; universals to universals; and particulars to particulars. Among those universals which apply to, or collect, particulars, I shall draw a rough distinction between

---

important function of the verb-like part, *viz.* that of indicating time, by means of variation in tense. I mention this objection only to pass it over; for it may be countered in many ways. It would be odd, even in practice, to use time-indication as a guide to the location of predicates. And there is nothing compelling in theory about the association of this function with a variation in the style of introduction of a particular range of terms.

[8] It will be noticed that I move from 'assert*ive* tying' to 'assert*ed* ties'. This move reveals the nature of the notions involved. Thus one who *characterizes* x as y (adjective) *asserts* that x *is characterized by* y (noun), and one who *instances* x as a y *asserts* that x *is an instance of* a y.

two types; and hence also between two kinds of non-relational tie which bind particulars and universals. This is the distinction between *sortal* and *characterizing* universals, and hence also between the sortal (or instantial) tie, and the characterizing tie. A sortal universal supplies of itself a principle for distinguishing and enumerating particulars which it collects. It presupposes no antecedent principle, or method, of individuating the particulars it collects. Characterizing universals, on the other hand, whilst they supply principles of grouping, even of counting, particulars, supply such principles only for particulars already distinguished, or distinguishable, in accordance with some antecedent principle or method. Roughly, and with reservations, certain common nouns for particulars introduce sortal universals, verbs and adjectives applicable to particulars introduce characterizing universals. Now it is not only characterizing universals which have the power to supply principles of grouping for particulars already distinguishable in accordance with some other principle or method. This power they share with particulars themselves. Thus, just as among particulars already distinguished as (historical) utterances (or catches at cricket), we may further group together those which are wise utterances (or difficult catches), so among such particulars we may further group together those which are Socrates' utterances (or Carr's catches). Socrates, like wisdom, may serve as a principle of grouping of particulars already distinguished as such in accordance with some other principle or method. I shall accordingly assume the right to speak of non-relational ties between particulars and particulars; and to this kind of tie I shall, in memory of Cook Wilson, give the name, 'the attributive tie'. In general, whenever a particular is bound to a universal by the characterizing tie, we can frame the idea of another particular bound to the first by the attributive tie; so to the characterizing tie between Socrates and the universal, *dying*, there corresponds the attributive tie between Socrates and the particular, his death.

Let us now compare the ways in which terms may collect each other by these three kinds of tie.

(1) One and the same particular may be sortally or instantly tied to a number of different sortal universals: thus Fido is a dog, an animal, a terrier. In general, the universals to which one and the same particular is sortally tied will have a characteristic relation to each other, which is sometimes described as that of sub- or super-ordination. Again, one and the same sortal universal may be instantially tied to a number of different particulars: Fido, Coco, and Rover are all dogs. Such particulars will have to each

other a general, or sortal, resemblance. We may say that while one particular may collect several universals by the instantial tie, and one universal may collect many particulars by the instantial tie, the principle of collection in each case is of quite a different kind. We may mark this difference by employing, in addition to the symmetrical form, 'x is instantially tied to y' (where x or y can be either particular or universal, so long as one is each), also the asymmetrical form, 'x is an instance of y' (where x must be particular and y universal).

(2) One and the same particular may be tied by a characterizing tie to many characterizing universals: thus Socrates is wise, is warm, is cold, fights, talks, dies. And one and the same characterizing universal may be tied by a characterizing tie to many different particulars: Socrates, Plato, Aristotle are all wise, all die. Via the characterizing tie, again, then, one particular collects (at different times) many universals, and one universal (at different times) many particulars. But again the principle of collection is different in each case. The principle on which one particular collects different characterizing universals at different times is supplied by the continuing identity of the particular (in which the most widely and generally, though not universally, distinguishable factor is what is vaguely referred to as spatio-temporal continuity); the principle on which one characterizing universal collects different particulars, at the same or different times, involves a certain characteristic resemblance between those particulars at those times. We may mark this difference by adding to the symmetrical phrase, 'x is joined by a characterizing tie to y', the asymmetrical phrase, 'x is characterized by y' (where x must be particular and y universal).

(3) When we come to consider the attributive tie, there is a difference in the situation. A given particular, say Socrates, may collect, by the characterizing tie, an enormous number of characterizing universals; correspondingly it may collect, by the attributive tie, an enormous number of particulars. Thus Socrates collects, by the characterizing tie, say *smiling* and *orating*, and correspondingly, by the attributive tie, a particular smile and a particular oration. But whereas the universals, *smiling* and *orating*, can collect, by the characterizing tie, any number of particulars of the same kind as Socrates, the particular smile and the particular oration cannot, by the attributive tie, collect any other particulars of the same kind as Socrates. Let us express this feature of attributive ties by speaking of the dependent member and the independent member of any such tie: the independent member may in general collect many particulars similar to

the dependent member, but the dependent member cannot collect any other particulars similar to the independent member. In addition to the symmetrical form, 'x is attributively tied to y', we may employ the asymmetrical form, 'y is attributed to x' (where y must be the dependent member).[9]

The object of this discussion of different kinds of non-relational ties was to prepare the ground for setting up another criterion for the subject–predicate distinction. Now there is an obvious analogy between the ways in which sortal and characterizing universals respectively collect the particulars they collect. This analogy does not extend to the ways in which particulars collect universals by instantial or characterizing ties; nor does it extend to the ways in which particulars collect other particulars by the attributive tie. Suppose now, on the strength of these analogies and disanalogies, we adopt the following ruling: the primary sense of 'y is predicated of x' is 'x is asserted to be non-relationally tied to y either as an instance of y or as characterized by y'. In view of the senses we have given to 'is an instance of' and 'is characterized by', this amounts to *ruling* that universals can be predicated of particulars, but not particulars of universals. The next step is to extend the sense of 'y is predicated of x', while preserving the analogies on which the primary sense is based. Thus, to allow that universals may be predicated of universals, we have to show that there are non-relational ties between universals and universals analogous to the characterizing or sortal ties between universals and particulars. And, of course, it is easy to find such analogies. Is not thinking of different species as species of one genus analogous to thinking of different particulars as specimens of one species? Again, the tie between different musical compositions, themselves non-particulars (types), and their common form (say, the sonata or the symphony) is analogous to the sortal tie between a particular and a universal. Or again, thinking of different hues

---

[9] There are some particulars which are the independent members of all the attributive ties they enter into. These may be called, simply, independent particulars. Aristotle seems to have thought that the only independent particulars (of at all a familiar kind) were fairly substantial things like horses and men. But there seems no reason for denying that some phenomena or occurrences less substantial than these may also rank as independent particulars. No doubt there will be borderline cases, i.e. cases where we should hesitate between saying that one particular is dependently attributed to another and saying that it is genuinely (e.g. causally) related to another. But it seems difficult to force the border quite as far as Aristotle would wish in the direction of the satisfyingly substantial particular; unless indeed we reinforce the present notion of an independent particular with further criteria (a procedure which has much to recommend it on other, though connected, grounds).

(colours) as bright or sombre, thinking of different human qualities as amiable or unamiable, is analogous to thinking of different particulars as characterized in such-and-such ways. In all these cases we think of universals collecting other universals in ways analogous to the ways in which universals collect those particulars which are instances of them or are characterized by them. But we cannot think of particulars collecting *either* universals *or* other particulars in ways at all analogous to these. A further slight extension of the sense of 'y is predicated of x' is required, to allow for the doctrine that particulars, though not simply predicable, may be parts of what is predicated. This may be most readily secured by a slight modification of the rules for 'is an instance of' and 'is characterized by'. The phrases, 'is an instance of' and 'is characterized by', as I have introduced them, are properly followed by, respectively, the designation of a sortal universal and the designation of a characterizing universal. We now rule that so long as the proper successors of these phrases are present, the principles of grouping which they introduce may be further modified in any way whatsoever, without detriment to the appropriateness of 'is an instance of' or 'is characterized by'. Thus one particular may be an instance, not only of a smile, but of a smile of Socrates, and another may be characterized, not only by being married, but by being married to John. So Socrates and John may be part of what is predicated, though not themselves predicable.

In this way, by taking as the fundamental case of y being predicated of x, the case in which x (a particular) is asserted either to be an instance of, or to be characterized by, y (a universal), and by proceeding thence to develop other cases by analogy or extension, we can build up a sense of 'to predicate' for which it is true that universals can both be simply predicated and have things predicated of them (i.e. be subjects), whereas particulars can never be simply predicated, though they can have things predicated of them (i.e. be subjects) and can be parts of what is predicated.

This procedure, then, yields us the second, or 'categorial', criterion for the subject–predicate distinction. In developing the first, or 'grammatical', criterion, I made no use of any distinction between types of terms, but concentrated solely on the presence or absence of the propositional symbolism, i.e. of the propositional style of term-introduction. In developing the categorial criterion, on the other hand, I make no reference to the location of the assertive symbolism, but build up the criterion solely on the basis of a distinction between types of terms. To all appearance, therefore, the two criteria are independent of each other. We must now enquire how far there is, in practice, a correspondence between what is predicated in the sense of the first criterion, and what is predicated in the sense of the second; and then seek to explain the degree of correspondence we find.

Tensions and affinities between these criteria. That the correspondence works well in general is obvious enough. It is all the more instructive to consider certain special cases, where tension develops between the grammatical and categorial requirements for a predicate, and where we find a rather remarkable linguistic resolution of the tension. We approach these cases indirectly, by way of some cases where there is no such tension.

Among characteristic linguistic forms of grammatically predicative expression are the following: an indicative form of a verb; an adjective preceded by an indicative form of the verb 'to be'; a noun preceded by the indefinite article preceded by an indicative form of the verb 'to be'. Thus we have 'Socrates smiles', 'Socrates is wise', 'Socrates is a philosopher'. In each of these examples a predicated universal is introduced by one of the characteristic linguistic forms. Both the categorial test and the grammatical test for what is predicated yield the same answer. In so far as these two tests are always to yield the same answer, we might expect that proper names of particulars would never admit of appearance in any of these simple forms. In practice, of course, we find that names of particulars admit quite freely of adjectival forms which can follow the verb 'to be': e.g. 'is English, Victorian, Napoleonic, American, Russellian, Christian, Aristotelian', etc.; they admit fairly freely of use as nouns after the indefinite article and the verb 'to be': e.g. 'is a Hitler, a Quisling' etc.; and they even sometimes admit of a verb-form: e.g. it might be jocularly said of a philosopher that he Platonizes a good deal. These cases, however, present no difficulty for one who wishes to insist on the correspondence between the category requirements and the grammatical requirements for predicates. Suppose 'N' is the relevant proper name of a particular. Then it does not generally seem that we use the forms 'x is N-ic (N-ian)', 'x is an N', 'x N-izes', to assert a non-relational tie between x and N. What, in such cases, the grammatical predicate-expression introduces and assertively links to x is not just the particular, N, but either a characterizing or sortal universal to which the particular has, for historical reasons, given its name (e.g. *being Napoleonic*) or one of those compounds of relational universal and particular which the extended category criterion allows us to count as predicable (e.g. in some contexts, 'being American' has the force of 'being manufactured in America' and 'being British' means 'being subject to the sovereign of Great Britain').

The point here is that language freely allows the use of proper names of particulars in simple grammatically predicative forms, just in those cases where the use of these forms has no tendency to make us say that we are predicating the particular; in the cases, in fact, where we can say that the term introduced by the grammatically predicative expression is a universal or a universal-cum-particular. Should anyone object to the use of the word 'universal' here, we can say instead: the principle of collection supplied in such a case by, e.g. Napoleon, is a resemblance principle of the kind which universals supply, and not a principle of the kind which the continuing identity of a particular supplies. The non-relational tie asserted by 'The gesture was Napoleonic' is a characterizing tie rather than an attributive tie: the things asserted to be bound by the tie are not the gesture and Napoleon, but the gesture and the resemblance principle of collection supplied by Napoleon. Generally, we are prepared to use such predicate-forms as 'is Napoleonic' only when we can regard Napoleon as supplying a principle of collection at least analogous to those supplied by universals. Thus the analogy on which our category-notion of predication is built up is preserved.

But now let us compare cases where we are prepared to use these forms with cases where we are strikingly unprepared to use them. Let us take first Ramsey's pair of sentences:

(1) Socrates is wise
(2) Wisdom is a characteristic of Socrates.

We should notice, first, that if we start off with the substantive, 'wisdom', to say what (1) says, then we do *not* proceed to 'is Socratic' or 'Socratizes', but proceed instead somewhat as in (2). Now the category test and the grammatical test alike require us to say of (1) that wisdom is predicated of Socrates, the subject of the predication. The category test seems to require us to say exactly the same thing of (2). For both sentences assert (do they not?) a characterizing tie binding the particular, Socrates, and the universal, wisdom. The grammatical test does not require us to say the same thing of (2). But language safeguards us from having, on this test, to say the *opposite* thing (i.e. that Socrates is predicated of wisdom) by introducing, as it were, a dummy universal, *being a characteristic (of)*. If we take this at its face value, we are able, adhering to the grammatical test, to purchase immunity from saying that Socrates is predicated of wisdom, and to say instead that what is predicated of wisdom is the compound of universal and particular, *viz. being a characteristic of Socrates*. What we find here is, as it were, an anxiety to preserve the grammatical predicate-place for the categorially predicable, even at the cost of faking universals to keep up appearances. For the general grammatical requirements of verb-like plus substantival elements would be satisfied by writing (2) in a form, such as 'Wisdom is Socratic (Socratizes)', which, since it interposes no dummy universal, would, on the grammatical criterion, require us to say that Socrates is predicated and would thus lead to an overt clash between the grammatical criterion and the category criterion.

Why do I speak of *faking* universals to avoid the overt clash? The answer lies in the previous section. But a part of it is obvious enough, if we ask why we do not similarly insist on

Socrates is characterized by wisdom

instead of

Socrates is wise.

To any such insistence we could raise an objection. It is a necessary feature of any term, particular or universal or particular-cum-universal, that it is capable of entering into a non-relational tie with (some) other terms, and any subject–predicate proposition is an assertion of a non-relational tie between terms. If we promote the tie to a term, or a part of a term, then we must regard the proposition as asserting a non-relational tie between the new terms, e.g. *Socrates*, and *being characterized by wisdom*. But if we *insist* on the promotion at the first stage, why not at the second, thus: 'Socrates is characterized by being characterized by wisdom'? And so on. We must stop at some point if we are to have a proposition. Why insist on starting?

But does not the same objection apply to the insistence on (2) as an alternative to 'Wisdom Socratizes'? It would, of course, apply, if we discounted the reason, the motive, for the preference. But we cannot discount it: the question of justification (explanation) of the drive to keep up appearances is still *sub judice*. Besides, we have an alternative way, permitted by the grammatical criterion, of looking at the matter. We can construe 'Wisdom is a characteristic of' as predicate-expression, and 'Socrates' as subject-expression, and see the whole sentence, not as an insisted-on alternative to 'Wisdom Socratizes', but as a permitted periphrasis for 'Socrates is wise'. But if we make this choice, then we must be clear that the other analysis which the grammatical criterion leaves open (*viz.* Subject: 'Wisdom'; Predicate: 'is a characteristic of Socrates') is no longer admitted to be an open alternative at all. That is, we must give up, grammar notwithstanding, the ambition so to frame this proposition that wisdom appears as a subject.

Faced with (2), then, either we can take the grammatical criterion at its face value, call 'wisdom' a subject-expression and then note that, in order to keep in line with the category criterion, we have to fake the dummy universal, *being a characteristic (of)*; or we can keep in line without faking anything—but in that case we have directly to strengthen the grammatical criterion with the category criterion and say that, appearances notwithstanding, no analysis of (2) is permissible which makes 'wisdom' the subject-expression.

Let us consider now another set of cases, in some respects analogous, in others more complicated. Sometimes, if we asked which of the kinds of non-relational tie I have distinguished was actually asserted by a proposition, the natural answer would be the attributive tie. But this seems to raise difficulties. For since the grammatically predicative expression carries the assertive symbolism and introduces a term, and is completed into an assertion by the subject-expression which also introduces a term, we should expect the respective terms these two expressions introduce to be precisely those which are asserted to be joined by whatever non-relational tie a proposition asserts to obtain. But the attributive tie joins only particulars to particulars. So, if the foregoing reasoning is sound, then in the assertion of attributive ties either nothing appears as a predicate or a particular does. But the idea that nothing appears as a predicate goes against the grammatical requirements, and the idea that a particular appears as a predicate goes against the category requirements. How does language deal with this situation? We are concerned, it must be remembered, with assertions in which one particular is asserted to be attributively tied to another, in which, as we sometimes actually say, one particular is attributed to another.

Examples of sentences of this kind are:

The blow which blinded John *was struck by* Peter.
The catch which got Compton out *was made by* Carr.[10]

---

[10] Sometimes the genitive case is used in such constructions: thus, 'The blow was Peter's', 'The catch was Carr's'.

The particulars asserted to be attributively tied are the blow and Peter in one case, the catch and Carr in the other. And appearances are this time saved by promoting the tie between the particular action and the particular agent into a quasi-relational-universal. The general scheme of such sentences is roughly:

The particular action—is performed/executed/done by—the particular agent.

It is easy to see that the would-be relational universal is no such thing, no genuine term. We cannot, for example, form a further term by compounding the particular action with the quasi-universal. The agent and his action are two different particulars; but his action and his doing of his action are not two different particulars. As before, if we insist, for its own sake, on the erection of tie into term at one stage, why not at another, i.e. why not insist on moving to 'The doing of the action—was executed by—the agent', and so on?

It might seem that, again as before, we have available another way of looking at these sentences. Must we see them as supplying dummy universals to keep up the façade of agreement between the grammatical requirements and the category requirements for a predicate? Can we not see them as permitted periphrases for sentences which raise no such problem, i.e. for sentences which are not naturally seen as assertions of attributive ties at all? In some simple cases, this choice is obviously open: e.g. 'He effected his escape' is simply a periphrastic way of saying 'He escaped'. And it is true that sentences are available which are, in a broad sense, variants on our problem sentences. Thus we can say: 'Compton was caught out by Carr', and 'John was blinded by being struck by Peter'. But do these sentences do quite the same job as the problem sentences? We can *speak* them so that they do—by stressing 'Carr' in one and 'Peter' in the other. The point is that the grammatical structure of the problem sentences is appropriate to the cases where the corresponding assertions carry certain presuppositions: that there was a catch which got Compton out, a blow which blinded John. The structure of the variant sentences is not similarly appropriate to these cases, though the force of presupposition can be preserved by suitable stressing of elements in the variant sentences. This means that there is a certain strain in construing the problem sentences as permitted periphrases for other sentences, sentences in which 'The blow which blinded John' and 'The catch which got Compton out' do not appear as claimants for the position of subject-expression. It is not merely whim which induces us to cast the terms these phrases introduce for the role of subjects of predication. In this fact we may detect the germ of another criterion for the subject–predicate distinction, a criterion which may turn out to form a bridge between those other two whose real and feigned correspondences we have been considering. This idea I shall develop in the next two sections.

I have described my examples crudely and questionably enough, and there is, I think, a rich field of interesting matter here towards which I have only gestured. What is, I think, unquestionable is that these examples show (to speak metaphorically) a kind of effort on the part of language to keep, or to seem to keep, in line two criteria for something being predicated, or appearing as a predicate: the grammatical criterion, according to which that which is predicated is introduced by a part of the sentence which carries assertive symbolism; and the category criterion according to which only universals, or complexes containing universals, never particulars *simpliciter*, can be predicated. It is as if there were felt to be a certain appropriateness in these two criteria corresponding, yielding the same result. It is the tendency which I thus metaphorically speak of in terms of effort or feeling, which we now have to try to explain.

The conditions of introduction of particular terms and universal terms into propositions. I think it is possible to explain this association, this affinity which the grammatical criterion and the category criterion appear to have for each other. I think, too, that the general lines of at least part of the explanation are clear and indisputable. The detailed elaboration of this part, however, seems to me a matter of great difficulty and complexity. Since I must be brief, what I say will necessarily be sketchy and incomplete.

Part of the answer to our question is to be found in a contrast between the conditions of introducing particular and universal terms respectively into propositions. The notion of term-introduction, which I have used throughout, is, of course, neutral as between the introduction of a term as a subject of predication and the introduction of a term as predicated. *But term-introduction, in either mode, essentially involves the idea of identification.* The term-introducing expression indicates, or is meant to indicate, what term (*which* particular, *which* universal) is introduced by its means. When we say 'John smokes', the first expression indicates what particular it is that is referred to, the second expression indicates what characteristic it is that is ascribed to him.

Let us first consider the conditions of introducing a particular into a proposition; and here I shall temporarily revert, for the sake of its familiarity, to the non-neutral terminology of 'referring'. We are to enquire into the conditions which must be satisfied in order for it to be the case that an identifying reference to a particular is made by a speaker and correctly understood by a hearer. One condition, evidently, is that there should be a particular which the speaker is referring to; another is that there should be a particular which the hearer takes him to be referring to; a third is that the speaker's particular should be identical with the hearer's. Let us pay attention to the first of these conditions. What does it involve? (What is concealed by the phrase, 'to which he is referring'?) Well, at least it involves this requirement, that (in the standard case—we need not consider others) there should be a particular answering to the description used by the speaker, if he uses a description. What if he uses a name? One cannot significantly use a name to refer to someone or something unless one knows who or what it is that one is referring to by that name. One must, in other words, be prepared to substitute a description for the name. So the case of name-using calls for only a minor modification of the condition stated. There must be a particular answering to the description which the speaker uses, or to the description which he is prepared to substitute for the name he uses, if he uses a name. But this condition is not enough. He is referring to just one particular. If we abstract from the force of the definite article in a given speech-situation, there may be many particulars which are fitted by the description the speaker uses or the description he would substitute for the name he uses. Of course the speaker, rightly, relies heavily on the context of the speech-situation. He says no more than is necessary. But we are now considering, not simply what he says, but the conditions of his doing what he does by what he says. For him to be referring to just one particular, it is not enough that there should be at least one particular which his description fits. There must be *at most* one such particular *which he has in mind*. But he cannot, for himself, distinguish the particular which he has in mind by the fact that it is the one he has in mind. So there must be some description he could give, though it need not be the description he does give, which applies uniquely to the one he has in mind and does not include the phrase, 'the one I have in mind'.[11] It might be maintained that this remark requires qualification by the addition of some such phrase as 'as far as he knows' after 'uniquely'; and this on the ground that the speaker's subsequent knowledge might embrace a second and distinguishable particular which, however, also answered to any putatively identifying description which he was able to give at the time of the original putative reference. But this argument is mistaken. If the situation as described should really arise (it would be a rare, but not impossible, one), then it would follow that the speaker really did not know at the time of the original putative reference what particular he was speaking of, that he really did not satisfy the conditions of making a genuine identifying reference, though he thought he did; for there would now be no answer to the question, *which* particular he was then referring to. If, on the other hand, he can now answer this question, then it follows that he could then have supplied some detail which would differentiate the particular referred to from the one his subsequent knowledge embraces, i.e. the situation as described would not really have arisen.

We may summarize all this by saying that in order for an identifying reference to a particular to be made, there must be some true empirical proposition known (in some not too exacting sense of this word) to the speaker, to the effect that there is just one particular which answers to a certain description. *Mutatis mutandis*, a similar condition must be satisfied for a hearer, in order for it to be the case that there is some particular which the hearer takes the speaker to be referring to. (The third condition of those I listed requires, not indeed that the speaker's and hearer's descriptions should be identical, but that each description should apply—uniquely—to one and the same particular.)

I have been using the terminology of identifying reference for the sake of its familiarity and convenience. We can substitute the neutral

---

[11] Such a description (call it an 'identifying description') may, of course, include demonstrative elements, i.e. it need not be framed in purely general terms. In general, indeed, it could not be so framed; it is impossible, in general, to free the identification of particulars from all dependence upon demonstratively indicatable features of the situation of reference. It should be added, moreover, that the identifying description, though it must not include a reference to the speaker's own reference to the particular in question, may include a reference to another's reference to that particular. If a putatively identifying description is of this latter kind, then, indeed, the question, whether it is a genuinely identifying description, turns on the question, whether the reference it refers to is itself a genuinely identifying reference. So one reference may borrow its credentials, as a genuinely identifying reference, from another; and that from another. But this regress is not infinite.

terminology of term-introduction without in any way altering the substance of what has been said.

Let us now enquire what similar conditions, if any, must be satisfied in order for a universal term (*such as particulars may either by characterized by, or be instances of*) to be successfully introduced into a proposition. *We find that there are no such parallel conditions which can be generally insisted on.* Suppose there is an adjectival form of expression, 'ϕ', for the universal in question. We are to look for some empirical proposition, if any can be found, which must be true in order for the universal term putatively introducible by 'ϕ' to be introduced at all. A sufficient condition of its introducibility would be the truth, known to the speaker, of the general empirical proposition that *something or other is ϕ*. But this cannot be generally insisted on as a necessary condition. For another equally sufficient condition, indeed one that is satisfied in the case of some universals, would be the truth of the empirical proposition that *nothing is ϕ*. If we form the disjunction of these two sufficient conditions, we may indeed be said to obtain a necessary condition: *viz.* that *either something is ϕ or nothing is ϕ*. But now we no longer have an empirical proposition, a fact about the world. We have a tautology.

It might be objected that we can find an empirical condition of the successful introduction of the universal term by means of the expression 'ϕ': *viz.* the condition that the proposition expressed in the words, 'something is ϕ' is, whether true or false, a significant empirical proposition, and is unambiguously understood by both speaker and hearer. But now the condition is in no sense parallel to, or on the same level as, that which we found to be necessary for the introduction of a particular. The required fact is not, in the required sense, a fact about the world. It is a fact about language. Parallels for it, i.e. facts about the significance and understanding of the words used, could be mentioned for the case of particular-introduction; but no parallel to the additional empirical requirements for the case of particular-introduction can be generally found for the case of universal-introduction.

It might again be objected that, in practice, empirical propositions of the form, 'something is ϕ', would not acquire their significance unless at least a preponderant proportion of them were also true. Therefore, it might be argued, the contrast between the conditions of particular-introduction and the conditions of universal-introduction is by no means as marked as I have claimed. The situation is, rather, that the introduction of a particular term universally presupposes, whilst the introduction of a universal term in general presupposes, the truth of some empirical proposition. But to this objection (apart from any cavils about the structure of the argument) there are two replies, of which the second, at least, is decisive.

The first reply consists in emphasizing differences between the kinds of presupposed empirical propositions. The kind of proposition the truth of which is universally required for the introduction of a particular term is a kind of proposition which states a quite definite fact about the world, something that might, as it were, belong to history. But the kind of proposition the truth of which may, in general, though not universally, be required for universal-introduction to be possible is a quite indefinite sort of proposition, the fact it states is a quite indefinite sort of fact. That something, somewhere, at some time, is or was red, or round, or wise, is not a fact which could belong to history.

The second reply nullifies the effect of the objection altogether. It is not only universally necessary that an empirical proposition of a sharply definite kind should be true in order for the introduction of a particular to be effected. It is also necessary for a proposition of that kind to be known to be true. For only so are the conditions of identifying reference to just one particular fulfilled; only so are the conditions of identification, on the speaker's or the hearer's part, fulfilled. Consider now how different it is with universal-introduction. It may be the case that the words used for identifying the universal terms introduced could acquire their meaning only if most of the universals so introduced were in fact instantiated. But once the words have acquired their meaning, however they acquire it, it is by no means necessary, in order for them to perform the function of identifying the universal term they introduce, that their users should know or believe empirical propositions to the effect that the universal terms in question are in fact instantiated. The users *will* generally know, or think, this. But *that* they should, is not a necessary condition of the expressions in question performing their identifying function. All that is necessary is that the users should know *what* the expressions mean, not *that* they acquired their meaning in virtue of the truth of some empirical proposition.

The vital contrast, then, may be summarily stated as follows. The identifying introduction of either a particular or a universal into discourse entails knowing what particular or what universal is meant (intended to be introduced) by the introducing expression. Knowing what particular is meant entails knowing (or, sometimes—in the case of the hearer—

learning, from the introducing expression used) some empirical fact which suffices to identify that particular, other than the fact that it is the particular currently being introduced. But knowing what universal is meant does not in the same way entail knowing any empirical fact: it merely entails knowing the language. (This is a *very* summary statement; it should not be regarded as a substitute for what it summarizes.)

But now a qualification must be made. I have said that it is a universally necessary condition of the introduction of any particular term into discourse, that there should exist, and be known, a true empirical proposition of a certain very definite kind, whereas it is not a necessary condition of the introduction of a universal term into discourse that there should exist, and be known, a true empirical proposition of any parallel kind. The qualification concerns the way in which the universal term is introduced. For if the universal term is introduced, not by means of some expression which identifies the universal term in virtue of its meaning, but by means of some expression which gives a description of the universal, then, indeed, for the introduction to be successfully so effected, it may be necessary that some empirical proposition is true. Thus the universal term, wisdom, may be introduced, not by means of the adjective, 'wise', or the substantive, 'wisdom', but by such a description as 'the quality most frequently attributed to Socrates in philosophical examples'. Or, again, a type of illness might be introduced, not as, say, 'influenza', but as 'the disease which kept John from work last week'. For this method of introduction to be successful, it must indeed be the case that there was a disease, just one disease, which, last week, kept John from work. The importance of this qualification will emerge shortly. It obviously does not contradict the main thesis, which, in the case of universal terms, has the form of the denial of a universal proposition.

Particulars the paradigm logical subjects. Now let us cease, for a moment, to speak of particulars and universals, and speak instead, and in general, of this distinction between: (1) expressions such that one cannot know what they introduce without knowing (or learning from their use) some distinguishing empirical fact about what they introduce; (2) expressions such that one can very well know what they introduce without knowing any distinguishing empirical fact about what they introduce. Both kinds of expression are in a certain sense incomplete. For introducing a term is not making a statement; it is only *a part* of making a statement. Yet expressions of the first kind have evidently a completeness, a self-sufficiency, which expressions of the second kind lack. Of expressions of class (1), one might say: although they do not explicitly state facts, they perform their role only because they present or represent facts, only because they presuppose, or embody, or covertly carry, propositions which they do not explicitly affirm. They necessarily carry a weight of fact in introducing their terms. But expressions of class (2) carry no weight of fact in introducing their terms. They can only *help* to carry a fact, and even this they can do—unless they form a part of a class (1)—only by being coupled with some other expression into an *explicit* assertion.

Let us now recall the grammatical criterion for a predicate-expression. The predicate-expression introduces its term in the coupling, propositional style, in the explicitly incomplete style which demands completion into an assertion. Now surely the manifest incompleteness of the assertive style of introduction—the demand to be completed into an assertion—answers exactly to the incompleteness of the second of the two kinds of expression I have just distinguished; it answers exactly to the failure of this kind of expression to present a fact on its own account. We have a contrast between something which in no sense presents a fact in its own right (but is a candidate for being part of a statement of fact), and something which does already in a sense present a fact in its own right (and is also a candidate for being part of a statement of fact). It is appropriate enough that in the explicit assertion constituted by both taken together, it should be the former which carries the propositional symbolism, the symbolism that demands completion into an assertion.

What we here propose, in effect, is a new, or mediating, criterion for the subject–predicate distinction. A subject-expression is one which, in a sense, presents a fact in its own right and is to that extent complete. A predicate-expression is one which in no sense presents a fact in its own right, and is to that extent incomplete. And we find that the new criterion harmonizes admirably with the grammatical criterion. The predicate-expression, on the new criterion, is one that can be completed only by explicit coupling with another. The predicate-expression, on the grammatical criterion, is precisely the expression which carries the symbolism demanding completion into an explicit assertion. We emphasize the harmony, the affinity, of these two criteria; and by fusing them, we return to and enrich, that contrast between the 'complete' and the 'incomplete' parts of the sentence which we discussed in expounding the 'grammatical' sense of the subject–predicate distinction. We find an additional depth in Frege's metaphor of the saturated and the unsaturated constituents.[12]

Not only does the new criterion harmonize admirably with the grammatical distinction. It also harmonizes, as the whole of the preceding section shows, with the category criterion. For, in the first place, the whole burden of that section was that particular-introducing expressions can never be incomplete in the sense of the new criterion, and thus can never be predicate-expressions on that criterion. This is part of what the category criterion requires. In the second place, it was shown in that section that universal-introducing expressions can be, and often are, incomplete in the sense of the new criterion, and thus can be, and often are, predicate-expressions; but also that universal-introducing expressions, when (e.g.) they identify the universal terms they introduce by description and not by meaning alone, can be complete in the sense of the new criterion, and thus can be, and sometimes are, subjects. This is the rest of what the category criterion requires.

These considerations seem to me to explain, at least in part, the affinity between the grammatical criterion and the category criterion for subjects and predicates. They explain, or help to explain, the traditional, persistent link in our philosophy between the particular–universal distinction and the subject–predicate (reference–predication) distinction. When once that association has been firmly established, and explained, at a fundamental level, we can allow a certain flexibility to enter our classifications at a more sophisticated level. Thus, in the statement, 'Generosity is a more amiable virtue than prudence', may we not want to say that generosity and prudence appear as subjects, and the universal-characterizing universal, *being a more amiable virtue (than)*, appears as a predicate? Yet the expressions, 'generosity' and 'prudence', do not possess the kind of completeness which our mediating criterion requires of subject-expressions: they identify their terms by meaning alone, they do not covertly present any fact. The solution of this problem is that, once the fundamental association has been made, the analogies I spoke of earlier may be allowed to carry the burden of further extensions of the problematic distinction. The analogies I mean in this case are those that hold between non-relational

---

[12] I do not say there are not further depths. At no point do I claim to be *interpreting* Frege.

(characterizing) ties binding particulars and universals on the one hand, and non-relational ties binding universals and universals on the other.

This is but one case, and a simple one. There are others, requiring different treatment, which I shall not now discuss. But there is one further piece of explanation which must be given. Another persistent element in the traditional theory is the doctrine that expressions introducing complex terms such as I have referred to as 'universals-cum-particulars', may be classified as predicate-expressions (e.g. 'is married to John'). Yet do not such expressions, by virtue of containing a part which introduces a particular, possess the completeness which—making all allowance for flexibility—I must presumably insist on counting as a disqualification for the status of predicate? The answer is that such expressions do not themselves, as wholes, possess this completeness, though each contains a part which does. The expression 'is married to John' does not, *as a whole*, present any fact; for it performs its term-identifying function just as successfully if no one is married to John as it does if someone is married to John. The expression 'John' carries, in use, its own presupposition of fact; but the expression 'is married to John' carries no further presupposition of fact of *its* own. All *it* presupposes is the tautology that either someone is married to John or no one is. So such complex expressions, taken as a whole, have the incompleteness that qualifies them to rank as predicates.

The general account I have sketched raises many more questions and problems than I have now space to consider. I shall conclude by referring briefly to one or two of these.

In the first place, the crucial idea of completeness remains vague. I have spoken of term-introducing expressions which are complete in the relevant sense as presenting or representing facts, or as presupposing or embodying or covertly carrying propositions. The variety of terminology may well seem suspicious. What precise account can be given of the relations between term-introducing expressions which are, in the relevant sense, complete, and the facts or propositions which confer upon them their completeness? How is the content of these facts or propositions determined by, or otherwise related to, the actual term-introducing expression used?

The variety of cases is too great to allow of a single answer to this question. In certain simple cases, the answer is simple enough. Suppose I say, pointing, 'That person there can direct you.' The expression, 'That person there', introduces (identifies) a particular. It is clear enough both what the fact is upon which the term-introduction rests, and what its relation is to the words used. The term-distinguishing fact is that there is just one person there, where I am pointing; if there is no one at whom I could be taken to be pointing, my putatively term-introducing expression fails of a reference and my statement fails of a truth value. In such cases, then, we have a clear enough sense of presupposition, and a clear enough indication of what is presupposed by the use of the term-introducing expression. But now consider a less simple case. What if our term-introducing expression is the proper name (ordinarily so-called) of a particular? Clearly it is not required, for term-introduction by such means, that there should be just one object or person which bears the name. Nor can we be satisfied, in the present context, with the answer that the presupposed fact is the fact that there is just one object or person which both bears the name and is being currently referred to by its means. For—to consider the case of the speaker alone—the previous argument requires the 'presupposed' fact to be some true empirical proposition known to the speaker which he might cite in order to indicate *which* particular he has in mind; and this cannot be the fact that there is just one he has in mind. But now if we find a fact which answers to this specification (i.e. which might serve to distinguish the one he has in mind), there is no longer any guarantee that the fact we find can be said to be presupposed, by the statement containing the term-introducing expression, in the simple sense of presupposition which we have just seen illustrated in the case of the statement beginning 'That person there'. It might, for example, be the case that there is just one child whom I saw before breakfast yesterday, and this might be the child whom I currently refer to as 'John'. But it will certainly not be the case that just this existential fact is presupposed, in the sense illustrated, by the statement I currently make about John.

Nevertheless I think it would be a mistake to conclude that the notion of presupposition is irrelevant to our question in the case of names. Consider the situation in which a reference is made, by name, to Socrates. By the argument of the previous section, both speaker and hearer, in this situation, satisfy the conditions for successful term-introduction if each knows some distinguishing fact or facts (not necessarily the same ones) about Socrates, facts which each is prepared to cite to indicate whom he now means, or understands, by 'Socrates'. But what is the relation between these facts and the name? Or, to put what is really the same question in another form, what are the conditions of my correctly describing them as 'facts about Socrates', where I use, and do not mention, the name? It is in relation to this question that the notion of presupposition is once more relevant. (Here I try to summarize a thesis which has been well argued by Mr. John Searle.[13]) Suppose we take a group of speakers who use, or think they use, the name 'Socrates' with the same reference. Suppose we then ask each member of the group to write down what he considers to be the salient facts about Socrates, and then form from these lists of facts a composite description incorporating the most frequently mentioned facts. Now it would be too much to say that the success of term-introduction within the group by means of the name requires that there should exist just one person of whom all the propositions in the composite description are true. But it would not be too much to say that it requires that there should exist one and only one person of whom some reasonable proportion of these propositions are true. If, for example, it should be found that there was just one person of whom half the propositions were jointly true, and just one person, a different one, of whom the other half of the propositions were jointly true, then, unless some indication were given of which Socrates was meant, it would become impossible to give a straightforward answer to the question, whether any particular 'proposition about Socrates' were true or false. It is true, perhaps, of Socrates$_1$ and not of Socrates$_2$. It is neither true nor false of Socrates *simpliciter*, for, it turns out, there is no such person.

We do not need, then, to give up, but rather to refine, the notion of a presupposition. To give a name to the refinement I have just illustrated, we might speak of a presupposition-set of propositions. The propositions making up the composite description of Socrates would form such a set. Neither the limits of such a set, nor the question of what constitutes a reasonable, or sufficient, proportion of its members will in general be precisely fixed for any putatively term-introducing proper name. This is not a deficiency in the notion of a presupposition-set; it is part of the efficiency of proper names.

It will be obvious that the range of actual cases is by no means exhausted by the two examples I have chosen: the example of a simple demonstrative-cum-descriptive indication on the one hand, and that of a proper name, such as 'Socrates', on the other. It cannot even be claimed that the

---

[13] In a forthcoming article. [John Searle, 'Proper Names', *Mind*, 67, 1958, pp. 166–73.]

proper name, in that use of it which I have discussed, is quite typical of its class, or that the account given can be quite simply extended to other cases of name-using. There is, accordingly, no hope of giving a simple general account of the relation between 'complete' term-introducing expressions and the term-distinguishing facts which must be known in order for term-introduction to be effected by their use. But, then, it is no part of my thesis that such an account can be given.

Having said this, we can safely, for the sake of a name, speak of such term-distinguishing facts or propositions as 'presupposed' by the use of those term-introducing expressions; and turn, in conclusion, to consider one more point. I have said that the success of any putatively term-introducing expression in introducing a *particular* term rests upon knowledge of some term-distinguishing fact. Very often, if we formulated such facts, the resulting statements would themselves contain expressions introducing particular terms. This need not fill us with fear of infinite regression. For we can always count on arriving, in the end, at some existential proposition, which may indeed contain demonstrative elements, but no *part* of which introduces (definitely identifies) a particular term, though the proposition *as a whole* may be said to present a particular term. (The simplest form of such a proposition is: 'There is just one so-and-so there.') But though the fact that the immediate presuppositions of most expressions introducing particular terms will themselves contain expressions introducing particular terms is not a fact that need fill us with fear of infinite regression, it is a fact that may well fill us with salutary caution. What it should caution us against is the idea that we are in any way bound, by adopting the explanations I have given, to consider presupposed propositions which contain no parts introducing particulars as the *only* presupposed propositions which are relevant to our theory. This is certainly not the case. All our theory requires is that expressions introducing particulars, unlike expressions introducing universals, should *always* be complete in a certain sense; and that sense is explained when it is shown how those expressions must always carry an empirical presupposition. The requirement that they should carry such a presupposition is satisfied just as fully in the case where the presupposed propositions themselves contain expressions introducing particulars as in the cases where they do not. It is no doubt reassuring to learn that, if we should embark on a journey through successive presuppositions, we can be sure of reaching an end.

But it is not to be supposed that such an end must, or can, be reached in a single step.

It might still be thought, however, that the position we have arrived at is theoretically unsatisfactory, in the following way. I have claimed to investigate the conditions of introducing a particular term into a proposition by means of a definitely identifying expression. I have asserted that the possibility of such term-introduction rests upon knowledge of some term-distinguishing fact. If we formulated propositions expressing such knowledge, they would be found either to contain expressions themselves introducing other particular terms, or at least to involve quantification over particulars. Now it can plausibly be argued that sentences involving quantification over particulars (e.g. 'There is just one so-and-so there') could have no place in language unless definitely identifying expressions for particulars (e.g. 'That so-and-so') also had a place in language. But if this is so, how can I claim to have stated the conditions which must be satisfied for the introduction of a particular by means of a term-introducing expression? For I cannot formulate my statement of conditions without tacitly supposing that language contains term-introducing expressions for particulars. So the account suffers from circularity.

This objection fails. It fails through not distinguishing between (1) an account of the conditions-in-general of the use in language of expressions introducing particular terms, and (2) a doctrine concerning the conditions of the use, on any particular occasion, of an expression introducing a particular term. Alternatively, the distinction overlooked by the objection might be described as that between (1) an account of the conditions of the introduction of particulars into *discourse* in general, and (2) an account of the conditions of the identifying introduction of a particular into a given *piece* of discourse. It is, of course, the second of these, and not the first, which I have advanced. Viewed in the first way, my account would indeed suffer from circularity; viewed in the second, it does not. It may well be felt that a doctrine of the second kind should be supplemented with some account of the first kind. I believe that such an account can be given, and that it reinforces, at a more fundamental level, the general kind of position I have here defended. But that is another matter.

To sum up, then. We set up, as a paradigm for reference, as a paradigm for the introduction of a subject, the use of an expression to introduce a particular, to introduce, that is, something the thought of which is in a sense complete, since it rests upon knowledge of a fact (or facts), and in a sense incomplete, in that, so introduced, the particular is thought of as a constituent of a further fact; and we set up, as a paradigm for the introduction of a predicate, the use of an expression to introduce a universal, to introduce, that is, something the thought of which has the same kind of incompleteness as that of a particular, but lacks its completeness. The two introduced terms are to be such that the assertion of a non-relational tie between them constitutes something once more complete, a complete thought; and the association of the symbolism of assertion with the universal rather than the particular we see as the mark of the lack, on the part of the thought of the former, of that completeness which the thought of the latter possesses.

Once the fundamental association is made, and explained, it is possible to explain those further extensions of the problematic distinction which, for example, allow universals to appear as logical subjects. On this matter, too, there is much more to be said than I have been able even to suggest.

5
'The Post-Linguistic Thaw'[1]

An Australian philosopher, returning in 1960 to the centre of English philosophy after an absence of more than a decade, remarked on, and regretted, the change he found. He had left a revolutionary situation in which every new move was delightfully subversive and liberating. He returned to find that, though the subject appeared still to be confidently and energetically cultivated, the revolutionary ferment had quite subsided. Where there had been, it seemed to him, a general and triumphant movement in one direction, there were now a number of individuals and groups pursuing divergent interests and ends, often in a relatively traditional manner.

His picture was a little over-simplified; but not grossly so. There did develop, in the late 1940s and the early 1950s, a new method, a new idea, in English philosophy which captured the imaginations of many of those who entered the field for the first time or returned to it after six years of an enforced intellectual sterility. In a curious way it combined, this new idea, magnitude of claim with modesty of pretension. The results it promised were to be achieved not by the inspiration of genius but by the careful and cooperative labours of men of sense.

Yet the results themselves were to be great. Foreseeably near were the total dissolution of ancient problems and the final extinction both of the avowedly metaphysical doctrines whose end had too often been announced before and of that traditional empiricism which had opposed to them the name of natural science and the reality of a weak metaphysics of its own. This clearing of ancient rubbish was to be accompanied by the delivery of the authentic treasure: the revelation, that is, of a whole world of infinite subtlety and diversity with its own fine and complex structure, a

---

[1] 'Editor's Note: Strawson deplored this title; see pp. 236–7 below.'

world which had always lain about us to be observed as soon as we ceased straining our eyes towards imaginary grandeurs and simplicities.

The means of both dissolution and revelation was a refined, thorough and, above all, a realistic awareness of the meanings of words. For the purposes of ordinary and of specialized discourse reasonably instructed adults had all mastered, had all *had* to master, a set of instruments of great subtlety, flexibility, and power. The thorough and unprejudiced study of the use which we actually made of these linguistic instruments in the course of our business with one another and the world would at last make it possible for us to understand the detailed structure of our actual conception of the world, and thereby free us from the philosophical fantasies or perplexities engendered by a reflection which was incomplete, uncontrolled, or obsessive.

Looked at in this cool and even light, much of the philosophy of the immediate and remoter past did indeed seem to consist of huge, bizarre mistakes, fantastic muddles, over-simplifications of an unbelievable grossness and crudity. Traditional problems shrivelled, traditional theories crumbled and 'linguistic' philosophers, treading a sure path, could pick their way—if they were careful and thorough—through swamps of controversy in which their perhaps more powerful but certainly less enlightened predecessors had become hopelessly and ridiculously bogged. A traditional Theory of Truth could scarcely survive a careful examination of the actual employment of the word 'true'; a traditionally conceived Problem of Knowledge looked like sheer misunderstanding by the side of a sufficiently thorough study of the use of the verb 'to know'. Error and misunderstanding could be regarded as finally disposed of when they were not only shown to be such but their very sources were, by the same operation, fully and clearly exposed.

The devastations wrought by the method were such as to inspire a kind of awe as well as an intense satisfaction. They also inspired a kind of hope which was not, at the time, absurd. It was possible to speculate about how long it would take to 'finish off' traditional philosophy; and a lecturer could conclude his lectures on the moral philosophy of the sophisticated Hume by remarking: 'Had Hume shown the same acumen in logic [i.e. epistemology] as he showed in morals... philosophy... would have been over... sooner.'

It is by no means as easy as is sometimes supposed to trace the sources of this captivating and, up to a point, brilliantly successful movement. Undeniably it had something in common with, and owed something to,

Logical Positivism. There was a community of attitude to many traditional problems and solutions. But the Logical Positivists moved to the assault rather lightly equipped with an over-simple theory of meaning, and operated, at least in England, from the flimsy base of an eighteenth-century empiricist ontology. No very elaborate exercises in the study of language actually at work were necessary to demonstrate the inadequacy of the first and the absurdity of the second.

And here the great figure of Wittgenstein comes to mind; for it was precisely in the name of the need to 'bring words back to their use in the language which is their original home' that he conducted his own exhausting battles against the belief in the adequacy of the Humean apparatus of impressions and ideas. Yet the direct influence of Wittgenstein on the development of linguistic philosophy after the war appears to have been small. His writings were known to few; and those not at that time the most active. Austin, who most clearly stated and most effectively vindicated the claims of the linguistic idea, owed no traceable debt to Wittgenstein; and the *idées maîtresses* which Professor Ryle handled with such brilliance of imagery and force of phrase seemed to derive, if from anywhere, then very distantly from Aristotle.

Nor was the atmosphere in which Professors Ryle and Austin conducted their researches the atmosphere of Wittgensteinian anguish ('Philosophy is hell'). Philosophy, rather, was complicated and fascinating; it was even allowed to be amusing. The publication of the *Philosophical Investigations* in 1953 revealed Wittgenstein clearly and generally as a philosopher of genius, many of whose thoughts, spoken in Cambridge, had somehow become assimilated to the very different style of Oxford; but it was impossible to say quite how. For though many had learnt much from the wartime and pre-war work of Professor Wisdom, who had constantly acknowledged his debt to Wittgenstein, it was now clear also how much Professor Wisdom's note was his own.

Whatever the sources of linguistic philosophy, its claims and methods could reasonably be expected to excite suspicion and hostility both from outside the world of academic philosophy and from within it. The reaction was a little belated. Many of the serious-minded were still reproaching academic philosophers, vaguely thought of as logical positivists, for excessive preoccupation with esoteric technicalities of logic at a time when it was the non-esoteric non-technicalities of ordinary speech which were actually absorbing their attention; and by the time the target was more accurately located, the scene was already changing in the way noted by the returning Australian.

Ultimately the full tide of denunciation rolled in. The linguistic philosophers were charged with dullness, triviality, pedantry, abdication, evasion, frivolity, complacency, conservatism, and obscurity. It remained an odd fact, discouraging to its critics, that a movement with these marked deficiencies was capable of exerting such an enormous attractive power wherever English was the language of philosophy, particularly in Australia and the United States of America. The influx from abroad of young students and established teachers of philosophy into Oxford, the home of dullness, continued at an unprecedented rate throughout the post-war period; and Oxford philosophers were invited in increasing numbers to export their product in person to the United States.

Neither the hostility nor the enthusiasm which the movement excited was in the least surprising. The atmosphere of particular and informal clarities in which the movement lived caused genuine bafflement and uneasiness in many whose conception of philosophy was more elevated than definite. What was clear seemed obscure to those whose unconscious demand was for obscurity, and the study of the familiar seemed contemptuously esoteric in a region where everything was expected to be strange. But to the genuine student of the subject, accustomed but not reconciled to pseudo-precise terminology and stale controversy, the new movement offered an unparalleled freshness of approach, and a real hope of replacing forever collapsing theories with actually ascertainable truths. This was sufficient reason for its appeal.

The self-conscious employment of the linguistic method produced brilliant and often amusing results. It destroyed much and revealed much. It should continue to play a great part in philosophy, acting as an indispensable control on extravagance, absurdity, and over-simplification; revealing more and more of the fascinating substructure of our thinking. But it no longer appears that it can, by itself, satisfy all the demands of philosophical enquiry. Above all, it cannot, by itself, satisfy the persistent philosophical craving for generality, for the discovery of unifying pattern or structure in our conception of the world.

That craving has often enough been nourished with illusion; and the generalizing philosopher of today is less likely than his predecessors to claim final or exclusive correctness for the pattern of connections he presents. Yet there seems no reason why it should not be possible from time to time to sketch out, in the style of the day, a fundamental order of conceptual connections discernible in human thinking, or to illuminate different particular areas of thought in a more systematic way than the linguistic method was able to promise by itself. In any case, the desire for generality is ineliminable from philosophy. Temporarily overlaid in some minds by the successes of the linguistic method, the desire inevitably re-asserted itself. One result, among others, was a more sympathetic understanding of the history of the subject. What had appeared in that first dazzling light simply as an array of crude mistakes could sometimes, after all, be sympathetically viewed as an attempt, not wholly unsuccessful, to establish a general structure such as the refinements of the new method were powerless to reveal by themselves.

Even in the heyday of the linguistic movement it is doubtful whether it numbered among its adherents or semi-adherents more than a substantial minority of British philosophers. It was associated primarily with one place—Oxford—and there it centred on one man—Austin, its most explicit advocate and most acute and whole-hearted practitioner. Its heyday was short. When a revolutionary movement begins to write its own history, something at least of its revolutionary impetus has been lost; and in the appearance of *The Revolution in Philosophy* (1956) and of Mr. G. J. Warnock's *English Philosophy since 1900* (1958) there were signs that eyes were being lifted from the immediate task, indications of pause and change.

Indeed, the pull of generality was felt by Austin himself, who, before he died, was beginning to work out a general classificatory theory of acts of linguistic communication. It is still too early to say what definite directions change will take. In spite of the work of Professor Ayer, who never attached value to the linguistic idea, and who, in his most recent book, *The Problem of Knowledge* (1956), continued to uphold a traditional empiricism with unfailing elegance and skill, it seems unlikely that he or others will work much longer in that vein.

There are portents, however, of a very different kind. One is the appearance of a persuasive study entitled *Hegel: A Re-examination* (1958) by Professor J. N. Findlay. Professor Stuart Hampshire's *Thought and Action*

(1959), with its linking of epistemology, philosophy of mind, and moral philosophy, is highly indicative of a trend from piecemeal studies towards bolder syntheses; it shows how the results of recent discussions can be utilized in a construction with both Hegelian and Spinozistic affinities. Mr. P. F. Strawson's *Individuals* (1959) suggests a scaled-down Kantianism, pared of idealism on the one hand and a particular conception of physical science on the other. The philosophy of logic and language takes on a tauter line and a more formal tone in the work of logicians who derive their inspiration mainly from Frege. Finally, some of the most successful work of the period has been in the philosophy of mind; and it seems reasonable to suppose that further studies will follow upon Professor Ryle's *Concept of Mind* (1949), Wittgenstein's *Investigations* (1953), and Miss Anscombe's *Intention* (1957), and that, in them, Ryle's explicit and Wittgenstein's implicit suggestions of systematization will be refined and reassessed.

The Australian philosopher had reason enough to claim that he found a changed situation. When knowledge of this fact of change finally filters through to those who habitually comment on the state of philosophy without any significant first-hand acquaintance with it, reactions of complacency may be expected. In the anticipated face of these it is worth reaffirming that the gains and advances made in the dozen years which followed the war were probably as great as any which have been made in an equivalent period in the history of the subject.

A new level of refinement and accuracy in conceptual awareness has been reached, and an addition to philosophical method has been established which will, or should, be permanent. It is not only within the sphere of concerns peculiar to the philosopher that the results of these advances show themselves. The province of jurisprudence offers an almost ideal ground for the application of a critical technique of which the essence is an accurate surveying of the actual operation of concepts. Professor Hart and Mr. Honoré have achieved one striking success in this field with the publication of *Causation in the Law* (1959); and in a brilliant series of lectures to be published under the title of *The Concept of Law* Professor Hart illuminates with the same clarity and accuracy the most general issues of jurisprudence.

There is no reason why philosophical prose should be more ugly and turgid than other prose; and the best philosophical writing in England has always had a place among the best writing in England. This tradition is maintained, in a variety of individual modes; in Professor Ayer's Augustan elegance; in Austin's wit and sharp lucidity; in Professor Wisdom's strange, persuasive cadence; in the graceful and ironic urbanity of Mr. Warnock; above all, perhaps, in Professor Ryle's masterly handling of a vivid and wide-ranging vocabulary and a taut and balanced sentence structure. These and others who have thought clearly and written well include some who belonged, some who half-belonged, and some who did not belong at all, to the linguistic movement. There are enough of the first to make it clear that one kind of sensitivity to the use of words need not exclude another.

6

Analysis, Science, and Metaphysics

It has been said, rightly, that English philosophy between the wars was dominated by the notion of analysis. One might say the same of English and American philosophy after the Second World War, but then one would have to add that the conception of analysis was entirely different from that held earlier. It is true, of course, that even before the Second World War, the word 'analysis' was given several different interpretations. Nevertheless, I think that a certain central idea was never far from the minds of all those who praised, or claimed to practise, the analytic method during this earlier period. This was the idea of translation, of an ideal paraphrase as the proper goal of philosophical analysis—even though this goal might itself be a mere ideal. On this conception of analysis, the principal philosophical problems would be resolved if one could translate sentences of ordinary language which contained problematic concepts by means of other sentences—expressions which would exhibit clearly the underlying complexities of these concepts; or if one could transpose ordinary sentences whose grammatical structure was misleading into a

---

Editor's note. This is a translation by Richard Rorty of a paper presented in French at the Royaumont Colloquium of 1958, which was first published in the proceedings of the colloquium, *La philosophie analytique* (Paris: Editions de Minuit, 1962), along with a transcription of the ensuing discussion. A translation of the discussion may be found in English in *The Linguistic Turn*, edited by R. Rorty (Chicago: University of Chicago Press, 1967, pp. 321–30). Rorty notes that 'Mr. Strawson's paper contains many sentences and paragraphs which occur, in English, in his essay in *The Philosophy of Rudolf Carnap*. At these points, I have followed the wording of the latter essay in my translation.' The essay is 'Carnap's Views on Constructed Systems versus Natural Languages in Analytical Philosophy', in the *Library of Living Philosophers* volume edited by P. A. Schillp (La Salle, IL: Open Court Publishing, 1963).

The original paper gives the date of the date of the colloquium as 1961, and it has also been dated to 1959 and 1960, but it seems that it actually took place in 1958. See 'Royaumont Revisited', by S. Overgaard, *British Journal for the History of Philosophy*, 18(5), pp. 899–924.

form which would exhibit clearly the true structure of the thoughts they expressed or of the facts they signified. Some among those who held this view thought that the new formal logic offered by *Principia Mathematica* would supply the general structure of the language of paraphrase, the general forms of the clarifying sentences. Some philosophers even thought they knew what the ultimate elements of analysis would turn out to be— what kind of terms would provide the content for these general forms. These primitive terms, they thought, would denote what was immediately presented to the senses—those ephemeral 'givens' beloved of British empiricists from the seventeenth century down to the present. Still other philosophers remained sceptical or neutral about these points, while nevertheless accepting the general notion that clarifying paraphrases were, ideally, what analysis should produce.

Toward the end of this earlier period, a sense of disillusion began to be felt by the analysts of this persuasion. On the one hand, Wittgenstein had begun to give lectures of a quite new sort at Cambridge. His ideas, as they spread beyond the small circle of his auditors, made it possible to envisage a more flexible and more fruitful philosophical method. On the other hand, the results of actual attempts to apply the method of analysis were disappointing. The sentences of ordinary language seemed to resist being forced into the moulds which had been shaped by men who had preconceived ideas about the proper form or the proper content of the clarifying paraphrases. Even translations which had, at first, seemed obviously successful began to be hedged about with doubts and qualifications, and were often in the end repudiated altogether. In the end, analysts began to feel a pervasive doubt about what they were doing. It seemed that one could only achieve a translation by sacrificing all or part of the meaning of the expression which one was trying to analyse. What was intended as analysis turned out to be falsification; or, if the original meaning was successfully conserved, fidelity was secured only at the cost of circularity.

If translation, as a philosophical method, cannot produce any sound results, it seems clearly necessary to abandon it. But it is possible, in abandoning it, to preserve something of what the analysts had originally intended. This can be done in either of two, apparently opposed, ways. Sentences of ordinary language fulfil our ordinary needs. In general, they leave nothing to be desired in the way of clarity for practical purposes, even though they leave much to be desired from the point of view of *philosophical* clarity. Thus the attempt to replace these sentences with clarifying paraphrases—clarifying in the sense that their form and their content would meet our need for philosophical understanding—was very natural. But since ordinary sentences resisted such translation, a choice had to be made. One could either retain the construction of clarifying paraphrases as one's goal, while admitting that these paraphrases could never have precisely the same meaning as the ordinary sentences they replaced, or else one could retain the goal of explaining the precise meaning of these expressions, while admitting that the construction of paraphrases in an ideal language would not produce this result. The first choice gives rise to the programme of linguistic constructionism, the second to that of description of linguistic usage. If one adopts the most rigorous and most highly developed form of the first programme, one will construct a formal system which uses, generally, the apparatus of modern logic and in which the concepts forming the subject matter of the system are introduced by means of axioms and definitions. The construction of the system will generally be accompanied by extra-systematic remarks in some way relating the concepts of the system to concepts which we already use in an unsystematic way. This is the method of 'rational reconstruction'; and indeed the system of elementary logic itself, which provides the general form of the system as a whole, can be regarded as a reconstruction of the set of concepts expressed by the logical constants of daily life. Following the other method seems very different. For it consists in the attempt to describe the complex patterns of logical behaviour which the concepts of daily life exhibit. It is not a matter of prescribing the model conduct of model words, but of describing the actual conduct of actual words; not a matter of making rules, but of noting customs. Obviously the first method has certain advantages. The nature and the powers of the apparatus to be used are clear. Its users know in advance what *sort* of thing they are going to make with it. The practitioner of the second method is not so well placed. Unless he is to be content with the production and juxtaposition of particular examples, he needs some meta-vocabulary in which to describe the features he finds. *Ex hypothesi*, the well-regulated meta-vocabulary of the first method is inadequate for his purposes. So he has to make his own tools; and, too often, hastily improvised, over-weighted with analogy and association, they prove clumsy, lose their edge after one operation, and serve only to mutilate where they should dissect.

I wish to examine in more detail these two apparently opposed methods. I shall compare their merits in respect of that philosophical clarification which they both hope to achieve. Obviously, the result of such a comparison will depend in part on the sense one gives to the notion of 'clarification'. One could interpret this word in such a way that there was no interesting question as to which of the two methods would be better for this purpose. Such a result would ensue, for example, from taking 'clarification' in the sense which Carnap seems to give it in the first chapter of *Logical Foundations of Probability*.[1] A pre-scientific concept is clarified in this sense if it is supplanted or succeeded by one which is more *exact* and more *fruitful*. The criterion of fruitfulness, according to Carnap, is that the concept should be useful in the formulation of many logical theorems or empirical scientific laws. The criterion of exactness is that the rules of the use of the concept should be such as to give it a clear place 'in a well-connected system of scientific concepts' (p. 7). Such a well-connected system, it seems, is a formal system which incorporates them. If one agrees with Carnap on all these points, then clearly the thesis that clarification can be best achieved by system-construction appears as an understatement.

Even if we abjure this last step, and think of clarification more vaguely as the introduction, for scientific purposes, of scientifically exact and fruitful concepts in place of some of those we use for all the other ordinary and extraordinary purposes of life, the issue between the two methods remains less than exciting. I am not competent to discuss the extent to which theoretical scientists either examine minutely the behaviour of words in ordinary language or construct axiom systems. It seems to me extremely improbable that they do much of the first; and I suspect (but may be quite wrong) that logicians exaggerate the extent to which they do, or ought to do, the second. But my incompetence in this area troubles me not at all. For however much or little the constructionist technique is the right means of getting an idea into shape for use in the sciences, it seems *prima facie* evident that to offer formal explanations of key terms of scientific theories to one who seeks philosophical illumination of essential concepts of non-scientific discourse is to do something utterly irrelevant—is a sheer misunderstanding, like offering a textbook on physiology to someone who says (with a sigh) that he wished he understood the workings of the human heart. In the case of many a philosophically troubling concept, indeed, it is hard to know in what direction to look for a scientifically

---

[1] Rudolf Carnap, Logical Foundations of Probability, second edition (Chicago, IL.: The University of Chicago Press, 1962).

satisfactory concept which stands to it in the required relation of correspondence or similarity. But the general conclusion holds even for those cases where there is a clear correlation. I may mention, for example, Carnap's own example of the clarification of the pre-scientific concept of warmth by the introduction of the exact and scientifically fruitful concept of temperature. Sensory concepts in general have been a rich source of philosophical perplexity. How are the look, the sound, the feel of a material object related to each other and to the object itself? Does it follow from the fact that the same object can feel warm to one man and cold to another that the object really is neither cold nor warm nor has any such property? These questions can be answered, or the facts and difficulties that lead to our asking them can be made plain; but not by means of formal exercises in the scientific use of the related concepts of temperature, wavelength, and frequency. Indeed the introduction of the scientific concepts may itself produce a further crop of puzzles, arising from an unclarity over the relations between two ways of using language to talk about the physical world, the relations between the quantitative and the sensory vocabularies. This unclarity is another which will scarcely be removed by exhibiting the formal workings of the quantitative concepts.

It is possible, however, to understand the idea of clarification, and of the contribution which system-construction may make to it, in a different and more philosophical way; in such a way, in fact, that the issue stated at the outset remains open, requires to be argued further. The partisan of constructionism may well concede that introducing exact concepts for scientific purposes is one thing, and clarifying ordinary concepts is another. He may also concede that the latter task is the peculiarly philosophical one. Conceding all this, he may still maintain that the latter task will be best fulfilled by system-construction. He can maintain that attempts to analyse the forms of ordinary discourse are inevitably futile, because of the untidiness, the instability, the disorder, and the complexity of ordinary language. In place of undertaking such an analysis, he may say, let us construct perspicuous models of this language (or at least of some parts of this language) in which all the *essential* logical relations between our ordinary concepts are evident, because they will have been freed from the incidental ambiguities of everyday speech. Such a model of language has the following features. First, it is intrinsically clear, in that its key concepts are related in precise and determinate ways, whereas, *ex hypothesi*, the ordinary concepts to be clarified do not have such precise and determinate relations to each other or to the other ordinary concepts in terms of which we might seek to explain them. Second, at least some of the key concepts of the system are, in important respects, very close to the ordinary concepts which are to be clarified. The system as a whole then appears as a precise and rigid structure to which our ordinary conceptual equipment is a loose and untidy approximation.

The way in which the debate could once more reach an uninteresting deadlock is the following. It could be maintained dogmatically on the one hand that nothing but the mastery of such a system would really *be* understanding, in a philosophical sense, of the concepts to be clarified. Or it might be maintained dogmatically on the other hand that since, *ex hypothesi*, the ordinary concepts to be examined do not behave in the well-regulated way in which the model concepts of the system are made to behave, there can be no real understanding of the former except such as may be gained by a detailed consideration of the way they do behave, i.e. by an investigation of the ordinary uses of the linguistic expressions concerned. Here the deadlock is reached by each party refusing to count as *understanding* a condition which is not reached by the method he advocates.

There may be something final about this deadlock. For there may here be something which is in part a matter simply of preference, of choice. Nevertheless, there are considerations which may influence choice. For surely, in deciding what to count as philosophical understanding, it is reasonable to remind ourselves what philosophical problems and *un*clarities are *like*. Such a reminder I shall briefly attempt later. But I shall partly anticipate it now, in mentioning some general difficulties which arise for the constructionist in the position he is now assumed to occupy.

The constructionist would of course agree that it is necessary to supply an interpretation for the linguistic expressions of his theory. This is not secured merely by the formal relationships between the constructed concepts which the theory exhibits. At some point it is necessary also to explain the meaning of the linguistic expressions for the constructed concepts in terms which do not belong to the theory and the meaning of which is taken as already known. So *some* extra-systematic remarks are essential. This point need not in itself raise any particular difficulty. So long as a small number of extra-systematic points of contact are clearly made, the meaning of the remaining elements follows from their clearly defined relationships within the system to those to which life has been given by the extra-systematic remarks. But if the constructionist claim to achieve clarification is to be vindicated, it is not sufficient, though it is necessary, that the interpretation of the linguistic expressions of his theory should be determined. For the claim to clarify will seem empty, unless the results achieved have some bearing on the typical philosophical problems and difficulties which arise concerning the concepts to be clarified. Now these problems and difficulties (it will be admitted) have their roots in ordinary, unconstructed concepts, in the elusive, deceptive modes of functioning of unformalized linguistic expressions. It is precisely the purpose of the reconstruction (we are now supposing) to solve or dispel problems and difficulties so rooted. But how can this purpose be achieved unless extra-systematic points of contact are made, not just at the one or two points necessary to fix the interpretation of the constructed concepts, but at *every* point where the relevant problems and difficulties concerning the unconstructed concepts arise? That is to say, if the clear mode of functioning of the constructed concepts is to cast light on problems and difficulties rooted in the unclear mode of functioning of the unconstructed concepts, then precisely the ways in which the constructed concepts are connected with and depart from the unconstructed concepts must be plainly shown. And how can *this* result be achieved without accurately describing the modes of functioning of the unconstructed concepts? But this task is precisely the task of describing the logical behaviour of the linguistic expressions of natural languages; and may *by itself* achieve the sought-for resolution of the problems and difficulties rooted in the elusive, deceptive mode of functioning of unconstructed concepts. I should not want to deny that in the discharge of this task, the construction of a model object of linguistic comparison may sometimes be of great help. But I do want to deny that the construction and contemplation of such a model object can *take the place* of the discharge of this task; and I want also to suggest that one thinks that it can only if one is led away from the purpose of achieving philosophical understanding by the fascination of other purposes, such as that of getting on with science.

Moreover, the general usefulness of systems of constructed concepts as objects of comparison with the unconstructed concepts in which our problems are rooted is necessarily limited. For the types or modes of logical behaviour which ordinary concepts exhibit are extremely diverse. To detect and distinguish them is a task in which one may well be hindered rather than helped by fixing one's eye too firmly on the limited range of types of logical behaviour which the concepts occurring in a formal system can there be shown to display. Such a system can only offer us relations between constructed concepts which have been fixed by stipulative definition. In this respect, system-construction reproduces the limitations and the narrowness of the original conception of analysis. Like it, it simply puts to one side a great number of widely different features of the functioning of our language—features which it is important to observe and describe with precision, if one wishes to resolve philosophical problems. One might put the point metaphorically as follows: living, linguistic beings have an enormous diversity of functions, only some of which can be reproduced by the computer-like machines which the constructionist can build.

It is still, however, too soon for us to say that we have reached a definitive judgement concerning the relative merits of the two methods. It is, in fact, impossible to make such a judgement without attempting a general description of philosophical problems, difficulties, and questions. It is rash to attempt such a general description, but at any rate this much will be broadly agreed: that they are problems, difficulties, and questions *about* the concepts we use in various fields, and not problems, difficulties, and questions which arise *within* the fields of their use. To say more is to risk the loss of general agreement. Nevertheless, I think it is possible roughly to distinguish, though not to separate, certain strands or elements in the treatment of this diverse mass of conceptual questions. First, and very centrally, we find the necessity of dealing with paradox and perplexity. For it often happens that someone reflecting on a certain set of concepts finds himself driven to adopt views which seem to others paradoxical or unacceptably strange, or to have consequences which are paradoxical or unacceptably strange. Or—the obverse of this—it may happen that someone so reflecting becomes unable to see how something that he knows very well to be the case can *possibly* be the case. In this situation the critical philosopher must not only restore the conceptual balance which has somehow been upset; he must also diagnose the particular sources of the loss of balance, show just how it has been upset. And these achievements are not independent of each other. It also seems to me possible to say in general what kind of thing the source of conceptual unbalance is. Such unbalance results from a kind of temporary onesidedness of vision, a kind of selective blindness which cuts out most of the field, but leaves one part of it standing out with a peculiar brilliance. This condition may take many different, though interconnected forms. The producer of philosophical paradox, or the sufferer from philosophical perplexity, is temporarily dominated by one logical mode of operation of expressions, or by one way of using language, or by one logical type or category of objects, or by one sort of explanation, or by one set of cases of the application of a given concept; and attempts to see, to explain, something which is different in terms of, or on analogy with, his favoured model. The distortions which result from such attempts are of equally many kinds. To correct the distortions, one must make plain the actual modes of operation of the distorted concepts or types of discourse; and, in doing this, one must make plain the differences between their modes of operation and those of the model concepts or types of discourse; and, in doing this, one must, if one can, make plain the sources of the blinding obsession with the model cases.

This, then, is one strand in the treatment of philosophical problems—one which is in itself quite complex. I call it central, partly because the need for it has in fact provided so strong an impetus to the whole activity. From it can be distinguished, though not separated, certain other strands. One is the attempt to explain, not just how our concepts and types of discourse operate, but why it is that we have such concepts and types of discourse as we do; and what alternatives there might be. This is not a historical enquiry. It attempts to show the natural foundations of our logical, conceptual apparatus, in the way things happen in the world, and in our own natures. A form which propositions exemplifying this strand in philosophy may often take is the following: if things (or we) were different in such-and-such ways, then we might lack such-and-such concepts or types of discourse; or have such-and-such others; or might accord a subordinate place to some which are now central, and a central place to others; or the concepts we have might be different in such-and-such ways. It might reasonably be maintained, or ruled, that full understanding of a concept is not achieved until this kind of enquiry is added to the activities of comparing, contrasting, and distinguishing which I mentioned first. Of course speculations of this kind are restricted in certain ways: they are limited by the kinds of experience and the conceptual apparatus we in fact have. But this is only the restriction to intelligibility; it leaves a wide field open to philosophical imagination.

The distinction I used above between the way things happen in the world, and our own natures, is here, though vague, important. For it is a part of our nature that, things other than ourselves being as they are, it is natural for us to have the conceptual apparatus that we do have. But human nature is diverse enough to allow of another, though related, use of philosophical imagination. This consists in imagining ways in which, without things other than ourselves being different from what they are, we might view them through the medium of a different conceptual apparatus. Here, then, is a third strand. Some metaphysics is best, or most charitably, seen as consisting in part in exercises of this sort. Of course, even when it can be so interpreted, it is not *presented* as a conceptual or structural revision by means of which we might see things differently; it is presented as a picture of things as they *really* are, instead of as they delusively seem. And this presentation, with its contrast between esoteric reality and daily delusion, involves and is the consequence of the unconscious distortion of ordinary concepts, i.e. of the ordinary use of linguistic expressions. So metaphysics, though it can sometimes be charitably interpreted in the way I suggest, in fact always involves paradox and perplexities of the kind I first mention; and sometimes embodies no rudimentary vision, but merely rudimentary mistakes.

Still other strands need to be distinguished. That examination of current concepts and types of discourse to which paradox and perplexity so commonly give the initial impulse can be pursued with no particular therapeutic purpose, but for its own sake. This is not to say that puzzlement is not in question here. One can, without feeling any particular temptation to mistaken assimilations, simply be aware that one does not clearly understand how some type of expression functions, in comparison with others. Or, having noticed, or had one's attention drawn to, a certain logico-linguistic feature appearing in one particular area of discourse, one may simply wish to discover how extensive is the range of this feature, and what other comparable features are to be found. Of course, the resulting enquiries may well pay therapeutic dividends. But this need not be the purpose for which they are undertaken. Here, then, is a fourth strand.

I think that there is a fifth philosophical aim to which those which I have so far sketched should be subordinated. So far, I have spoken of metaphysics as if its principal aim were the reformation of concepts, and its most frequent achievement their deformation. I have contrasted reforming metaphysics with descriptive analysis. However, we should recognize the existence of another sort of metaphysics, one which shares the descriptive aim of analysis. The descriptive metaphysician resembles the descriptive analyst in that he wishes to make clear the actual behaviour of our concepts, rather than to change them. His enterprise differs from that of the analyst only in scope and in level of generality. But this difference is important. An analytical examination of a certain area of human thought—an analysis, say, of the concept of memory, or of cause, or of logical necessity—may, and should, take a great deal for granted, presuppose a great deal. To clarify a particular part of our conceptual apparatus, there is no need to make a profound study of the general structure of that apparatus. But the goal of descriptive metaphysics will consist precisely in the exhibition of that structure. It will try to show how the fundamental categories of our thought hang together and how they relate, in turn, to those formal notions (such as existence, identity, and unity) which range through all categories. Obviously the conclusions which descriptive metaphysics reaches must not conflict with those arrived at by a careful descriptive analysis. Still, it is not evident that the tools and the method of descriptive analysis can suffice by themselves to do the job which descriptive metaphysics attempts.

If these are the tasks of philosophy, what can we now say about the pretensions of the two heirs of the classical programme of analysis—the two contrasting methods of philosophical clarification which we have been examining? It seems to me that the roles of these two methods become clear when we consider the first and the fourth objectives of philosophical enquiry which I have distinguished. The description of the modes of functioning of actually employed linguistic expressions is of the essence of the fourth aim; and it is simply the least clouded form of a procedure which is essential to the achievement of the first. Here the arguments put forward above apply. To observe our concepts in action is necessarily the only way of finding out what they can and cannot do. The right kind of attention to the ordinary use of expressions provides a means of refutation of theories founded on mistaken assimilations; it provides a description of the actual functioning of the problematic concepts, to take the place of the mistaken theory; and, finally, it helps, or may help, with the diagnosis of the temptations to the mistakes. This last it may do because the analogies which seduce the philosopher are not, in general, private fantasies; they have their roots in our ordinary thinking, and show themselves in practically harmless, but detectable ways, in ordinary language—both in its syntactical structure and in the buried metaphors which individual words and phrases contain. I have already acknowledged that system-construction may have an ancillary role in achieving these two types of aim, and given reasons for thinking that it must remain ancillary—and limited. Model objects of linguistic comparison may help us to understand the given objects; but it is dogmatism to maintain that the construction of model objects is the best or the only means of achieving such understanding.

In the case of those exercises of philosophical imagination which I have referred to as the second and third strands, the case is somewhat different. To understand the foundation of our concepts in natural facts, and to envisage alternative possibilities, it is not enough to have a sharp eye for linguistic actualities. Nor is system-construction a direct contribution to the achievement of the first of these two, i.e. to seeing why we talk as we do. But it may be to the second, i.e. to imagining how else we might talk. The constructionist may perhaps be seen as an enlightened reforming metaphysician—one who, perhaps wistfully, envisages the possibility of our situation and our need for communication so changed and simplified that such a well-regulated system of concepts as he supplies is well-adapted to both. It is only when the claim to exclusiveness is made on behalf of the constructionist method, and of particular constructions, that one must begin to query the enlightenment. But, again, this claim may be softened to the expression of a preference—which leaves one no more to say.

There remains the fifth strand in the philosophical enterprise. It is obviously interlaced with the others, and cannot be detached from them. Still, it imposes its own demands. It is possible to stick to the scrupulous examination of the actual behaviour of words, and to claim that this is the only sure path in descriptive philosophy. But it seems to me that if we do no more than this, then the relations and the structures which we shall discover will not be sufficiently general, or sufficiently far-reaching, to satisfy our urge for full metaphysical understanding. For when we ask ourselves questions about the use of a certain expression, the answers we give ourselves, revealing as they are at a certain level, presuppose, rather than exhibit, the general structural elements which the metaphysician wishes to discover. This does not mean that the metaphysician can ignore either the conclusions or the methods of descriptive analysis. On the contrary, these methods and conclusions serve as an indispensable control in the working-out of properly metaphysical solutions. But neither do these methods suffice, of themselves, to arrive at such properly metaphysical conclusions. For myself, I can offer no general recipe for achieving the sort of comprehension I have in mind here. It would indeed be the vainest of dreams to imagine that the structure which descriptive metaphysics wishes to discover could be crystallized in any formal system.

To conclude, then. There is not just one thing which is legitimately required of the philosopher who would increase our conceptual understanding. In particular, it is certainly not *enough* to say that he should describe the functioning of actually employed linguistic expressions. For simply to say this would not be to give any indication of the sort of description he should provide. That indication is given when it is shown how description of the right sort may bear upon our conceptual confusions and problems. Next we see how more may be required of him than the resolution of these confusions with the help of those descriptions; how a more systematic classification and ordering of the types of discourse and concept we employ may be sought; how a fuller understanding of both may be gained by enquiring into their foundation in natural facts; how room may here be found for the envisaging of other possibilities; how he may, in the end, strive for the goal of a descriptive metaphysics. If the philosopher is to do all or only some of these things, it is true that he cannot stop short at the literal description, and illustration, of the behaviour of actually used linguistic expressions. Nevertheless, the actual use of linguistic expressions remains his sole and essential point of contact with the reality which he wishes to understand, conceptual reality; for this is the only point from which the actual mode of operation of concepts can be observed. If he severs this vital connection, all his ingenuity and imagination will not save him from lapses into the arid or the absurd.

7

Bennett on Kant's Analytic

Mr Bennett, as was to be expected, has written a first-rate book on Kant's Analytic.[1] It is vivid, entertaining, and extremely instructive. It will be found of absorbing interest both by those who already know the *Critique* and by those—if there are any such—who have a developed interest in philosophy, yet no direct acquaintance with Kant. These last it will surely drive to the text and, as surely, will drive them to approach it in a truly philosophical spirit. Bennett's Kant is not a giant immersed, or frozen, in time. He is a great contemporary—a little out of touch, admittedly, with recent developments in mathematics and physics—but one with whom we can all argue, against him, at his side, or obliquely to him. And so Bennett does argue, continuously, fiercely, and fruitfully; and summons to join in the argument, at appropriate moments, those older contemporaries, Locke, Leibniz, Berkeley, and Hume, and those younger contemporaries, Wittgenstein, Ryle, Ayer, Quine, Quinton, Warnock, the present reviewer, and others. This is splendid, and a necessary corrective to that extraordinary isolation in which Kant tends to be islanded, partly, indeed, by his own unique qualities, but partly by oceans of the wrong kind of respect. Bennett, continuously engaging his great antagonist, shows the right kind.

The discussions in Bennett's book follow in general the order of the main divisions of the *Critique*, from the Introduction to the end of the Analytic; the only significant displacement is of the chapter on Phenomena and Noumena, which is briefly alluded to at a fairly early stage. But *Kant's Analytic* is far from being a section-by-section commentary. Rather, it consists of two clearly distinguishable things, one a unity, the other a

---

[1] Jonathan Bennett, *Kant's Analytic* (Cambridge: Cambridge University Press, 1966).

plurality. There is, first, a single main line of argument concerned with the limiting conditions on anything which we could conceive of as a possible experience. This line of argument Bennett presents as both acceptable in itself and having a reasonable measure of correspondence with parts of Kant's own doctrine. It is set out mainly in Bennett's Chapters 3, 4, 8, 14, and 15. Second, there is a series of discussions of issues raised in, or suggested by, the text—discussions which are more or less detachable from the main line of argument and more or less independent of each other. It is largely, though not exclusively, in connection with these several units of discussion that Bennett's nearer contemporaries are summoned to join in the argument. The discussions range over a great variety of topics: the analytic–synthetic distinction; the nature of geometry; the possession, acquisition, and application of general concepts; the unity of space; the distinction between 'formal' and 'material' concepts; the dispensability of definite singular terms; the analysis of the notion of causal necessity; the distinction between intensive and extensive magnitudes; the notion of continuity of sensation, time, and change; the private-language argument; and many others. The general quality of these fairly short, pungent discussions is high; the best are brilliantly lucid and persuasive. Strung together on the thread of Kant's text, they contribute much to that sense of freshness and contemporaneity which I have mentioned.

I select for discussion a few among the many questions which invite it. '*Unobviously analytic.*' Bennett accepts the notion of analyticity as a property of sentences-in-a-use which express truth solely in virtue of meaning. He thinks, however, that Kant tends to conceive this notion too narrowly, tending to restrict its application to cases of obvious or 'elementary' analyticity. As a result, Kant is driven to the mystery of the synthetic a priori and thence to an even greater mystery, the vain and extravagant invocation of noumenal machinery. We might have been spared this if Kant had taken more account of the existence, besides obviously analytic truths, of truths which are unobviously analytic. Not that this would be the appropriate label for the theorems of Euclidean geometry, about which (Bennett holds) Kant is clearly wrong, since they have, simply, the status of propositions of a physical, hence disconfirmable, theory. But 'the most interesting truths which Kant calls synthetic a priori... are unobvious analytic truths about the conditions under which certain distinctions can be made, or under which certain concepts can have a significant use, affirmative or negative' (p. 42).

Now what is the unobviously analytic? Bennett's discussion (pp. 7–8) points to a clear answer, reminiscent, in its way, of Descartes's account of intuition and deduction, of Locke's account of intuitive and demonstrative knowledge. By a series of steps, themselves involving nothing but the elementarily analytic, we may establish something as unobviously analytic: the unobviousness comes from the complexity (that is, length) of the procedures, the analyticity from the dependence on nothing but the elementarily analytic.

Unfortunately, it is far from obvious that the 'interesting truths' for which Bennett is inclined to claim the status of the unobviously analytic conform to this model. Indeed, it is rather obvious that Bennett does not even think they do. Thus he favours, and argues for, the view that 'objectivity requires spatiality' (that the distinction between the objective and the subjective, the outer and the inner, requires for its application that experience be of a world which is '"spatial" in a fairly strong sense'). He says of this view that it is, if true, analytic, though unobviously so. But he also says that it is a view which can never be conclusively proved—'one is at the mercy of the overlooked possibility' (p. 43)—and that this is a feature it shares with all interesting truths of its kind. If we try, then, to think of any such view as unobviously analytic (in the sense of pp. 7–8), we have to suppose that there are other truths which are both elementarily analytic (hence 'obvious') and yet curiously elusive, so that we can never get our hands on them to complete the demonstration of unobvious analyticity.

This seems difficult, and the difficulty may encourage us to look for another way of conceiving the unobviously analytic. We find in Bennett no other account of a clarity comparable with that of the inadequate account. We do find, however, something else to the purpose, in the shape of a readiness to admit at least one limiting truth about human experience to what is declared to be a completely different category. Thus 'the temporality of the given is a fact which, *although contingent*, cannot be thought away' (italics mine); the claim that there might be (for example, God might have) atemporal knowledge of reality is 'a claim which we do not understand: we cannot see what it comes to or how to fill in any details'; 'we cannot talk or think about what it would be like' (pp. 48–50).

I doubt if the word 'contingent' in the first of these passages really does anything more than register Bennett's reluctance to invoke analyticity at this point. If we leave it out, then what difference can we find between the quoted descriptions of the truth that experience is temporal and the description of those other limiting truths which Bennett is inclined to classify as unobviously analytic, though incapable of conclusive proof? Well, we might say: more steps in *argument* are involved in the other cases. That is true. And perhaps some of these steps are elementarily analytic. But not all can be, since conclusive proof is unavailable. Now Bennett does not think that the fact that temporality is a limiting condition on anything we can conceive of as a possible experience requires, or permits, explanation by means of noumenal machinery. So there seems to be no *general* need to force limiting truths about experience into the category of the unobviously analytic. But then is there *any* need?

I am not voicing a general scepticism about the notion of analyticity. Far from it. My scepticism is simply about the utility of invoking the notion to preserve the respectability of our metaphysics.

Transcendental Idealism and Phenomenalism. Bennett identifies Kant's transcendental idealism with phenomenalism, of which he whole-heartedly approves. Is the identification correct? Should we share the approval? Well, Kant's transcendental idealism certainly includes as at least part of itself a form of phenomenalism regarding bodies in space. If this part were clearly detachable from the rest, we might think the issue of the correctness of the identification comparatively trivial. But is it clearly detachable? Bennett acknowledges the fact that Kant has a doctrine of the ideality of inner, as well as of outer, sense—a doctrine according to which we are not aware of ourselves as we are in ourselves, but only as we appear. But Bennett has a short two-stage way with this aspect of transcendental idealism. Stage 1 is: 'I here reject Kant's unhappy notion that, just as outer experience is one's encounter with an objective realm, inner experience is one's encounter with oneself' (p. 45). Stage 2 is: 'Transcendental idealism about subjective time is not false but trivial.... Phenomenalisms are designed to operate *across* the subjective/objective borderline' (p. 52). Now it can hardly be thought that Kant himself regarded the doctrine of the ideality of inner sense as *trivially* true. He at least must have held that this part of the thesis of transcendental idealism was connected in the way of identity with the opposition between ourselves as we are in ourselves and ourselves as we appear to ourselves in inner sense (that is, in time). Is there any reason for thinking that he would have held the corresponding connection to be any less essential in the case of the doctrine of outer sense? We must surely rather think that Kant's phenomenalism regarding bodies in space does have (for him) an essential connection with the opposition between how things are in temselves and how they appear in *outer* sense (that is, in space). These oppositions we may well, in both cases, find unintelligible, and in consequence reject transcendental idealism. But then why should we preserve the phenomenalism regarding bodies in space, which transcendental idealism includes?

Because, Bennett will say, it is true in itself, however disreputable its critical connections. Perhaps this is where the terminological difficulties begin—difficulties, now, about the meaning of 'phenomenalism'. Bennett refers, protectively, to this doctrine as 'that least understood and oftenest "refuted" of philosophical theories' (p. 193). But if all those years of a full, free use of the terminology of *logical construction* (of material objects out of sensory states), of *analysis* or *reduction* (of statements about the former into, or to, statements about the latter) have not helped us to understand the doctrine correctly, how will Bennett's full, free use of this terminology help us to understand it now? And he does use it fully and freely (cf. esp. pp. 22, 23, 127, 216). At one point, opposing transcendental idealism, as understood by him, to transcendental realism, he says *of the latter* that it 'denies that non-mental statements reduce to mental ones' and 'gives to the concept of a non-mental (*sc.* physical) item an irreducible place in our conceptual scheme' (p. 23). But one thought that what Kant had supremely done was to show that such a concept *does* have such a place. Of course, when we step outside our ordinary conceptual scheme into the rarefied atmosphere of the critical philosophy as a whole, then we are supposed to see that this scheme, though empirically inescapable, does not present things as they are in themselves; and then, and therefore, we are supposed to embrace the phenomenalistic idealism which the transcendental variety includes. The idea that phenomenalism imposes itself independently of the full apparatus of transcendental idealism seems to be both mistaken in itself and hardly a Kantian view.

It may well be, however, that I am in part misunderstanding Bennett here rather than disagreeing with him.

The main line of argument. The main line of argument concerns the limiting conditions on any experience which any of us could 'intelligibly suppose' (cf. p. 124) he might find himself enjoying. This may perhaps be shortened to: the limiting conditions on the experience of a self-conscious being. The theses are:

(1) The data of experience are temporal (Ch. 4).

(2) Self-consciousness requires knowledge of some of one's own past states (Ch. 8).
(3) The general applicability of the concept of the past requires that experience include experience of the objective (Ch. 14).
(4) Most particular applications of the concept of temporal order among past experiences require the backing of objective considerations (Ch. 15).
(5) Objectivity requires 'spatiality' (Ch. 3).

I have already remarked on Bennett's view of the status of (1). Thesis (2) is regarded by Bennett as the main salvageable contribution of the Transcendental Deduction; (3) as obtainable by a reconstruction of the Refutation of Idealism; and (4) as the conclusion of a kind of latent argument underlying the manifest content of the Second Analogy. For (5), in which 'spatiality' is given a rather formal sense, Bennett sets out an independent argument early in his book, in place of Kant's regular, unargued transition from 'outer' to 'spatial'.

Given Bennett's view of the status of (1), a minor problem arises about that of (2). (1), it is asserted, is contingent; (2), it is implied, is unobviously analytic. But (2) seems to imply (1), at least as far as self-conscious beings are concerned. Perhaps the difficulty could be met by declaring that it is the conditional, *if* (1) *then* (2), which is analytic; or by declaring that an amended (1), including a reference to self-consciousness, is itself analytic. In the latter case, the original, 'contingent' (1), might, it seems, be put on the shelf. There are other possibilities. One of them, as already hinted, is to discard these categorizations as dubiously useful in this area.

Bennett's distribution of achievement, as between the Analytic of Concepts (that is, mainly, the Transcendental Deduction) and the Analytic of Principles (that is, mainly, the Refutation of Idealism and the Analogies) is not altogether convincing nor, perhaps, entirely consistent. He says, in more than one place, that the object of the Transcendental Deduction is to establish that a self-conscious being must be a concept-using being, and that concept-using requires judgement about the past. The step is mediated by Bennett's version of the theory of transcendental synthesis: 'transcendental synthesis' is best understood by reference to the capacity for that kind of application of complex concepts which involves giving weight to criteria-of-identity-over-time. Now it seems clear that Kant himself regarded whatever exercise of conceptual capacities was required for self-consciousness as necessarily linked to the notion of experience of an objective world (experience of the world *as* an objective world); and that *he* regarded this general link as already made out in the Transcendental Deduction. But Bennett will not have it that any such link is made out there. The whole burden of actually establishing that experience must be of the objective is held to fall on the reconstructed Refutation of Idealism. But then we must ask how Bennett's notion of the application of complex concepts involving criteria-of-identity-over-time finds a place in *his* version of what is actually achieved in the Deduction. In so far as Bennett answers this question, he does so by reference to the subject's employment of criteria of *self*-identity. But it is hard to see what this comes to when he adds that, for the 'subject' of the Transcendental Deduction—so to speak—the question whether something was a past mental state of his would be simply equivalent to the question whether it occurred at all.

Roughly speaking, Bennett represents the line of argument as follows: (*a*) the thought 'This is how it is with me *now*' requires the thought 'That is how it was with me *then*'; (*b*) the general concept of *the past* will have no application unless experience involves the application of concepts of the objective. He says that (*a*) is what is brought out by the Transcendental Deduction, and (*b*) is what we can glean from a reconstruction of the Refutation of Idealism. But if the reason (*b*) is true is that only under the stated condition will concepts of the requisite kind of complexity be applied; and if the exercise of the capacity for applying such concepts is precisely what is required for self-consciousness in general; then isn't the requirement that experience be of the objective already contained—as Kant seems to have thought and Bennett seems to deny—in the argument of the Transcendental Deduction, which insists on synthesis as the condition of self-consciousness? The weight that falls on the Refutation of Idealism, if this *is* denied, seems to be a heavy one indeed for a passage added as an afterthought.

It is impossible in this limited space to do more than thus baldly expose one's doubts; so I must add that this linear version of Bennett's argument does nothing like justice to the subtlety and force of his exposition or to the great illumination to be gained from these sections of his book.

As regards (4) above, Bennett shows great ingenuity in finding in the Second Analogy a much better argument than any which, on the face of it, it seems to contain; and makes a good case, too, for holding that he did not really put the sixpence in the pudding himself.

Substance. Bennett's treatment of the First Analogy is interesting, but puzzling. 'The Analogy', he says, 'takes for granted that we have to do with objective states of affairs and says something about how these are divided up into objects and their states or properties' (p. 187)—that is, into 'substances' and 'determinations of substances'. He takes Kant's fundamental claim to be that every objective happening is an alteration—that is, a change of, or in, something which persists throughout the change. Bennett points out, quite correctly, that if this claim is reasonably construed, it does not involve the consequences either (1) that there are things which last forever or (2) that 'objects' which suffer destruction are really only properties or states of everlasting things. Kant, on the other hand, seems to draw the first conclusion and also, by implication, the second.

There are oddities on the way to these correct judgements. I give one instance. One of the questions which Bennett considers is the question whether we might not order our experience differently from the way in which we do order it, according only a property-like status in some instances in which we in fact accord a thing-like status. He says that we might indeed do this, though it is more efficient to proceed as we do. He discusses an imagined example of what, by all possible tests, would appear to qualify as the 'annihilation' of a material object, and says that we could, though at a cost in convenience, retell the whole story in terms of change in the properties of other things. He says he excludes from consideration the sort of existence change (that is, cessation of existence of a thing) which is 'really only an alteration of the [thing's] parts, as when a book is destroyed by burning' (p. 188). But in so far as the question at issue is the feasibility of the kind of conceptual reordering which Bennett seems to have in mind, it is not even clear what it *means* to say that such cases are excluded from consideration. Can it be that Bennett thinks that the answer to the question is *obviously* affirmative for any type of object, granted that we have to do with none but ordinary cases, that it becomes a *difficult* question only when we confront the imagined case of annihilation? Or is it simply that altogether distinct questions are being confused here? The import of Bennett's question about conceptual reordering, and that of his answer to it, are in any case not clear. How much is meant, for example, by loss of conceptual 'efficiency' or 'convenience'? Are these notions at all adequate to what he has in mind? Or again, since Bennett presumably does not wish to suggest that *all* sorts of ordinary objects could simultaneously be 'reconceptualized' as, or in terms of, properties of other things, one might have expected some account of a possible non-arbitrary basis for selective reconceptualization; but no such principle is even hinted at.

It would be ungrateful, and unjust, to conclude on a carping note. I have selected for criticism some outstanding points on which doubt may reasonably be felt. There are others. But there are many more points where one feels nothing but gratitude and admiration for clarity of exposition and fertility and penetration in argument. This is a rich book, and it will permanently modify any careful reader's understanding of the *Critique* and of the matters with which it deals.

8

Does Knowledge Have Foundations?

The history of philosophy is full of unhappy or unsatisfactory metaphors. One of the least happy must be the metaphor which some empiricists employed when, to represent the relation of certain favoured classes of propositions to propositional knowledge in general, they called the favoured propositions the *foundations* of knowledge. Foundations, whatever else they may be, are *durable*, relatively to the structures raised upon them. They persist. They are laid down before building proper begins and they often remain long after the ruin or demolition of the edifice they support. But the propositions selected by the empiricist as the foundations of knowledge are essentially perishable. They are, at any moment, for any experiencing subject, just those propositions which might serve as reports of what he is currently observing or experiencing. Their essential character is that of reports of *present* observation or experience; and no proposition can survive in that character beyond the moment it relates to.

To criticize a metaphor is not, *ipso facto*, to criticize a doctrine, not even the doctrine the metaphor is meant to make vivid for us. So we ought to try to detach the doctrine from the metaphor and discover what it literally amounts to. And even if the doctrine is muddled, as the metaphor suggests it may very well be, there is often a philosophical truth at the bottom of a philosophical muddle; and so, if there is a muddle in the case, we should try to find out whether there is a truth as well.

It is not very easy to detach the doctrine from the metaphor; but it is clearly, or fairly clearly, a doctrine about the relation of evidential support, about the relation which one proposition has to another when it serves as part of the reasons or grounds for accepting the other as true. Suppose someone is making a case for the truth of a certain proposition, arguing in favour of its truth; or suppose someone is trying to arrive for himself at the truth on a certain matter on which he has not yet a settled opinion, on the basis of matters on which he already has a settled opinion. In a situation of either of these kinds, the metaphor of foundations is not altogether out of place. For the man, arguing with another or, as it were, with himself, will normally be assuming, or taking for granted, the truth of a good many other propositions. It would be not unreasonable to call these explicit premises and implicit assumptions of his argument. His argument *is* a sort of structure which rests upon *them*. They are taken as accepted before the construction begins and they have to remain in place throughout the process; if one of them is knocked out, the structure is in danger of collapsing.

In the case of a particular argument or train of reasoning, then, there are indeed some propositions which serve as support for others and are not themselves regarded as in need of support. This is a platitude, I think, which no one would wish to dispute. But of course the doctrine we have to consider is not this platitude. It differs from it in at least two ways. Accepting the platitude does not commit one to maintaining that there is any one particular species or class of propositions which serve as foundation-propositions (as explicit premises or implicit assumptions) in all sound arguments or trains of reasoning. On the contrary, it is quite obvious that foundation-propositions in particular arguments or trains of reasoning may include propositions of any and every class. The doctrine we are to consider, however, does select one class of propositions as *the* foundation-class of propositions: the class I have already mentioned. It might, in fact, be better to call it one *type* of proposition rather than one class of proposition; for the sets of propositions which, according to the doctrine, qualify as foundation-propositions are different not only from moment to moment, but also from observer to observer at any moment. The class of propositions which, for one observer at a given moment, could count as reports of what he currently observes may indeed have some members in common with the class of propositions which would have this same status for another observer at that moment. But obviously this will be so only for observers in pretty much the same observational situation; and even for such observers as these the two classes will not be identical in membership.

Here, then, is one difference between the doctrine and the platitude. The platitude allows propositions of any type to serve as foundation-propositions. The doctrine selects just one type of proposition as foundation-propositions. The other difference is this. The platitude relates to particular arguments or trains of reasoning. The doctrine relates to something less circumscribed and less easily identifiable: it relates to knowledge in general.

Now nothing is simply known: whatever is known is known to, or by, somebody. For any person at any moment there is a more or less extensive body or set or system of propositions which he either knows or at least thinks he knows. The membership of this body or system is perhaps a little indefinite at the edges in so far as there are some propositions which he will only hesitantly claim to know. And its composition will change over time, as some things are forgotten and others learned. But throughout most of an individual's life, the gains normally outweigh the losses. The individual builds up, cumulatively, a progressively richer picture of the world and its working. We may speak intelligibly of an individual's belief-system, a gradually changing and on the whole steadily growing body of belief.

The doctrine we have to consider is the doctrine that the perishable propositions of the empiricist's favoured class stand in a special relation to the more durable propositions of any such system—or at least to those of them that the individual whose system it is can properly be said to *know*. The doctrine is that the perishable propositions constitute the *ultimate* evidential support, the *ultimate* reasons (or grounds or justification) for accepting the durable propositions. It is still not clear, however, what this means. As it stands, it is just so many words. By considering some things it scarcely can mean, we might come closer to discovering what, if anything, it does mean.

One thing it scarcely could mean is that when any person in fact knows some durable proposition to be true, then some perishable proposition of the empiricist's favoured type constitutes the reason, or the ultimate reason, which that person actually has for believing the durable proposition. This would be a preposterous thesis. In the first place the membership of any individual's class of perishable propositions is always tiny and always changing and can have no bearing whatever on any but at most an insignificant fragment of his total belief-system; and even when a perishable proposition *does* momentarily serve as someone's reason for believing a true durable proposition, it is normally a condition of its doing so that the person in question should have other true beliefs not thus supported. (Thus my reason for thinking at a certain moment that the petrol tank is empty or nearly empty may be my current observation that the petrol gauge reads zero. But my ability even to make this observation, let alone appreciate its significance, depends on beliefs of mine for which current observation supplies no reason at all.) In the second place, the thesis presupposes a picture of the nature of an individual's belief-system which is itself a gross distortion of the facts of mental life. The picture is that of a kind of hierarchical structure of beliefs with higher members resting on lower members which are the individual's evidence for them or his reasons for believing them and lower members resting on still lower members until we come to the lowest level of all. But it is quite false that an individual's belief-system or set of beliefs is organized in any such way. This is not, of course, to say that members of an individual's belief-set lie entirely loose and separate in his mind, like items in a badly packed suitcase. On the contrary they are *connected*, in numerous and complex ways. But they are not organized like an argument or an army of arguments. Of many propositions it is true that the more securely fixed they are in one's belief-system, the less appropriate it seems to ask what one's reasons are for believing them. What are my *reasons* for thinking that my daughter's name is Julia, that the French for rabbit is 'lapin', or that Napoleon was defeated at Waterloo? One might say: these are things I know too well to have *reasons* for believing.

Before we leave the preposterous thesis, it might be worth enquiring whether we could make it a little less preposterous by extending the empiricist's class of foundation-propositions to include not only propositions stating what the individual currently observes but also propositions stating what he can remember observing in the past. On this amendment, foundation-propositions would no longer be thought of as essentially perishable in character; they could survive for an individual for as long as he could remember making the observation which engendered them. This is a slight improvement, in that the class of foundation-propositions at anyone's command at any moment is greatly enlarged. But the thesis is still preposterous. Of all the things one knows it is but an insignificant proportion of which one could truthfully say: my reason, or my basic reason, for believing this proposition is such-and-such an observation which I recall making. And of course the enlargement of the foundation-class does nothing to meet the objection that the presupposed picture of the individual's belief-system is wholly unrealistic.

We may take it, then, that the foundationalist thesis is not a thesis about how an individual's belief-system, in so far as it is also a knowledge-system, is organized in his mind. Could it be a thesis about how all those parts of his belief-system which are indeed knowledge *come to have a place* in his belief-system?, i.e. the thesis that everything he knows which is not itself a proposition of the foundational kind he came to know as a result of *inference* from propositions which were of the foundational kind *or* as a result of inference from propositions which he earlier came to know in this way *or* as a result of inference from propositions *some* of which he earlier came to know in this way and *some* of which were themselves of the foundational kind. This thesis is also preposterous; and since a succession of victories over preposterous theses would be tedious, I will not discuss it further.

Points made so far include the general point that a hierarchical picture of a reasoned structure is unrealistic both as a picture of how an individual's belief-system is organized in his mind and as a picture of how the system is built up. I earlier remarked, however, that *at some times* and *for some purposes*—e.g. when we are arguing for, or trying to reach, a conclusion—*some parts* of an individual's belief-system *are* organized as reasoned structures; and that in these cases it does make sense to talk of the foundations of the structures. Would a possible interpretation of the empiricist doctrine be the thesis that in all such cases, if the argument really justified its conclusion, then its foundations would always be propositions of the empiricist's favoured sort? This thesis would be much weaker and more limited than its predecessors and would also, as earlier remarked, be obviously false. I mention it only to distinguish it from another thesis which is not so clearly limited and not so clearly false.

Part of this thesis is that there is no proposition about the world or its working which is in principle immune from question, that all beliefs whatever are in principle open to challenge or criticism. And the other part of the thesis is that when a belief is seriously questioned, any rational procedure for settling the question one way or another must involve giving the questioner (or his giving himself) some reason for thinking that the belief or its contradictory is true; and this can be done only by putting the questioner (or by his putting himself) in a position to make relevant observations—to hear something or to see something. So there is a sense in which the acceptability of the questioned proposition (or its contradictory) rests ultimately on propositions stating what the questioner sees or hears in such situations. This would hold for *any* proposition which was both challenged and sustained after challenge. And any proposition whatever is open to challenge. So actual and possible propositions stating what is seen and heard in observation situations do ultimately, and in a sense, lie at the basis of the acceptability of all acceptable propositions.

The points made in this version of the doctrine seem, with some trimming of rhetoric and some modification perhaps, to be themselves acceptable points. Yet it is worth setting beside them some other points which tend, as it were, to diminish their impact. One of these other points I have made, in a slightly different context, already. It is that many of the observations regarded as relevant to some disputed belief are observations that the observer could not even make, let alone appreciate the relevance of, were it not for the presence in his belief-system of many other beliefs or assumptions which are not themselves in question at the moment of observation. Another point is this. Very often the testing-procedure, in the case of a disputed belief, consists in looking up an authoritative text, or an atlas, say, or in consulting some other person who is presumed to know the truth of the matter. It is worth considering the relative roles of observation and assumption in such a case. The only function of the observation is to give the observer access to *someone else's* past or present *belief* about the matter in hand. That the observation achieves this result is itself a belief which itself involves a quite complicated set of assumptions; and the belief that this result, once achieved, settles the question at issue is a belief that the beliefs of the authority in question are themselves reliable. Yet a third point is this. It is said that no proposition is in principle immune from question. But the only questions we need take seriously are serious questions. And we should note that almost any serious question, seriously asked in the spheres of history or natural science or practical affairs, presupposes an enormous framework or background of things taken to be known. (Consider the background of knowledge involved in seriously questioning, say, the historicity of Jesus.) Doubts and questions arise within frameworks of knowledge and assumption. And about the general frame of all these frameworks no serious doubt or question is, or could be, ever raised. This means that philosophical scepticism about, say, the external world, other minds, or the reality of the past, does not, in the present sense, count as serious questioning at all.

I think we have reached the point at which we can give up the doctrine of foundations. In no form does it help us very much to get what we want, which is, presumably, a realistic picture of our knowledge-structures and belief-systems as they are—a picture which must, of course, among other things, show how propositions of present and remembered observation fit into the structures. One thing which emerges, I hope, from what has so far been said is the great importance, *at any stage at which reasons, criticism, inference are in question*, of bodies of pre-existing knowledge or belief to provide an indispensable background for these reflective operations. The formation of such a corpus, in the case of each individual—the formation of that individual's world-picture—is, of course, the outcome of his exposure to, and interaction with, the world, including the training and instruction he receives from other members of his community; and that such exposure involves observation, seeing and hearing, is another platitude which is not in question. Even after the power of critical and self-conscious reflection has clearly emerged, the process whereby the individual's picture of the world is enlarged, modified, filled in, is still quite largely a matter of unreflective adjustment to, or accommodation of, the same sort of influences as operate in the earlier formative periods. There are two presumptions which underlie the whole process, regarded as a process of building up structures of knowledge. The first is that the picture which a man builds up for himself of that part of the world-scene and its history of which he has continuous and intimate first-hand experience will *generally* be, within the terms available to him, a substantially accurate picture. We might call this the presumption of first-hand authority. The second is that when someone purports to communicate information to another or to others, it will *generally* be in good faith. This we might call the presumption of general truthfulness. The first of these presumptions may be a part of what gives the foundationalist doctrine such appeal as it has.

Actually the word 'presumption' is too weak a word for these two conditions. They are not merely fortunate contingencies which make the acquisition and spread of knowledge *easier*. They are closer to being conceptual truths, conditions for the possibility of the existence and application of our concepts of knowledge, accuracy, truth.

I said earlier that at the bottom of a philosophical muddle there often lies a philosophical truth. So far the only truths we have been able to dig out from the ruins of the foundationalist metaphor seem rather platitudinous. There is the rather specific platitude that when a seriously contested belief is being checked, one has to make some observation, even if it is only a matter of looking at a text or listening to what someone says. And there is the rather general platitude that first-hand experience of the world and its ways, or the receiving of information and instruction about it from others, also as a matter of necessity involves observing—looking and listening, or, at least, seeing and hearing. This seems rather a disappointing result; so perhaps we should inquire whether there isn't more to be said, or even whether these platitudes themselves can't be so turned as to catch the eye with more of a philosophical glitter to them.

So let me turn the platitudes a little. At any moment, we may say, our knowledge (or belief) system *has* to accommodate the beliefs which current experience *forces on us* at that moment. This may, and generally will, involve no strain; and, as already implied, what our current experience does force on us in the way of belief is a function of the character of the pre-existent system. Again, the accommodation may be effected by some conflicting belief's discreetly sinking out of sight, to reaffirm itself when the moment is past; or by a temporary failure of sensitivity to logical strain; though, on this last point, it should be added that, in view of the inextricable involvement with each other of belief about the world and action in it, we cannot for long harbour inconsistent beliefs on matters that really concern us without severe stress and loss of power to achieve effective action. In any case, there is nothing temporary about the general necessity of this kind of accommodation to current experience. It is a necessity which is always with us; and always was with us, from the time when we could first be credited with beliefs at all; so that from that time onwards all subsequent states of our belief-system are the outcome of the ongoing process of accommodation to the unceasing pressures of experience.

We can turn the platitude here just a little further. We mustn't turn it too far, or we shall find ourselves trapped once more in the errors of classical empiricism, struggling once again in the bogs of problematic idealism or phenomenalism. But we can safely turn it a little further by remarking that the picture of a belief-system responding to the continuous pressures of experience doesn't sufficiently bring out the closeness of the relation between belief and experience at the point of contact. Beliefs involve concepts and the concepts which figure in our most primitive and least theoretical beliefs only acquire meaning for us, only *are* concepts for us as being just those concepts which enter most intimately and immediately into our experience of the world. They are what—special training apart—we experience the world as exemplifying, what we *see* things and situations *as* cases of. Correlatively experience is awareness of the world *as* exemplifying *them*. We should not say that belief at this level is formed on the basis of, or as the result of the pressures of, experience. Rather we should say that, at this level, belief, concept, and experience are *merged*; that seeing and believing are, at this level, one. Of course this would be an exaggeration; for judgement may sometimes be suspended, or we may sometimes reasonably refuse, as we say, to believe what our senses tell us. But it is only an exaggeration; and a corrigible one. One of the mistakes of the classical empiricists was to suppose that the concepts in question were concepts of simple sensory qualities. But they are not; they are concepts of objects and people and *their* qualities and relations.

I think perhaps it is this intimate and necessary relation of belief, concept, and experience—belief about the world, concepts of the objective, and experience of the world—that is the most interesting *philosophical* truth at the bottom of the muddle about foundations; but of course it is not necessary, in order to accommodate *this* truth, to embrace an unrealistic picture of the structure, organization, and evolution of our knowledge—or belief-systems.

Something other than philosophical illumination, however, may accrue from the foundational doctrine. Whatever its theoretical defects—and in so far as it hovers uneasily between the preposterous and the platitudinous, those defects are not minor—it may yet have a certain practical value. Muddled theories may be the vehicle of excellent precepts: in this case, of a caution against credulity, an encouragement to criticism, a reminder that though not every accepted belief or purported piece of information can be checked, or tested, against the evidence of our eyes and ears, some can be and many should be. For the presumptions which I mentioned as conditions of the possibility of our concept of knowledge are only *general* presumptions. They allow plenty of room for the formation, and for the unwitting or deliberate propagation, of false belief.

I would like to end with two quotations. The first is from Wittgenstein and runs:

When we first begin to *believe* anything, what we believe is not a single proposition, it is a whole system of propositions. (Light dawns gradually over the whole.)

The second is from Austin, and I put it in in case what I have said seems rather messy and complicated instead of neat and simple. It runs:

Well, it is complicated a bit; but life and truth and things do tend to be complicated. It's not things, it's philosophers, that are simple.

9
Knowledge and Truth

When a philosopher undertakes to discuss the nature of truth, it usually happens that we very quickly find him talking about something else: linguistic meaning, perhaps, or the nature of knowledge. The reason for this is that the perfectly general question about the nature of truth is only too easily answered. Presumably we know what truth in general is if we know in general what it is for a statement or belief to be true. Well, a statement is true if and only if things are as one who makes that statement thereby states them to be. A belief is true if and only if things are as one who holds that belief thereby holds them to be. This answer is sometimes given the form of a schema: the statement or belief that p is true if and only if p. The schema covers every conceivable case of truth because it allows of any grammatically admissible filling. Thus if someone says that Peter is bald, what he says is true if and only if Peter is bald. If someone believes that $7 + 5 = 12$, what he believes is true if and only if $7 + 5 = 12$. And so on.

The answer is unassailable but frustrating. Surely in raising the general question we wanted something more substantial than this thin and trivial-seeming formula. Perhaps we wanted to know about the nature of those things—thoughts, propositions, statements, or beliefs—which we call true or false. Or, hot for certainties as we are, perhaps, we wanted to know about the general conditions under which we may be said to *know* that one of these things is true. And so we find our philosopher turning to these other matters. In particular, recently, under the title of Theories of Truth, philosophers and logicians have been conducting investigations into the general types of *linguistic structures* by mastering which we are able to say and understand the true and false things we do say and understand.

This is not an unnatural turn to take. If it were not for language, truth would amount to very little, because thought would amount to very little—propositional thought, at least, the kind to which the notion of truth is appropriate. Beyond a certain not very advanced point, what we can't say we can't think. But our languages put at our disposal a limitless potential of thought. They do so because to understand a language is to know, in advance, the significance, of limitless sentences and combinations of sentences; even though we shall only ever use or read or hear a comparatively insignificant proportion of them. A central problem which confronts the theorist of meaning is that of explaining the individual language-user's understanding of the potentially limitless range of the sentences of his language. Evidently the problem cannot be solved at all without crediting the speaker with some kind of mastery of a structure of general rules or principles of combination of linguistic elements. Such a mastery, taken together with a grasp of a finite vocabulary of elements, (individually learned), must contain in itself the possibility of this limitless understanding. The specific problem for the theorist of semantic structure is to disclose the principles of combination involved and make clear their semantic force.

It might be questioned whether the title of truth-theory is appropriate to these investigations. But it is not inappropriate. For the central consideration in understanding the significance of sentences is a grasp of their truth conditions. To understand a sentence is to know what thought it expresses or is capable, in given contextual circumstances, of expressing; and to know this is to know what we would be believing if we took that thought to be *true*. So the theorist's task can almost equally well be described as that of displaying the limited set of principles which generate the truth conditions of the limitless sentences of a language.

Almost as well described; but not quite as well. I said that an enquiry into the nature of truth tends to turn, on the one hand, into an enquiry into the nature of meaning, on the other hand into an enquiry into the nature of knowledge. These are not independent enquiries. A theory of meaning must be, I have implied, a theory of understanding. It must not only show how the meanings of sentences are systematically determined by the meanings of constituent words and constructions. It must be able to show how we *understand* meanings as so determined. Understanding a sentence is knowledge of its truth conditions. But the claim to know what the truth conditions of a sentence were would be an empty claim if accompanied by a total disclaimer of the ability to recognize when those truth conditions were fulfilled. More exactly, it would be nonsense to claim to know the truth conditions of a sentence but to admit to having no idea what would justify one in either affirming or denying that the conditions were fulfilled. Now a general theory of the justifying conditions for affirming or denying propositions is just what has been traditionally understood as a theory of knowledge. And so a theory of meaning points to a theory of knowledge. But it may, as I shall try to show, be a slightly misleading pointer.

Let me first return to our simple answer to the general question about the nature of truth. It might be said that the answer is not quite so empty as I suggested. Someone says or believes, say, that Peter is bald. What he says or believes is true if and only if Peter is bald. Does not this formula at least make the point that, as Austin once expressed it, it takes two to make a truth? For the formula incorporates a twofold reference: a reference, on the one hand, to a believing or a saying, on the other hand, to that in the world which the statement or belief is about. And it invites us to see the truth as consisting in a certain correspondence or fit between these two things. Moreover, at least in the case of a simple statement like 'Peter is bald', we can give a quite precise sense to this notion of correspondence or fit—as a word-to-world relation. Such a statement fits the world—or its appropriate bit of the world—if the particular item referred to by the subject-term has the general characteristic assigned to it by the predicate-term. Or in other words: a statement coupling particular name and general predicate is true if and only if the named item satisfies the predicate. Of course not all statements are of this simple form. But any theory which sets out to show systematically how the truth conditions of sentences of more elaborate construction are determined must be erected on the basis of precisely such simple forms as this. So such sentences lie at the foundation of a semantic theory of truth, a theory of meaning for a language.

And do they not also lie at the foundations of a theory of knowledge? The ability to recognize some particular individual, perceptually encountered, as possessing some general characteristic seems, on the face of it, fundamental both to linguistic understanding and to knowledge in general. And it is just this simple form of sentence which is best adapted to recording such recognitions; though to be sure, this is not all the simple form is fit for. So, perhaps, we can represent the theory of knowledge and the theory of meaning as two aspects of a single theory, having a common base or point of departure and yielding between them all that we can hope for by way of a substantial theory of truth.

However, caution is required. I want to mention two ways in which, if we are not careful, the embrace of these encouraging thoughts may lead us into error. I imagined someone finding it a merit of the simple formula I began with that it incorporated a twofold reference—to a saying or believing on the one hand, to that in the world which the statement or belief was about on the other; and hence envisaging truth as a kind of word-to-world correspondence, best understood in semantical terms. We might call this the realist interpretation of the formula; and my first point is that an incautious commitment to this interpretation, too simply understood, involves the risk of either adopting too narrow a conception of truth on the one hand or of falling into mythology on the other. We say that Peter is bald; that $7 + 5 = 12$; that John ought to look after his sick brother; and so on. All these things we call true. And our thin formula, thinly understood, covers them all. We say and believe that $7 + 5 = 12$; and $7 + 5$ does $= 12$; so what we say and believe is true. But if we now impose the realist interpretation on our formula, matters are not so straightforward. We are in no difficulty with 'Peter is bald'. There is Peter, his head but sparsely adorned with hair, an object in the world, visibly in a condition which fully satisfies the semantic condition for the truth of our statement. But what relations and dispositions of what things in the world make it *true* that $7 + 5 = 12$ or that *if* Peter is bald, *then* Peter is bald? Again, John and his sick brother are doubtless in the world; the former's activity of caring for the latter may be so as well; but where in the world shall we find the relation signified by 'ought'?

There are two well-known responses to these difficulties, both of which show the power of the realist conception of truth. One is to declare that mathematical equations, the tautologies of logic, and moral judgements are not, strictly speaking, statements or propositions at all, and hence are not, strictly speaking, true or false. They are to be assimilated, rather, to rules or imperatives. They relate to the ordinary natural world; but they relate to it, not as statements about it, but as recipes for action within it.

The other and opposite reaction is to embrace Platonism in mathematics and logic, and non-natural qualities in the sphere of morals. The philosopher who follows this course does not, like his opponent, limit the concept of truth; instead he extends the concept of reality or the world. He imagines or invents a realm of perfect immutable mathematical objects, the relations between which are simply reflected or mirrored in the truths of mathematics; or, as Moore did, he imagines a layer of non-natural qualities supervening upon the qualities or relations to be found in nature.

Both reactions are unsatisfactory. The first all too cavalierly ignores or overrides the coverage of the concept of truth that we actually have. 'It is true that p if and only if p'—the unassailable formula that we began with—is no less hospitable to moral judgements and mathematical propositions than it is to records of common observation or history or propositions of natural science. At the very least this fact calls for explanation. The second reaction does indeed offer an explanation. But the explanation it offers is spurious; and a spurious explanation is worse than none at all.

If both reactions are unsatisfactory and they share a common motivation, it is that common motivation which we must question. We must look with a critical eye at that realist conception, that simple notion of correspondence, which encourages one party to limit the extent of truth to what is thought of as the world and encourages the other party to extend the limits of the world to fit what is acknowledged as the truth. Not that we need abandon the simple realist conception altogether. Obviously there are some cases which it fits very well. We should rather take these cases as a starting point, as the primary or basic cases of truth; and then seek to explain how we intelligibly and properly extend the notion of truth beyond these limits and apply it to utterances which play a different and often more complex role in our lives and our thoughts.

Obviously I have not the time, even if I had the power, to undertake now a comprehensive explanation on these lines. I turn instead to another point at which caution is required—all the more so, perhaps, if we envisage such a progressive explanation of the coverage of the concept of truth. I spoke a little earlier of the capacity to recognize a particular situation or individual, with which one is perceptually confronted, as being of a certain general kind or as possessing a certain general character; and I remarked that this capacity seemed fundamental both to linguistic understanding and to knowledge in general. Fundamental to linguistic understanding; for how else should the basic connections of meaning, the basic semantic links between word and world, be established? And fundamental to knowledge; for on what other basis could knowledge be developed, on what other *foundations* could the structure of beliefs which each of us counts as his knowledge of the world be erected?

So at least we rhetorically ask. And so we are encouraged—or some empiricist philosophers are encouraged—to embrace a certain picture of knowledge in general. Consider those propositions which for any experiencing subject, at any moment, are just the propositions which might serve as reports of the results of his exercise of this fundamental capacity of perceptual recognition: reports, that is, of current observation. Surely these propositions must be as fundamental as that capacity. They must be the *foundations* of knowledge.

But now we must ask what this could mean. We must ask what is the doctrine that lies behind the metaphor. In the context of a particular argument or train of reasoning the metaphor of *foundations* has a clear sense. A man starts from certain explicit premises and makes certain implicit assumptions, and argues or reasons, on this basis, to his conclusion. His argument *is* a sort of structure which *rests upon* these premises and assumptions. They are taken as accepted before the construction begins and they have to remain in place throughout the process; if one of them is knocked out, the structure is in danger of collapsing. In such a particular argument or train of reasoning, then, there *are* foundation-propositions; propositions which serve as support for others and are not themselves at the moment regarded as in need of support.

Evidently in such a context foundation-propositions are not just of one special kind; they may be of any kind. The doctrine we are to consider, however, does not relate to particular arguments. It relates to knowledge in general. It seems it must be the doctrine that one special class of propositions, namely observation propositions, constitute the *ultimate* evidential support, the *ultimate* reasons (or grounds or justification) for our accepting as true everything else we can properly be said to know.

It is still not wholly clear what this means. One thing it might mean is this: that when any person in fact knows some non-observation proposition to be true, then some observation-proposition constitutes the *reason*, or the *ultimate* reason, which that person actually *has* for believing the non-observation proposition.

Unfortunately this is a quite preposterous thesis. It is only slightly less preposterous if one extends the class of observation propositions to include not only propositions stating what the individual currently observes, but also propositions stating what he can remember observing in the past. The thesis is preposterous in several ways. First, of all the things one knows, it is but an insignificant proportion of which one could truthfully say: my reason, or my basic reason, for believing this proposition is such-and-such an observation which I am either making now or can recall making in the past. Second, even when someone can cite an observation as his reason for believing some other proposition, it is normally a condition of its serving as a reason that the person in question should have other true beliefs which are not thus supported. (Thus my reason for thinking at a certain moment that my petrol tank is empty may be my current observation that the petrol gauge reads zero. But my ability even to make this observation, let alone appreciate its significance, depends on beliefs of mine for which current or remembered observation supplies no reason at all.) Finally, the thesis presupposes a picture of an individual's belief-system which is itself a gross distortion of the facts of mental life.

The picture is that of a kind of hierarchical structure of beliefs with higher members resting on lower members which are the individual's evidence for them, or his reasons for believing them, and lower members resting on still lower members until we come to the lowest level of all. But it is quite false that an individual's belief-system or set of beliefs is organized in any such way. This is not, of course, to say that members of an individual's belief-set lie entirely loose and separate in his mind, like items in a badly packed suit-case. On the contrary, they are *connected* in numerous and complex ways. But they are not organized like an argument or an army of arguments. Of many propositions it is true that the more securely fixed they are in one's belief-system, the less appropriate it seems to ask what one's reasons are for believing them. What are my reasons for thinking that my daughter's name is 'Julia', that the French for rabbit is 'lapin', or that Napoleon was defeated at Waterloo? One might say: these are things I know too well to have *reasons* for believing.

As a picture of how an individual's belief-system is organized in his mind, the foundationalist thesis is, then, totally unrealistic.

Can we find for it any less unrealistic interpretation? It is often remarked that none of our beliefs about the world and its working is in principle immune from challenge or question; and when any one of our beliefs is seriously questioned, any rational procedure for settling the question will normally involve putting ourselves in a position to make some relevant observation. So observation propositions, it may be said, are at least the ultimate *checkpoints* of knowledge.

This is a more modest claim. Checkpoints are not foundations. Yet the impact of even this more modest claim is diminished once we realize that the observational checkpoints cannot function as such without assistance. Thus, many of the observations regarded as relevant to some disputed belief are observations that the observer could not even make, let alone appreciate the relevance of, were it not for the presence in his belief-system of many other beliefs or assumptions which are not themselves in question at the moment of observation. Again, the function of relevant observation, in the case of disputed belief, is very often simply to give the observer access to the past or present *belief* of someone else regarded as authoritative on the matter in question. That the observation in such a case achieves the desired result is itself a belief involving a quite complicated set of further assumptions, and while we may grant that no proposition in our belief-system is in principle immune from question, yet we must note that almost any serious question, seriously asked in the spheres of history or natural science or practical affairs, presupposes an enormous framework or background of things taken to be known. In general, at any stage at which *reasons*, *criticism*, *inference* are in question, bodies of pre-existing knowledge or belief provide an indispensable background for these reflective operations; and it is against such a background that observation propositions play their checking role.

Presumably we require of any theory of knowledge that it should give us a realistic picture of the general character of our knowledge-structures and belief-systems—including, or at least making room for, an account of how they develop and how they may rationally be modified. Such a picture must, of course, among other things, show how propositions of present and remembered observation fit into the structure. So far the only truth about these propositions which we have been able to dig out from the ruins of the foundationalist metaphor is the rather specific platitude that when a seriously questioned belief is being checked, one has to make some observation, even if it is only a matter of looking at a text or listening to what someone says.

But there is a more general truth to be recovered from these ruins. Evidently the formation of the individual's corpus of belief—the formation of his world-picture—is the outcome of his exposure to, and interaction with, the world, including the training he receives from other members of his community; and evidently such exposure involves observation, seeing and hearing. At some point in this process there emerges the power of critical and self-conscious reflection. Perhaps we should not say that the individual has a body of *beliefs before* this power emerges; certainly we should not say that this power emerges *before* he has a body of beliefs. As Wittgenstein put it: 'When we first begin to *believe* anything, what we believe is not a single proposition, it is a whole system of propositions. (Light dawns gradually over the whole.)' But the point to be stressed now is the ongoing and continuous character of the individual's exposure to the world. At any moment, we may say, our knowledge (or belief) system has to accommodate the beliefs which our current experience *forces on us* at that moment. This may, and generally will, involve no strain; and, as already implied, what our current experience does force on us in the way of belief is a function of the character of the pre-existent system. But the necessity of this kind of accommodation to current experience is a necessity which is always with us; and always was with us, from the time when we could first be credited with beliefs at all; so that from that time onwards all subsequent states of our belief-system are the outcome of the ongoing process of accommodation to the unceasing pressures of experience.

These, then are the elements of truth which we can, and must, retain from the foundationalist thesis. Let me conclude by remarking that we can perhaps retain something else as well: not so much a theoretical insight as a practical precept: a caution against credulity; an encouragement to criticism; a reminder that though not *every* accepted belief or purported piece of information can be checked or tested against the evidence of our eyes and ears, some can be so tested and many should be. We cannot coherently question everything at once; a radical and all-pervasive scepticism is senseless; but one of the things we learn from experience is that selective scepticism is wise.

10

Scruton and Wright on Anti-Realism

Both symposiasts agree that a theory of meaning for a language should also be a theory of understanding, i.e. it should yield an account of what a speaker's understanding of the language consists in.[1] They both refer to truth-theories, of a kind familiarly advocated: theories which implicitly represent the speaker's understanding of the declarative sentences of the language as consisting in knowing, in effect, under what conditions those sentences would be true (or: under what conditions utterance of those sentences would yield truth), irrespective of whether it could be *conclusively* ascertained that those conditions held or did not hold. Mr Scruton is inclined to say that such a theory could be correct as far as it went, but would not be complete or adequate; that it would require *supplementation* by an account, which might be more grateful to the verificationist ear, of the criteria which an understanding speaker would use for the application of certain predicates of the language, *viz*. those which were treated as primitive by the theory. However, such supplementation, he suggests, would constitute no challenge to the realist framework of the theory.

Mr Wright suggests that this view of Scruton's shows a misunderstanding of what a truth-theory purports to supply. Such a theory states the satisfaction-conditions of primitive predicates quite explicitly, and indeed it is on this basis that it delivers the truth conditions of sentences. So why, Wright enquires, if the truth-theory requires any supplementation at all,

---

[1] This address was delivered by Prof. Strawson on Sunday, 11 July, 1976, as Chairman of the symposium 'Truth Conditions and Criteria' by Mr Roger Scruton and Mr Crispin Wright during the annual Joint Session of this Society and the Mind Association at the University of Warwick; see *Aristotelian Society, Suppl. Vol.* 50, 1976, pp. 193–245. At the request of members, the address is here presented in the form in which it was originally delivered.

should it require supplementation only in the case of primitive predicates? Why not, for example and crucially, in the case of quantifiers too? The enquiry is pertinent, and its pertinence leads one to suppose that Wright's suggestion of a misunderstanding on Scruton's part may well be correct. But Wright's own position on the matter of supplementation is also open to question. He seems to think that if a truth-theory delivered an account of what the understanding speaker knows, then such a theory should be in no need of supplementation at all—it would already embody a full account of speaker's understanding. But this is by no means clear. To say what a speaker knows is not of itself to give an account of what his knowing it in practice consists in, of how his knowledge is manifested in his use of the language.

A rational speaker's grasp of his language is *manifested* in, *inter alia*, his responding in certain ways to the recognizable situations with which he is and has been confronted. So much is agreed on all hands, and is part of the reason why the theory of knowledge and the theory of understanding are inseparable. But Mr Wright seems to take it as evident that the rational speaker's response to such situations can in *no* case be *governed* by a certain kind of conception—a conception of a state of affairs, of a condition of truth, which, for one reason or another, in fact or in principle, is not, or is no longer, or is not for the speaker, accessible to direct observation or memory. But this question—whether the rational speaker's response can be so governed—is just the question at issue; and one has the impression that Mr Wright quite handsomely begs it. For on this crucial point I do not find that he produces any real argument. He suggests that no one who takes seriously the connection between meaning and use can dissent from his view. But this is not at all obvious. It *is* obvious enough that, as Wright puts it, 'grasp of the sense of a sentence cannot be displayed in *response* to unrecognisable conditions'. No truth-theorist needs to dispute this tautology. It is enough for the truth-theorist that the grasp of the sense of a sentence can be displayed in response to *recognizable* conditions—of various sorts: there are those which conclusively establish the truth or falsity of the sentence; there are those which (given our general theory of the world) constitute evidence, more or less good, for or against the truth of the sentence; there are even those which point to the unavoidable absence of evidence either way. The appropriate response varies, of course, from case to case, in the last case being of the form, 'We shall never know whether p or not'. Perhaps Wright objects to this because he thinks we oughtn't to *have* a general theory of the world which extends further, so to speak, than we can see. But this is a matter in which we have no option; and any theory of meaning had better adapt itself to the fact even at the cost of sacrificing a dogma or two.

I have not so far spoken as if it was anything but reasonably clear what the issue between the verificationist or anti-realist and his truth-theoretical opponent amounted to. But in fact I am very hazy about exactly where the actual lines of disagreement are supposed to be drawn. And this point at least must remain *un*clear just so long as it remains unclear where the limits of possible conclusive verification are supposed to fall; unclear just in which cases, and why, what the one party regards as the truth condition of a sentence is seen by the other as verification-transcendent and therefore as something either wholly dubious or at least as having no role to play in the explanation of the speaker's understanding of the sentence. So we need to know *at least* what is to count as falling within the range of 'recognisable situations', what is to count as conclusive verification, *whose* capacity in fact or in principle to do the recognizing is in question, what importance, if any, to attach to the disjunction 'in fact or in principle', and what 'in principle' means. My own impression is not that we are in the presence of a single clear-cut issue, but rather that we are in a confused area in which several well-worn philosophical problems are jostling each other as well as a number of new, and perhaps gratuitous, perplexities. Certainly the route *into* the area is relatively new: the new anti-realism starts from certain views on mathematical truth and mathematical discourse and seeks to generalize them to the extent of advancing counterpart views on discourse concerning the natural world. Of mathematics I am quite incompetent to speak. But there is a certain initial air of paradox about this approach; for I suppose that part at least of the appeal of anti-realist views about pure mathematics lay precisely in the *contrast* between the content of that science and the subject matters of history, geography, natural science, and ordinary chat; that it lay precisely in the view that the notion of a realm of facts waiting to be explored, some parts of which might, indeed would, remain undisclosed or be irrecoverably lost sight of, (a matter at best of speculation or uncertain inference)—that any such notion was quite improperly imported into mathematics from its natural home, *viz.* the natural world.

However, general complaints of unclarity or initial paradox don't advance discussion of any issue very much, so I should like to refer to one or two particular cases. I take first the ancient case of the sentence 'John is in pain', spoken of John by another. Mr Wright, if I have understood him correctly, attributes to his opponent the view that the sentence (or statement) has a truth condition which, from the speaker's point of view, is necessarily verification-transcendent, but which nevertheless governs the speaker's use of the sentence. The speaker's knowledge of these truth conditions, on this view, constitutes his grasp of its meaning. What is Mr Wright's alternative view of the relation of truth condition to meaning in this case? There seem to be three possibilities:

(1) The sentence has no *truth condition* at all; it is just a right thing to say in a certain range of circumstances, and knowing its meaning is practical knowledge of what those circumstances are.
(2) The sentence has truth conditions, and knowing its meaning is practical knowledge of these; but its truth conditions (at least for everyone except John) are nothing other than the disjunction of the circumstances aforementioned.
(3) The sentence has a truth condition, but this has nothing to do with its meaning (at least for anyone except perhaps John); anyone else can understand the sentence without knowing what its truth condition is.

I have arranged the possibilities in order of decreasing attractiveness. The last has the consequence that someone could have a complete grasp of the meaning of what he said without knowing what he was saying, i.e. asserting—an unappealing thought. The second amounts to a behaviourist, or some other variety of physicalistic, reductionism—with perhaps the additional feature that the predicate 'in pain' has a different sense in the mouth of a self-ascriber from that which it has in the mouth of an other-ascriber. The first—which denies that the sentence has a truth condition at all—is the least unattractive; but it has the unsatisfactory feature that it leaves one with no account of what the speaker, in uttering the sentence, is actually doing. It is really no good simply saying that he is making an 'assertoric use' of the sentence when it has just been denied that there is anything he actually asserts in uttering it. Something different, or at least something further, must be said. Thus, for example, Ramsey, when he denied the propositional status of variable hypotheticals (open generalizations), was ready with an alternative account: they are not judgements, he said, but rules for judging. They could be adopted or rejected, but not, strictly speaking, asserted or denied. Or Mackie, who denies truth value to conditionals, at least in their core meaning, offers an account of what one is doing in uttering them. It is not my purpose here either to endorse or to criticize such accounts. The point is that *some* alternative account of what the speaker is doing in saying 'John is in pain' must also be forthcoming if the sentence is denied a truth value; and the truth is that no remotely plausible account is, in this case, available. Indeed the correct and only plausible account of the whole matter is precisely the one which Wright rejects. It *is* part of what it is now fashionable to call our general *theory* of the world that we regard other people as subject to roughly the same range of sensations as we are painfully or joyously or indifferently aware of in ourselves; and it is in no way contrary to reason to regard ourselves—as in any case we cannot help doing—as justified in certain circumstances in ascribing to John a particular state of feeling which we cannot in the nature of the case experience ourselves, and his being in which is therefore, if such is the standard invoked, necessarily verification-transcendent. The seas of argument may wash for ever around these rocks of truth; but the rocks are not worn away.

 I consider another kind of case—the case of statements about the past, a past remote enough to be beyond the reach of the memory of anyone now living. An example would be: 'Lord Anglesey had his leg shot off at Wellington's side' or 'Charles Stuart walked bareheaded to his place of execution'. On the day in question, or the next day, such a sentence may be uttered by someone on the strength of observation or remembered observation of an occurrence or series of occurrences which the sentence itself describes and which can fairly be identified, at least for such a speaker, as fulfilling its truth condition. For us the situation is different. We not only were not, but, given the dates of our births, are in principle debarred from having been, in a position to make any such observation. If we assert such a sentence, it has to be on the strength of the historical evidence. Exactly the same question arises for the anti-realist in this case as in the case of 'John is in pain': i.e. what is the relation, as far as *we* are concerned, between truth condition and meaning? The same range of answers is available as before: no truth condition at all, truth condition absorbed into evidence, or truth condition irrelevant to meaning. But the point most worth emphasizing in this case is that whichever answer is chosen has the consequence that the sentence in our mouths has a different *meaning* from that which it has in the mouths of those who were in fact or in principle—though I confess to being unclear as to what principle—in a position to recognize that condition as obtaining which the sentence appears to describe. I think this conclusion about difference of meaning—indeed difference of kind of meaning—must be unacceptable. And in particular it must be unacceptable to anyone who rightly cherishes the doctrine that the meaning of a sentence is determined by the meanings of its constituents and the way in which they are combined in the sentence. For he will surely be reluctant to locate an *ambiguity* anywhere either in the constituents or in the construction of these sentences (at least as uttered by any Englishman). I have taken an example from the relatively recent past; but it would be a matter of no great difficulty, especially if we dwell upon the point about the relation between sentence-meaning and sentence-composition, to mount an argument carrying a truth condition conception of meaning as far back in the past as you please.

I should like to consider some other and more difficult kinds of example, but it would take time and I fear I should exceed a chairman's licence if I did so. The general point I have wanted to make is this. The conception of verification-transcendent truth conditions—at least in one or another of the relatively stringent senses of 'verification-transcendent' which Wright's anti-realist seems to favour—this conception, and its link with that of meaning, is an essential part of a general view of the world which is in no way contrary to reason and to which we are in any case inescapably committed. This does not mean for one moment that we have to sacrifice any of the real gains secured to us in the past under the banner of a more modest verificationism. In particular, it does not mean that any *concepts*, or pretended concepts, plain or fancy, for which it is claimed that they have, or might have, application *in* the world, are immune from empiricist criticism. Nor does it mean that we are committed in advance to saying, of every type of sentence which is declarative in form and introduces no dubious concept, that the meaning of any sentence of the type is wholly, or even in part, a matter of truth conditions, strictly understood. The notions of truth, assertion, and fact have areas of unproblematic application which are a good deal more comprehensive than Wright's anti-realist seems prepared to allow; but it does not follow that these areas are simply coextensive with the range of use of declarative sentences. Where the application of these notions *is* problematic, it is certainly our business to show how this is so and how the use of the types of sentence concerned is related to that of statements which are unproblematically true or false. But we have to do this in detail, case by case and bearing in mind all the time the general framework of our thought. Few things are more implausible than the idea that we can be rapidly forced into a wholesale revision *either* of our metaphysics *or* of our logic by a dogmatic interpretation of the observation, in itself irreproachable, that our understanding of a language is manifested only in our use of it.

11
Perception and its Objects

I

Ayer has always given the problem of perception a central place in his thinking. Reasonably so; for a philosopher's views on this question are a key both to his theory of knowledge in general and to his metaphysics. The movement of Ayer's own thought has been from phenomenalism to what he describes in his latest treatment of the topic as 'a sophisticated form of realism'.[1] The epithet is doubly apt. No adequate account of the matter can be simple; and Ayer's account, while distinguished by his accustomed lucidity and economy of style, is notably and subtly responsive to all the complexities inherent in the subject itself and to all the pressures of more or less persuasive argument which have marked the course of its treatment by philosophers. Yet the form of realism he defends has another kind of sophistication about which it is possible to have reservations and doubts; and, though I am conscious of being far from clear on the matter myself, I shall try to make some of my own doubts and reservations as clear as I can. I shall take as my text Chapters 4 and 5 of *The Central Questions of Philosophy*; and I shall also consider a different kind of realism—that advocated by J. L. Mackie in his book on Locke.[2] There are points of contact as well as of contrast between Ayer's and Mackie's views. A comparison between them will help to bring out the nature of my reservations about both.

According to Ayer, the starting point of serious thought on the matter of perception consists in the fact that our normal perceptual judgements always 'go beyond' the sensible experience which gives rise to them; for those judgements carry implications which would not be carried by any

---

[1] A. J. Ayer, *The Central Questions of Philosophy* (London: Weidenfeld and Nicolson, 1973), chs 4 and 5, pp. 68–111.

[2] J. L. Mackie, *Problems from Locke* (Oxford: Clarendon Press, 1976), chs 1 and 2, pp. 7–71.

'strict account' of that experience.[3] Ayer sees ordinary perceptual judgements as reflecting or embodying what he calls the common-sense view of the physical world, which is, among other things, a realist view; and he sees that view itself as having the character of 'a theory with respect to the immediate data of perception'.[4] He devotes some space to an account of how the theory might be seen as capable of being developed by an individual observer on the basis of the data available to him; though he disavows any intention of giving an actual history of the theory's development. The purpose of the account is, rather, to bring out those features of sensible experience which make it possible to employ the theory successfully and which, indeed, justify acceptance of it. For it is, he holds, by and large an acceptable theory, even though the discoveries of physical science may require us to modify it in certain respects.

Evidently no infant is delivered into the world already equipped with what Ayer calls the common-sense view of it. That view has to be acquired; and it is open to the psychologist of infant learning to produce at least a speculative account of the stages of its acquisition. Ayer insists, as I have remarked, that his own account of a possible line of development or construction of the common-sense view is not intended as a speculative contribution to the theory of infant learning. It is intended, rather, as an analysis of the nature of mature or adult perceptual experience, an analysis designed to show just how certain features of mature sensible experience vindicate or sustain the common-sense view which is embodied or reflected in mature perceptual judgements. Clearly the two aims here distinguished—the genetic–psychological and the analytic–philosophical—are very different indeed, and it will be of great importance not to confuse them. In particular it will be important to run no risk of characterizing mature sensible experience in terms adequate at best only for the characterization of some stage of infantile experience. It is not clear that Ayer entirely avoids this danger.

What is clear is that if we accept Ayer's starting point, if we agree that our ordinary perceptual judgements carry implications not carried by a 'strict account' of the sensible experience which gives rise to them, then we must make absolutely sure that our account of that experience, in the form it takes in our mature life, is indeed strict—in the sense of strictly

---

[3] Ayer, *Central Questions*, pp. 81, 89.   [4] Ibid., p. 88.

correct. Only so can we have any prospect of making a correct estimate of the further doctrines that the common-sense view of the world has the status of a *theory* with respect to a type of sensible experience which provides *data* for the theory; that this experience supplies the *evidence* on which the theory is based;[5] that the common-sense view can be regarded as *inferred* or at least inferrable from this evidence; and that our ordinary perceptual judgements have the character of *interpretations*,[6] in the light of theory, of what sensible experience actually presents us with.

But can we—and should we—accept Ayer's starting point? I think that, suitably interpreted, we both can, and should, accept it. Two things will be required of a strict account of our sensible experience or of any particular episode or slice of sensible experience: first, as I have just remarked, that it should in no way distort or misrepresent the character of that experience as we actually enjoy it, i.e. that it should be a true or faithful account; secondly, that its truth, in any particular case, should be independent of the truth of the associated perceptual judgement, i.e. that it should remain true even if the associated perceptual judgement is false. It is the second requirement on which Ayer lays stress when he remarks that those judgements carry implications which would not be carried by any strict account of sensible experience; or, less happily in my opinion, that in making such judgements we take a step beyond what our sensible experience actually presents us with. But it is the first requirement to which I now wish to give some attention.

Suppose a non-philosophical observer gazing idly through a window. To him we address the request, 'Give us a description of your current visual experience', or 'How is it with you, visually, at the moment?' Uncautioned as to exactly what we want, he might reply in some such terms as these: 'I see the red light of the setting sun filtering through the black and thickly clustered branches of the elms; I see the dappled deer grazing in groups on the vivid green grass . . .'; and so on. So we explain to him. We explain that we want him to amend his account so that, without any sacrifice of fidelity to the experience as actually enjoyed, it nevertheless sheds all that heavy load of commitment to propositions about the world which was carried by the description he gave. We want an account which confines itself strictly within the limits of the subjective episode, an

---

[5] Ibid., p. 89.   [6] Ibid., p. 81.

account which would remain true even if he had seen nothing of what he claimed to see, even if he had been subject to total illusion.

Our observer is quick in the uptake. He does not start talking about lights and colours, patches and patterns. For he sees that to do so would be to falsify the character of the experience he actually enjoyed. He says, instead, 'I understand. I've got to cut out of my report all commitment to propositions about independently existing objects. Well, the simplest way to do this, while remaining faithful to the character of the experience as actually enjoyed, is to put my previous report in inverted commas or *oratio obliqua* and describe my visual experience such as it would have been natural to describe in these terms, had I not received this additional instruction. Thus: "I had a visual experience such as it would have been natural to describe by saying that I saw, etc.... [or, to describe in these words, 'I saw... etc.'] were it not for the obligation to exclude commitment to propositions about independently existing objects." In this way [continues the observer] I *use* the perceptual claim—the claim it was natural to make in the circumstances—in order to characterize my experience, without actually making the claim. I render the perceptual judgement internal to the characterization of the experience without actually asserting the content of the judgement. And this is really the best possible way of characterizing the experience. There are perhaps alternative locutions which might serve the purpose, so long as they are understood as being to the same effect—on the whole, the more artificial the better, since their artificiality will help to make it clearer just to what effect they are intended to be. Thus we might have: "It sensibly seemed to me just as if I were seeing such-and-such a scene" or "My visual experience can be characterized by saying that I saw what I saw, supposing I saw anything, *as* a scene of the following character...".'

If my observer is right in this—and I think he is—then certain general conclusions follow. Our perceptual judgements, as Ayer remarks, embody or reflect a certain view of the world, as containing objects, variously propertied, located in a common space and continuing in their existence independently of our interrupted and relatively fleeting perceptions of them. Our making of such judgements implies our possession and application of concepts of such objects. But now it appears that we cannot give a veridical characterization even of the sensible experience which these judgements, as Ayer expresses it, 'go beyond', without reference to those judgements themselves; that our sensible experience itself is thoroughly permeated with those concepts of objects which figure in such judgements. This does not mean, i.e. it does not follow directly from this feature of sensible experience, that the general view of the world which those judgements reflect must be true. That would be too short a way with scepticism. But it does follow, I think, that our sensible experience could not have the character it does have unless—at least before philosophical reflection sets in—we unquestioningly *took* that general view of the world to be true. The concepts of the objective which we see to be indispensable to the veridical characterization of sensible experience simply would not be in this way indispensable unless those whose experience it was initially and unreflectively took such concepts to have application in the world.

This has a further consequence: the consequence that it is quite inappropriate to represent the general, realist view of the world which is reflected in our ordinary perceptual judgements as having the status of a *theory* with respect to sensible experience; that it is inappropriate to represent that experience as supplying the *data* for such a theory or the *evidence* on which it is based or from which it is *inferred* or *inferrable*; that it is inappropriate to speak of our ordinary perceptual judgements as having the character of an *interpretation*, in the light of theory, of the content of our sensible experience. The reason for this is simple. In order for some belief or set of beliefs to be correctly described as a theory in respect of certain data, it must be possible to describe the data on the basis of which the theory is held in terms which do not presuppose the acceptance of the theory on the part of those for whom the data *are* data. But this is just the condition we have seen not to be satisfied in the case where the so-called data are the contents of sensible experience and the so-called theory is a general realist view of the world. The 'data' are laden with the 'theory'. Sensible experience is permeated by concepts unreflective acceptance of the general applicability of which is a condition of its being so permeated, a condition of that experience being what it is; and these concepts are of realistically conceived objects.

I must make it quite clear what I am saying and what I am not saying here. I am talking of the ordinary non-philosophical man. I am talking of us all before we felt, if ever we did feel, any inclination to respond to the solicitations of a general scepticism, to regard it as raising a problem. I am saying that it follows from the character of sensible experience as we all actually enjoy it that a common-sense realist view of the world does not in general have the status of a theory in respect of that experience; while

Ayer, as I understand him, holds that it does. But I am not denying that to one who has seen, or thinks he has seen, that sensible experience might have the character it does have and *yet* a realist view of the world be false, to *him* the idea may well present itself that the best way of accounting for sensible experience as having that character is to accept the common realist view of the world or some variant of it. *He* might be said to adopt, as a theory, the doctrine that the common realist view of the world is, at least in some basic essentials, true. But this will be a philosopher's theory, designed to deal with a philosopher's problem. (I shall not here discuss its merits as such.) What I am concerned to dispute is the doctrine that a realist view of the world has, for any man, the status of a theory in relation to his sensible experience, a theory in the light of which he interprets that experience in making his perceptual judgements.

To put the point summarily, whereas Ayer says we take a step beyond our sensible experience in making our perceptual judgements, I say rather that we take a step back (in general) from our perceptual judgements in framing accounts of our sensible experience; for we have (in general) to include a reference to the former in framing a veridical description of the latter.

It may seem, on a superficial reading, that Ayer had anticipated and answered this objection. He introduces, as necessary for the characterization of our sensible experience, certain concepts of types of pattern, the names for which are borrowed from the names of ordinary physical objects. Thus he speaks of visual leaf patterns, chair patterns, cat patterns, and so on.[7] At the same time, he is careful, if I read him rightly, to guard against the impression that the use of this terminology commits him to the view that the employment of the corresponding physical-object concepts themselves is necessary to the characterization of our sensible experience.[8] The terminology is appropriate (he holds) simply because those features of sensible experience to which the terminology is applied are the features which govern our identifications of the physical objects we think we see. They are the features, 'implicitly noticed',[9] which provide the main clues on which our everyday judgements of perception are based.

This is ingenious, but I do not think it will do. This we can see more clearly if we use an invented, rather than a derived, terminology for these

---

[7] Ibid., p. 91. [8] Ibid., p. 96. [9] Ibid., p. 91.

supposed features and then draw up a table of explicit correlations between the invented names and the physical-object names. Each artificial feature name is set against the name of a type of physical object: our perceptual identifications of seen objects as of that type are held to be governed by implicit noticings of that feature. The nature and significance of the feature names is now quite clearly explained and we have to ask ourselves whether it is these rather than the associated physical-object terms that we ought to use if we are to give a quite strict and faithful account of our sensible experience. I think it is clear that this is not so; that the idea of our ordinary perceptual judgements as being invariably based upon, or invariably issuing from, awareness of such features is a myth. The situation is rather, as I have already argued, that the employment of our ordinary, full-blooded concepts of physical objects is indispensable to a strict, and strictly veridical, account of our sensible experience.

Once again, I must make it clear what I am, and what I am not, saying. I have been speaking of the typical or standard case of mature sensible and perceptual experience. I have no interest at all in denying the thesis that there also occur cases of sensible experience such that the employment of full-blooded concepts of physical objects would not be indispensable, and may be inappropriate, to giving a strict account of the experience. Such cases are of different types, and there is one in particular which is of interest in the present connection. An observer, gazing through his window, may perhaps, by an effort of will, bring himself to see, or even will-lessly find himself seeing, what he knows to be the branches of the trees no longer *as* branches at all, but as an intricate pattern of dark lines of complex directions and shapes and various sizes against a background of varying shades of grey. The frame of mind in which we enjoy, if we ever do enjoy, this kind of experience is a rare and sophisticated, not a standard or normal, frame of mind. Perhaps the fact, if it is a fact, that we can bring ourselves into this frame of mind when we choose may be held to give a sense to the idea of our 'implicitly noticing' such patterns even when we are not in this frame of mind. If so, it is a sense very far removed from that which Ayer's thesis requires. For that thesis requires not simply the possibility, but the actual occurrence, in all cases of perception, of sensible experience of this kind. One line of retreat may seem to lie open at this point: a retreat to the position of saying that the occurrence of such experiences may be *inferred*, even though we do not, in the hurry of life, generally notice or recall their occurrence. But such a retreat would be the final irony. The items in question would have changed their status radically: instead of data for a common-sense theory of the world, they would appear as consequences of a sophisticated theory of the mind.

This concludes the first stage of my argument. I have argued that mature sensible experience (in general) presents itself as, in Kantian phrase, an *immediate* consciousness of the existence of things outside us. (*Immediate*, of course, does not mean *infallible*.) Hence, the common realist conception of the world does not have the character of a 'theory' in relation to the 'data of sense'. I have not claimed that this fact is of itself sufficient to 'refute' scepticism or to provide a philosophical 'demonstration' of the truth of some form of realism; though I think it does provide the right starting point for reflection upon these enterprises. But that is another story and I shall not try to tell it here. My point so far is that the ordinary human commitment to a conceptual scheme of a realist character is not properly described, even in a stretched sense of the words, as a theoretical commitment. It is, rather, something given with the given.

II

But we are philosophers as well as men; and so must examine more closely the nature of the realist scheme to which we are pre-theoretically committed and then consider whether we are not rationally constrained, as Locke and Mackie would maintain we are, to modify it quite radically in the light of our knowledge of physics and physiology. Should we not also, as philosophers, consider the question of whether we can rationally maintain any form of realism at all? Perhaps we should; but, as already remarked, that is a question I shall not consider here. My main object, in the present section, is to get a clear view of the main features of our pre-theoretical scheme before considering whether it is defensible, as it stands, or not. I go in a somewhat roundabout way to work.

I have spoken of our pre-theoretical scheme as realist in character. Philosophers who treat of these questions commonly distinguish different forms of realism. So do both Ayer and Mackie. They both mention, at one extreme, a form of realism which Mackie calls 'naive' and even 'very naive', but which might more appropriately be called 'confused realism'. A sufferer from confused realism fails to draw any distinction between sensible experiences (or 'perceptions') and independently existing things (or 'objects perceived') but is said (by Mackie expounding Hume) to credit the former with persistent unobserved existence.[10] It should be remarked that, if this is an accurate way of describing the naive realist's conception of the matter, he must be very confused indeed, since the expression 'unobserved' already implies the distinction which he is said to fail to make. Speaking in his own person, Mackie gives no positive account of the naive realist's view of things, but simply says that there is, historically, in the thought of each of us, a phase in which we fail to make the distinction in question.[11] It may indeed be so. The point is one to be referred to the experts on infantile development. But in any case the matter is not here of any consequence. For we are concerned with mature perceptual experience and with the character of the scheme to which those who enjoy such experience are pre-theoretically committed. And it seems to me as certain as anything can be that, as an integral part of that scheme, we distinguish, naturally and unreflectively, between our seeings and hearings and feelings—our perceivings—of objects and the objects we see and hear and feel; and hence quite consistently accept both the interruptedness of the former and the continuance in existence, unobserved, of the latter.

At the opposite extreme from naive realism stands what may be called scientific or Lockian realism. This form of realism credits physical objects only with those of their properties which are mentioned in physical theory and physical explanation, including the causal explanation of our enjoyment of the kind of perceptual experience we in fact enjoy. It has the consequence that we do not, and indeed cannot, perceive objects as they really are. It might be said that this consequence does not hold in an unqualified form. For we perceive (or seem to perceive) objects as having shape, size, and position; and they really do have shape, size, and position and more or less such shape, size, and position as we seem to perceive them as having. But this reply misconstrues the intended force of the alleged consequence. We cannot in sense perception—the point is an old one—become aware of the shape, size, and position of physical objects except by way of awareness of boundaries defined in some sensory mode—for example, by visual and tactile qualities such as scientific realism denies to the objects themselves; and no change in, or addition to, our sensory equipment could alter this fact. To perceive physical objects as, according

---

[10] Mackie, *Problems*, p. 67.   [11] Ibid., p. 68.

to scientific realism, they really are would be to perceive them as lacking any such qualities. But this notion is self-contradictory. So it is a necessary consequence of this form of realism that we do not perceive objects as they really are. Indeed, in the sense of the pre-theoretical notion of perceiving—that is, of immediate awareness of things outside us—we do not, on the scientific–realist view, perceive physical objects at all. We are, rather, the victims of a systematic illusion which obstinately clings to us even if we embrace scientific realism. For we continue to enjoy experience *as of* physical objects in space, objects of which the spatial characteristics and relations are defined by the sensible qualities we perceive them as having; but there are no such physical objects as these. The only true physical objects are items systematically correlated with and causally responsible for that experience; and the only sense in which we *can* be said to perceive them is just that they cause us to enjoy that experience.

These remarks are intended only as a *description* of scientific realism. I do not claim that they show it to be untenable. I shall return to the topic later.

In between the 'naive' and the 'scientific' varieties, Ayer and Mackie each recognize another form of realism, which they each ascribe to 'common sense'. But there is a difference between Ayer's version of common-sense realism and Mackie's. For Mackie's version, unlike Ayer's, shares one crucial feature with scientific realism.

The theory of perception associated with scientific or Lockian realism is commonly and reasonably described as a representative theory. Each of us seems to himself to be perceptually aware of objects of a certain kind: objects in space outside us with visual and tactile qualities. There are in fact, on this view, no such objects; but these object appearances can in a broad sense be said to be representative of those actual objects in space outside us which are systematically correlated with the appearances and causally responsible for them. The interesting feature of Mackie's version of common-sense realism is that the theory of perception associated with it is no less a representative theory than that associated with Lockian realism. The difference is simply that common sense, according to Mackie, views object appearances as more faithful representatives of actual physical objects than the Lockian allows: in that common sense, gratuitously by scientific standards, credits actual objects in space outside us with visual and tactile as well as primary qualities. As Mackie puts it, common sense allows 'colours-as-we-see-them to be *resemblances* of qualities actually in the things'.[12] On both views, sensible experience has its own, sensible objects; but the common-sense view, according to Mackie, allows a kind of resemblance between sensible and physical objects which the scientific view does not.

I hope it is already clear that this version of common-sense realism is quite different from what I have called our pre-theoretical scheme. What we ordinarily take ourselves to be aware of in perception are not resemblances of physical things but the physical things themselves. This does not mean, as already remarked, that we have any difficulty in distinguishing between our experiences of seeing, hearing, and feeling objects and the objects themselves. That distinction is as firmly a part of our pre-theoretical scheme as is our taking ourselves, in general, to be immediately aware of those objects. Nor does it mean that we take ourselves to be immune from illusion, hallucination, or mistake. We can, and do, perfectly adequately describe such cases without what is, from the point of view of the pre-theoretical scheme, the quite gratuitous introduction of sensible objects interposed between us and the actual physical objects they are supposed to represent.

The odd thing about Mackie's presentation is that at one point he shows himself to be perfectly well aware of this feature of the real realism of common sense; for he writes, 'What we seem to see, feel, hear and so on . . . *are seen as real things without us*—that is, outside us. We just see things as being simply there, of such-and-such sorts, in such-and-such relations . . . .'[13] He goes on, of course, to say that 'our seeing them so is logically distinct from their being so', that we might be, and indeed are, wrong. But he would scarcely dispute that what is thus *seen as* real and outside us is also *seen as* coloured, as possessing visual qualities; that what is *felt as* a real thing outside us is also felt as hard or soft, smooth or rough-surfaced—as possessing tactile qualities. The real realism of common sense, then, does indeed credit physical things with visual and tactile properties; but it does so not in the spirit of a notion of representative perception, but in the spirit of a notion of direct or immediate perception.

Mackie's version of common-sense realism is, then, I maintain, a distortion of the actual pre-theoretical realism of common sense, a distortion which wrongly assimilates it, in a fundamental respect, to the Lockian

---

[12] Ibid., p. 64.   [13] Ibid., p. 61.

realism he espouses. I do not find any comparable distortion in Ayer's version. He aptly describes the physical objects we seem to ourselves, and take ourselves, to perceive as 'visuo-tactual continuants'. The scheme as he presents it allows for the distinction between these items and the experiences of perceiving them and for the causal dependence of the latter on the former; and does so, as far as I can see, without introducing the alien features I have discerned in Mackie's account. It is perhaps debatable whether Ayer can consistently maintain the scheme's freedom from such alien elements while continuing to represent it as having the status of a 'theory' in relation to the 'data' of sensible experience. But, having already set out my objections to that doctrine, I shall not pursue the point.

Something more must be said, however, about the position, in the common-sense scheme, of the causal relation between physical object and the experience of perceiving it. Although Ayer admits the relation to a place in the scheme, he seems to regard it as a somewhat sophisticated addition to the latter, a latecomer, as it were, for which room has to be made in an already settled arrangement.[14] This seems to me wrong. The idea of the presence of the thing as accounting for, or being responsible for, our perceptual awareness of it is implicit in the pre-theoretical scheme from the very start. For we think of perception as a way, indeed the basic way, of informing ourselves about the world of independently existing things: we assume, that is to say, the general reliability of our perceptual experiences; and that assumption is the same as the assumption of a general causal dependence of our perceptual experiences on the independently existing things we take them to be of. The thought of my fleeting perception as a *perception* of a continuously and independently existing thing implicitly contains the thought that if the thing had not been there, I should not even have *seemed* to perceive it. It really should be obvious that with the distinction between independently existing objects and perceptual awareness of objects we already have the general notion of causal dependence of the latter on the former, even if this is not a matter to which we give much reflective attention in our pre-theoretical days.

Two things seem to have impeded recognition of this point. One is the fact that the correctness of the description of a perceptual experience as the perception of a certain physical thing *logically* requires the existence of that

---

[14] Ayer, *Central Questions*, pp. 87–8.

thing; and the *logical* is thought to exclude the *causal* connection, since only logically distinct existences can be causally related. This is not a serious difficulty. The situation has many parallels. Gibbon would not be the historian of the decline and fall of the Roman Empire unless there had occurred some actual sequence of events more or less corresponding to his narrative. But it is not enough, for him to merit that description, that such a sequence of events should have occurred and he should have written the sentences he did write. For him to qualify as the *historian* of these events, there must be a causal chain connecting them with the writing of the sentences. Similarly, the memory of an event's occurrence does not count as such unless it has its causal origin in that event. And the recently much canvassed 'causal theory of reference' merely calls attention to another instance of the causal link which obtains between thought and independently (and anteriorly) existing thing when the former is rightly said to have the latter as its object.

The second impediment is slightly more subtle. We are philosophically accustomed—it is a Humean legacy—to thinking of the simplest and most obvious kind of causal relation as holding between types of item such that items of both types are observable or experienceable and such that observation or experience of either term of the relation is distinct from observation or experience of the other: i.e. the causally related items are not only distinct existences, but also the objects of distinct observations or experiences. We may then come to think of these conditions as constituting a requirement on all primitive belief in causal relations, a requirement which could be modified or abandoned only in the interests of theory. Since we obviously cannot distinguish the observation of a physical object from the experience of observing it—for they are the same thing—we shall then be led to conclude that the idea of the causal dependence of perceptual experience on the perceived object cannot be even an implicit part of our pre-theoretical scheme, but must be at best an essentially theoretical addition to it.

But the difficulty is spurious. By directing our attention to causal relations between *objects* of perception, we have simply been led to overlook the special character of perception itself. Of course, the requirement holds for causal relations between distinct objects of perception; but not for the relation between perception and its object. When x is a physical object and y is a perception of x, then x is *observed* and y is *enjoyed*. And in taking the enjoyment of *y* to be a perception of *x*, we *are* implicitly taking it to be caused by *x*.

This concludes the second phase of my argument. I have tried to bring out some main features of the real realism of common sense and of the associated notion of perception. From the standpoint of common-sense realism we take ourselves to be immediately aware of real, enduring physical things in space, things endowed with visual and tactile properties; and we take it for granted that these enduring things are causally responsible for our interrupted perceptions of them. The immediacy which common sense attributes to perceptual awareness is in no way inconsistent either with the distinction between perceptual experience and thing perceived or with the causal dependence of the former on the latter or the existence of other causally necessary conditions of its occurrence. Neither is it inconsistent with the occurrence of perceptual mistake or illusion—a point, like so many others of importance, which is explicitly made by Kant.[15] Both Ayer and Mackie, explicitly or implicitly, acknowledge that the common-sense scheme includes this assumption of immediacy—Mackie in a passage I have quoted, Ayer in his description of the common-sense scheme. Unfortunately, Mackie's acknowledgement of the fact is belied by his describing common-sense realism as representative in character and Ayer's acknowledgement of it is put in doubt by his describing the common-sense scheme as having the status of a theory in relation to sensible experience.

III

It is one thing to describe the scheme of common sense; it is another to subject it to critical examination. This is the third and most difficult part of my task. The main question to be considered, as already indicated, is whether we are rationally bound to abandon, or radically to modify, the scheme in the light of scientific knowledge.

Before addressing ourselves directly to this question, it is worth stressing—indeed, it is essential to stress—the grip that common-sense non-representative realism has on our ordinary thinking. It is a view of the world which so thoroughly permeates our consciousness that even those

---

[15] Kant, 'The Refutation of Idealism', in *Critique of Pure Reason*, B274–9.

who are intellectually convinced of its falsity remain subject to its power. Mackie admits as much, saying that, even when we are trying to entertain a Lockian or scientific realism, 'our language and our natural ways of thinking keep pulling us back' to a more primitive view.[16] Consider the character of those ordinary concepts of objects on the employment of which our lives, our transactions with each other and the world, depend: our concepts of cabbages, roads, tweed coats, horses, the lips and hair of the beloved. In using these terms we certainly intend to be talking of independent existences and we certainly intend to be talking of immediately perceptible things, bearers of phenomenal (visuo-tactile) properties. If scientific or Lockian realism is correct, we cannot be doing both at once; it is confusion or illusion to suppose we can. If the things we talk of really have phenomenal properties, then they cannot, on this view, be physical things continuously existing in physical space. Nothing perceptible— I here drop the qualification 'immediately', for my use of it should now be clear—is a physically real, independent existence. No two persons can ever, in this sense, perceive the same item: nothing at all is publicly perceptible.

But how deep the confusion or the illusion must go! How radically it infects our concepts! Surely we mean by a cabbage a kind of thing of which most of the specimens we have encountered have a characteristic range of colours and visual shapes and felt textures; and not something unobservable, mentally represented by a complex of sensible experiences which it causes. The common consciousness is not to be fobbed off with the concession that, after all, the physical thing has—in a way—a shape. The way in which scientific realism concedes a shape is altogether the wrong way for the common consciousness. The lover who admires the curve of his mistress's lips or the lover of architecture who admires the lines of a building takes himself to be admiring features of those very objects themselves; but it is the visual shape, the visually defined shape, that he admires. Mackie suggests that there is a genuine *resemblance* between subjective representation and objective reality as far as shape is concerned;[17] but this suggestion is quite unacceptable. It makes no sense to speak of a phenomenal property as *resembling* a non-phenomenal, abstract property such as physical shape is conceived to be by scientific

---

[16] Mackie, *Problems*, p. 68.   [17] Ibid., chs 1 and 2, *passim*.

realism. The property of looking square or round can no more resemble the property, so conceived, of being physically square or round than the property of looking intelligent or looking ill can resemble the property of being intelligent or being ill. If it seems to make sense to speak of a resemblance between phenomenal properties and physical properties, so conceived, it is only because we give ourselves pictures—phenomenal pictures—of the latter. The resemblance is with the picture, not the pictured.

So, then, the common consciousness lives, or has the illusion of living, in a phenomenally propertied world of perceptible things in space. We might call it the lived world. It is also the public world, accessible to observation by all: the world in which one man, following another's pointing finger, can see the very thing that the other sees. (Even in our philosophical moments we habitually contrast the colours and visual shapes of things, as being publicly observable, with the subjective contents of consciousness, private to each of us, though not thereby unknowable to others.)

Such a reminder of the depth and reality of our habitual commitment to the common-sense scheme does not, by itself, amount to a demonstration of that scheme's immunity from philosophical criticism. The scientific realist, though no Kantian, may be ready, by way of making his maximum concession, with a reply modelled on Kant's combination of empirical realism with transcendental idealism. He may distinguish between the uncritical standpoint of ordinary living and the critical standpoint of philosophy informed by science. We are humanly, or naturally—he may say—constrained to 'see the world' in one way (i.e. to think of it as we seem to perceive it) and rationally, or critically, constrained to think of it in quite another. The first way (being itself a causal product of physical reality) has a kind of validity at its own level; but it is, critically and rationally speaking, an inferior level. The second way really is a correction of the first.

The authentically Kantian combination is open to objection in many ways; but, by reason of its very extravagance, it escapes one specific form of difficulty to which the scientific realist's soberer variant remains exposed. Kant uncompromisingly declares that space is in us; that it is 'solely from the human standpoint that we can speak of space, of extended things etc.';[18] that

---

[18] Kant, 'Refutation of Idealism', in *Critique*, B42.

things as they are in themselves are not spatial at all. This will not do for the scientific realist. The phenomenally propertied items which we take ourselves to perceive and the apparent relations between which yield (or contribute vitally to yielding) our notion of space, are indeed declared to have no independent reality; but, when they are banished from the realm of the real, they are supposed to leave behind them—as occupants, so to speak, of the evacuated territory—those spatially related items which, though necessarily unobservable, nevertheless constitute the whole of physical reality. Ayer refers in several places to this consequence; and questions its coherence.[19] He writes, for example, 'I doubt whether the notion of a spatial system of which none of the elements can be observed is even intelligible.'

It is not clear that this difficulty is insuperable. The scientific realist will claim to be able to abstract the notion of a position in physical space from the phenomenal integuments with which it is originally and deceptively associated; and it is hard to think of a conclusive reason for denying him this power. He will say that the places where the phenomenally propertied things we seem to perceive seem to be are, often enough, places at which the correlated physically real items really are. Such a claim may make us uneasy; but it is not obvious nonsense.

Still, to say that a difficulty is not clearly insuperable is not to say that it is clearly not insuperable. It would be better to avoid it if we can. We cannot avoid it if we embrace unadulterated scientific realism and incidentally announce ourselves thereby as the sufferers from persistent illusion, however natural. We can avoid it, perhaps, if we can succeed in combining elements of the scientific story with our common-sense scheme without downgrading the latter. This is the course that Ayer recommends[20] and, I suspect, the course that most of us semi-reflectively follow. The question is whether it is a consistent or coherent course. And at bottom this question is one of identity. Can we coherently identify the phenomenally propertied, immediately perceptible things which common sense supposes to occupy physical space with the configurations of unobservable ultimate particulars by which an unqualified scientific realism purports to replace them?

I approach the question indirectly, by considering once again Mackie's version of common-sense realism. According to this version, it will be

---

[19] Ayer, *Central Questions*, pp. 84, 86–7, 110.   [20] Ibid., pp. 110–11.

remembered, physical things, though not directly perceived, really possess visual and tactile qualities which resemble those we seem to perceive them as possessing; so that if, *per impossibile*, the veil of perception were drawn aside and we saw things in their true colours, these would turn out to be colours indeed and, on the whole, just the colours with which we were naively inclined to credit them. Mackie does not represent this view as absurd or incoherent. He just thinks that it is, as a matter of fact, false. Things *could* really be coloured; but, since there is no scientific reason for supposing they are, it is gratuitous to make any such supposition.

Mackie is surely too lenient to his version of common-sense realism. That version effects a complete logical divorce between a thing's being red and its being red-looking. Although it is a part of the theory that a thing which is, in itself, red has the power to cause us to seem to see a red thing, the logical divorce between these two properties is absolute. And, as far as I can see, that divorce really produces nonsense. The ascription of colours to things becomes not merely gratuitous, but senseless. Whatever may be the case with shape and position, colours are visibilia or they are nothing. I have already pointed out that this version of common-sense realism is not the real realism of common sense: *that* realism effects no logical divorce between being red and being red-looking; for it is a perceptually direct and not a perceptually representative realism. The things seen as coloured are the things themselves. There is no 'veil past which we cannot see'; for there is no veil.

But this does not mean that a thing which is red, i.e. red-looking, has to look red all the time and in all circumstances and to all observers. There is an irreducible relativity, a relativity to what in the broadest sense may be called the perceptual point of view, built in to our ascriptions of particular visual properties to things. The mountains are red-looking at this distance in this light; blue-looking at that distance at that light; and, when we are clambering up them, perhaps neither. Such-and-such a surface looks pink and smooth from a distance; mottled and grainy when closely examined; different again, perhaps, under the microscope.

We absorb this relativity easily enough for ordinary purposes in our ordinary talk, tacitly taking some range of perceptual conditions, some perceptual point of view (in the broad sense) as standard or normal, and introducing an explicit acknowledgement of relativity only in cases which deviate from the standard. 'It looks purple in this light,' we say, 'but take it to the door and you will see that it's really green.' But sometimes we do something else. We shift the standard. Magnified, the fabric appears as printed with tiny blue and yellow dots. So those are the colours it really is. Does this ascription contradict 'it's really green'? No; for the standard has shifted. Looking at photographs, in journals of popular science, of patches of human skin, vastly magnified, we say, 'How fantastically uneven and ridgy it really is.' We study a sample of blood through a microscope and say, 'It's mostly colourless.' But skin can still be smooth and blood be red; for in another context we shift our standard back. Such shifts do not convict us of volatility or condemn us to internal conflict. The appearance of both volatility and conflict vanishes when we acknowledge the relativity of our 'reallys'.

My examples are banal. But perhaps they suggest a way of resolving the apparent conflict between scientific and common-sense realism. We can shift our point of view within the general framework of perception, whether aided or unaided by artificial means; and the different sensible-quality ascriptions we then make to the same object are not seen as conflicting once their relativity is recognized. Can we not see the adoption of the viewpoint of scientific realism as simply a more radical shift—a shift to a viewpoint from which no characteristics are to be ascribed to things except those which figure in the physical theories of science and in 'the explanation of what goes on in the physical world in the processes which lead to our having the sensations and perceptions that we have'?[21] We can say that this is how things really are so long as the relativity of this 'really' is recognized as well; and, when it is recognized, the scientific account will no more conflict with the ascription to things of visual and tactile qualities than the assertion that blood is really a mainly colourless fluid conflicts with the assertion that it is bright red in colour. Of course, the scientific point of view is not, in one sense, a point of *view* at all. It is an intellectual, not a perceptual, standpoint. We could not occupy it at all, did we not first occupy the other. But we can perfectly well occupy both at once, so long as we realize what we are doing.

This method of reconciling scientific and common-sense realism requires us to recognize a certain relativity in our conception of the real properties of physical objects. Relative to the human perceptual standpoint the grosser physical objects are visuo-tactile continuants (and within

[21] Mackie, *Problems*, p. 18.

that standpoint the phenomenal properties they possess are relative to particular perceptual viewpoints, taken as standard). Relative to the scientific standpoint, they have no properties but those which figure in the physical theories of science. Such a relativistic conception will not please the absolute-minded. Ayer recommends a different procedure. He suggests that we should conceive of perceptible objects (i.e. objects perceptible in the sense of the common-sense scheme) as being literally composed of the ultimate particles of physical theory, the latter being imperceptible, not in principle, but only empirically, as a consequence of their being so minute.[22] I doubt, however, whether this proposal, which Ayer rightly describes as an attempt to *blend* the two schemes can be regarded as satisfactory. If the impossibility of perceiving the ultimate components is to be viewed as merely empirical, we can sensibly ask what the conceptual consequences would be of supposing that impossibility not to exist. The answer is clear. Even if there were something which we counted as perceiving the ultimate particles, this would still not, from the point of view of scientific realism, count as perceiving them as they really are. And nothing could so count; for no phenomenal properties we seemed to perceive them as having would figure in the physical explanation of the causal mechanisms of our success. But, so long as we stay at this point of view, what goes for the parts goes for any wholes they compose. However gross those wholes, they remain, from this point of view, imperceptible in the sense of common sense.

Ayer attempts to form one viewpoint out of two discrepant viewpoints; to form a single, unified description of physical reality by blending features of two discrepant descriptions, each valid from its own viewpoint. He can seem to succeed only by doing violence to one of the two viewpoints, the scientific. I acknowledge the discrepancy of the two descriptions, but claim that, once we recognize the relativity in our conception of the real, they need not be seen as in contradiction with each other. Those very things which from one standpoint we conceive as phenomenally propertied we conceive from another as constituted in a way which can only be described in what are, from the phenomenal point of view, abstract terms. 'This smooth, green, leather table-top', we say, 'is, considered scientifically, nothing but a congeries of electric charges widely

---

[22] Ayer, *Central Questions*, p. 110.

separated and in rapid motion.' Thus we combine the two standpoints in a single sentence. The standpoint of common-sense realism, not explicitly signalled as such, is reflected in the sentence's grammatical subject phrase, of which the words are employed in no esoteric sense. The standpoint of physical science, explicitly signalled as such, is reflected in the predicate. Once relativity of description to standpoint is recognized, the sentence is seen to contain no contradiction; and, if it contains no contradiction, the problem of identification is solved.

I recognize that this position is unlikely to satisfy the determined scientific realist. If he is only moderately determined, he may be partially satisfied, and may content himself with saying that the scientific viewpoint is superior to that of common sense. He will then simply be expressing a preference, which he will not expect the artist, for example, to share. But, if he is a hardliner, he will insist that the common-sense view is wholly undermined by science; that it is shown to be false; that the visual and tactile properties we ascribe to things are nowhere but in our minds; that we do not live in a world of perceptible objects, as understood by common sense, at all. He must then accept the consequence that each of us is a sufferer from a persistent and inescapable illusion and that it is fortunate that this is so, since, if it were not, we should be unable to pursue the scientific enterprise itself. Without the illusion of perceiving objects as bearers of sensible qualities, we should not have the illusion of perceiving them as space-occupiers at all; and without that we should have no concept of space and no power to pursue our researches into the nature of its occupants. Science is not only the offspring of common sense; it remains its dependant. For this reason, and for others touched on earlier, the scientific realist must, however ruefully, admit that the ascription to objects of sensible qualities, the standard of correctness of such ascription being (what we take to be) intersubjective agreement, is something quite securely rooted in our conceptual scheme. If this means, as he must maintain it does, that our thought is condemned to incoherence, then we can only conclude that incoherence is something we can perfectly well live with and could not perfectly well live without.

12
Liberty and Necessity

A first reading of the *Ethics* may leave the reader with a sense of strain or paradox. This is not because Spinoza both denies freedom of decision and celebrates freedom of mind. Even though all things follow with absolute necessity from the nature of God, there is nothing immediately paradoxical in distinguishing some of the conditions that thus follow with the honorific name of 'freedom'. What creates a first sense of strain is the fact that Spinoza recommends, urges, the following of a path—which he describes as a difficult path—to the achievement of such a condition, while assuring us that we have no choice in the matter, but only the illusion of choice. The strain can be accommodated. Spinoza understands that the illusion is inescapable. This knowledge, and perhaps his own subjection to the illusion, causes him to set out what can rationally be seen only as description in a form which will tend to promote in his fellows, or in some few of them, a state of affairs he himself values highly, desires to see more generally realized. Now a further effort of accommodation is required. Spinoza evaluates human propensities and conditions with some confidence. Yet he maintains that to a mind wholly free, a mind that truly comprehended the nature of things, all distinctions of value would lack application; they would not even be intelligible. We are to believe *both* that nothing is truly good or truly evil *and* that the supreme good is to approximate as nearly as possible that condition in which it would be understood that this is so. Again the accommodation can be made. We can reconstrue, reinterpret, the evaluations as descriptions of the causes and effects of certain human dispositions; note the effect such a description may itself have on some minds; note also the naturalness of the employment of a terminology which, by hypothesis, reflects the limitations of our own (and the author's) understanding; and *feel* the effect ourselves.

So the exercise is, in its way, superbly managed. The combination of total naturalism with a unique elevation of tone is, rather against the probabilities, splendidly brought off. Yet questions remain, both about the freedom which is declared to be illusion and about the freedom which is equated with blessedness and said to increase proportionately with increase of understanding. Spinoza attributes the illusion of freedom to our consciousness of our actions, decisions, and desires and our ignorance of their causes. Here are two theses: first, that the sense of freedom is illusory, because it entails a belief which is incompatible with the universal reign of natural causality; second, that the sense of freedom is caused in a certain way. Both theses are questionable. That we have a sense of freedom, that we necessarily act, as Kant says, under the *idea* of freedom, is generally allowed. That this sense entails a belief incompatible with the universal reign of natural causality is frequently denied; by Kant for dubiously intelligible reasons; by others for more pedestrian reasons. The pedestrian compatibilist will maintain, not that free actions are free from all causality, but that they are free from certain kinds of causality—the causality, he will say, of constraint; and he will be ready enough to illustrate what he means by this with examples of physical force or intrusive psychological compulsion.

One who, on this ground, questions the first thesis is under an obligation of consistency to question also the second—the thesis about the causal source of the sense of freedom. He can scarcely allow that knowledge of causes would make those causes constraining which were not so before; and he would surely be hardly more willing to allow that such knowledge would cause an authentic sense of freedom to be displaced by an illusion of constraint. So, it seems, he must deny that the sense of freedom is caused by ignorance of causes. And then, in all intellectual decency, he may feel obliged to give another account of the source of that sense.

Can these requirements be met? At one level at least, they can. Men are not generally ignorant of the immediate causes of their actions: they often enough know what combinations of desire, preference, belief, and perception prompt them to act as they do. Not all their reasons are rationalizations. As for the remoter causes of their actions, i.e. the causes of their own desires, dispositions, and preferences, they will often enough have a reasonably accurate notion of the sources of these as well, acknowledging both the general determining power of education, training, environment, and heredity and the specific influence of this or that element of these determining forces. Blank ignorance of causes does not exist; so the sense of freedom cannot be attributed to such ignorance. Whence, then, does this sense arise? Or, better perhaps, what does it consist in?

Here one can only sketch an answer. First, we should consider that our desires and preferences are not, in general, something we just note in ourselves as alien presences. To a large extent they *are* we. The point gains force from the very fact of exceptions to it: i.e. from the presence in some subjects, sometimes, of dispositions and desires which they do experience as intrusive compulsions. In respect of them, there is no sense of freedom, but its absence is not attributable to knowledge of their causes; on the contrary, the sufferers from such compulsions may suffer also from just such ignorance of their causes as Spinoza would declare to be the source of the sense of freedom.

Second, we should consider the experience of deliberation and relate this experience to the point that our desires and preferences are not, in general, something we just note in ourselves as alien presences. A corollary of this point is that, in the experience of deliberation, we are not mere spectators of a scene in which—setting aside the element of reckoning, of calculation—contending desires struggle for mastery with ourselves as prize. This image may sometimes be appropriate, but it is not the image appropriate to the standard experience of deliberation. That experience heightens our sense of self;[1] in the higher-order desire which determines what we call our choice we identify ourselves the more completely; and this is why we call it our choice.

Finally, we should consider the experience of agency. When a basic action of ours issues by a normal causal route from a specific intention of so acting, which itself issues from a combination of relevant belief and desire, then we have immediate knowledge, not only that our action has been such as we intended to perform, but also that it has been performed intentionally. As has been pointed out by recent writers in the theory of action, it can sometimes happen that someone acts as he intended to act yet does not perform that action intentionally. The action may issue causally from the appropriate combination of desire and belief, but the causal route from desire and belief to action may be of the wrong kind. The anticipatory thought of action may, for example, so disturb or unnerve us that we

---

[1] For my appreciation of the connection between the two, I am indebted to some unpublished work on self-determination by Galen Strawson.

find ourselves *unintentionally* making just such a bodily movement as we *intended* to make—as letting go the rope which holds up the fellow mountaineer, in a famous example of Professor Davidson. In such cases the experience of agency is lacking. The cases are worth mentioning in order to emphasize the fact that the experience is normally present, and to remind us of what it is like.

Here, then, is a part at least of the phenomenology of the sense of freedom. The fact that we find ourselves in our desires and preferences and do not, in general, find them as alien presences within ourselves; the experience of deliberation which heightens and strengthens our sense of self; and the constantly repeated experience of agency—all these contribute to, perhaps constitute, the sense of freedom. Experiencing it ourselves, we attribute it also to others.

Suppose it is acknowledged that the sense of freedom, so regarded, experienced in ourselves and attributed to others, is a natural fact; not, in general, causally threatened by knowledge of particular causes, nor logically threatened by a general belief in the reign of universal causality; not logically threatened because not a belief and hence not a belief incompatible with that general belief. Yet the sense of freedom, this natural fact, is closely linked with other attitudes to ourselves and others, with other feelings towards ourselves and others and with other concepts which we apply to ourselves and others; and it is often argued that the justification of some of these attitudes and feelings, and of the application of some of these concepts, requires, and is seen by us to require, the truth of beliefs which *are* incompatible with the general belief in the universal reign of causality. Spinoza speaks of the notions of sin and merit, praise and blame, and of allied emotions. In general, we may say, what are at issue are the notions, attitudes, and feelings associated with moral judgement, with the idea of moral desert. Now it certainly is generally held—it is a thesis, one might say, of the common moral consciousness—that the appropriateness of these attitudes and feelings, the applicability of these notions, requires, in respect of any occasion on which these attitudes and notions are in question, that the agent *could have acted otherwise* than he did act on that occasion. But—so the argument runs—if the thesis of determinism is true, then it is not true of any agent on any occasion that that agent could have acted otherwise than he did act on that occasion. Hence, if the thesis of determinism is true, the attitudes and notions in question are never appropriate.

Is the thesis of the common moral consciousness correctly interpreted in this line of reasoning? Is it, in any case, a line of reasoning which Spinoza accepts, or could consistently accept, as it stands? The reasoning depends heavily on the notions of 'appropriateness' or 'justification' of attitudes; and these notions, being alien to the profoundly naturalistic and descriptive style of Spinoza's thought, must at least be reinterpreted in terms of causes and effects. To put it crudely: the thesis that a certain attitude is justified only if a certain belief is true amounts, in its Spinozistic reconstrual, to the thesis that a certain attitude is causally dependent on a certain belief. Reinterpreting the reasoning in these terms, we must ask whether our proneness to the attitudes and feelings, and to the application of the concepts associated with moral judgement, is in fact dependent on beliefs incompatible with the truth of determinism.

The question returns us, with a difference, to the common moral consciousness. When, in a context of moral appraisal, the common moral consciousness delivers the judgement 'He could have acted otherwise' (have ϕ-d, say, instead of ψ-ing, as he did), is this judgement really equivalent to 'There was no sufficient natural impediment or bar, *of any kind whatsoever, however complex*, to his acting otherwise' (to his ϕ-ing, say, instead of ψ-ing)? I find it difficult, as others have found it difficult, to accept this equivalence. The common judgement of this form amounts rather to the denial of any sufficient natural impediment *of certain specific kinds or ranges of kinds*. For example, 'He could (easily) have helped them (instead of withholding help)' may amount to the denial of any lack on his part of adequate muscular power or financial means. Will the response, 'It simply wasn't in his nature to do so' lead to a withdrawal of moral judgement in such a case? I hardly think so; rather to its reinforcement.

There is another reason, equally familiar, for questioning the proposed equivalence. Acceptance of the equivalence commits one to the view that the practice of moral appraisal is either rationally grounded on, or causally dependent on, the conscious or tacit rejection of the thesis of determinism. But when those who accept the equivalence are invited to enlarge on the question, how a belief in the absence of determining causes explains or justifies the practices and attitudes in question, their answers are singularly insufficient. It is hard to see how randomness, or a belief in randomness, could either explain or justify any such thing; and attempts to formulate the appropriate belief in other terms have never resulted in anything but either high-flown nonsense or psychological descriptions which are in no way inconsistent with the thesis of determinism. No one has ever been able to state intelligibly what that state of affairs, that condition of freedom, which has been supposed to be necessary to ground our moral attitudes and judgements, would actually consist in. The question, 'If we believe in such a condition, what exactly are we believing?', remains unanswered and, I think, unanswerable.

Some who have faced this fact, but also have felt, or thought they felt, an irreconcilable tension between the reign of causality and the holding of moral attitudes, have concluded that there is something inherently confused about moral attitudes. This conclusion echoes Spinoza.

Nevertheless it is the wrong conclusion to draw; or, at least, drawn in this way and for this reason, it is wrongly drawn. Our proneness to moral attitudes and feelings is a natural fact, just as the sense of freedom is a natural fact. I have remarked that they are linked, and it is time to say more about the link. In speaking of the sense of freedom, I connected it closely with the sense of self. Our desires, decisions, actions are not in general felt as alien, as things that simply happen in, or to, us, like a pain or a blow. They are we. Our awareness of them is awareness of ourselves. I remarked that we attribute to others this same sense of freedom and this same sense of self. We see others as other selves, and are aware that they so see each other. But this is not a matter of a conclusion drawn by analogical reasoning. In a variety of ways, inextricably bound up with the facts of mutual human involvement and interaction, we *feel* towards each other as to other selves; and this variety is just the variety of moral and personal reactive attitudes and emotions which we experience towards others and which have their correlates in attitudes and emotions directed towards ourselves.[2] Of all, or most, of these emotions or attitudes, whether self-directed or other-directed, Spinoza himself treats in the *Ethics*. He treats of them as natural facts, bringing unparalleled psychological insight to bear on the detailed analysis of their causes and effects. For this analysis one can have nothing but admiration. What I have been concerned to dispute is the thesis that these emotions and attitudes, together with the associated sense of freedom, of self and of other selves, rest upon a belief, or beliefs, incompatible with the doctrine of the universal reign or natural causality.

---

[2] I have written at greater length of these attitudes in 'Freedom and Resentment', included in *Freedom and Resentment* (London: Methuen, 1974).

But we must again distinguish. There is the thesis that these emotions and attitudes, together with the sense of freedom, rest upon *false belief*. And there is the thesis that this cluster of associated feelings rests upon *ignorance*: upon ignorance of the actual causes of desires, dispositions, and actions. Clearly the two theses are logically independent. The second could be true even if the first were false. Earlier I summarily rejected the second thesis, as far as the sense of freedom was concerned, as well as the first. At least I rejected it in its full generality, arguing that we could have a reasonably accurate notion of the causal sources of our desires and dispositions and those of others—as well as of our actions, and theirs—without being in the least disposed, as a result of this knowledge, to lose our sense of these desires, dispositions, and actions as truly ours (or theirs), to lose our sense of our (or their) selves and our (or their) freedom in respect of them; whereas, on the other hand, we could sometimes experience as alien compulsions, in respect of which we had no sense of freedom, certain desires and dispositions of the causes of which we were truly ignorant, which we were quite at a loss to account for.

Yet further consideration of the second thesis is called for. I have spoken of a kind of non-specialist knowledge which we have of the sources of human dispositions, desires, and actions. We explain ourselves and others to ourselves and others in terms which we might call human and social terms. We refer to inherited traits, to social influences, to the effect of education, training, and experience, to the particular circumstances in which people find themselves. We speak of character and personality and the influences which form and modify them. We can develop considerable subtlety and expertise in this kind of knowledge. But it remains a relatively vague and inexact kind of knowledge; and there must be few who suppose that it will ever be anything else.

But we are also, and increasingly, able to view ourselves in a quite different kind of light—that of the physical and biological sciences; to see ourselves, in that light, as genetically programmed mechanisms of immense complexity, mechanisms constantly modified by their own history and responding, in constantly modified ways, to sensory inputs with behavioural outputs. The scope for the development of these sciences is no less immense than the complexity of the mechanisms which we must take ourselves to be; and we are only at the threshold of this development. Nevertheless the knowledge which these sciences deliver and promise differs in a fundamental respect from that knowledge of the causation of human behaviour which I have just spoken of; for it is, as far as it goes, *exact* knowledge. Let us suppose, then, that we were able to give complete causal explanations of human behaviour, including our own, in terms belonging to these exact sciences. Suppose, in a spirit entirely Spinozistic, that we were able to identify every thought, feeling, original impulse to action, with—or as the 'mental' aspect or correlate of—some complex physical state of which we could, in turn, determine the sufficient physical causes, tracing the latter as far back as we needed or wished to. Might we not then be said to have replaced our present, inexact, inadequate knowledge and understanding of the causes of our desires, dispositions, and actions with adequate knowledge and understanding? And might not such adequate knowledge remove the basis of the sense of freedom and the sense of self and hence of the associated moral and personal attitudes and emotions—thus vindicating the thesis that these last did indeed rest, if not on absolute ignorance, then at least on inadequate knowledge, of causes?

The suggestion involves obvious minor complications, inasmuch as such mental items as the sense of agency, say, or the sense of guilt, must themselves be supposed to have physical correlates and physical causes; so that it would at least be necessary to suppose substantial modifications in the mechanism itself to result from knowledge of its workings. But it is pointless to dwell on these complications. For the question which contains the suggestion is unanswerable. It is unanswerable because the supposition which gives rise to it could not conceivably be fulfilled. X, let us say, notices that Y's last remark has caused embarrassment to Z and, wishing to spare Z's feelings, X himself makes a remark intended to change the direction of the conversation. Can we seriously contemplate the possibility of being able to give, in terms belonging exclusively to the exact physical sciences, a complete causal account of the origin of precisely *this* complex of thought, feeling, and action on X's part? And of every other piece of human behaviour of even such modest complexity as this? The idea is absurd; and not because there would not be world enough and time to work out the solutions to such particular problems, as there is not world enough and time to work out the particular causal conditions of every movement of a leaf on the surface of a stream. It is more fundamentally absurd because there is no practical possibility of establishing the general principles on which any such calculation would have to be based. This does not mean that we must absolutely deny the existence of underlying psychophysical correlations even in such cases as these. It does mean that the idea of such correlations, in such cases, must remain merely an idea—something without effect, quite empty in a practical point of view. So for the explanation of X's behaviour, we must have recourse to the inexactitudes of: 'That is the sort of man he is—and he has a tenderness for Z—and he is that sort of man partly because he was brought up in *that* society—and Z appeals to him because . . .'; and so on.

There is, of course, more to be said about the scope of physical explanations of human behaviour. In particular, two points must be made. First, if the fine connections, envisaged above, between the language of the exact sciences on the one hand and the language of mind and behaviour on the other, are unattainable, grosser connections *are* attainable. Many general kinds of dependence of the mental and behavioural on the physical are well enough known. We can modify perception, stimulate memory, reduce or enhance aggression, depression, or sexual drive, say, by chemical or electrical means. A great extension of this kind of knowledge is to be foreseen; and knowledge of such dependences, and of the availability of techniques for exploiting them, may surely, *in certain cases*, contribute to inhibiting those personal and moral attitudes and reactions whose basis is at issue, or at least to lessening their force. So why, it may be asked, should *this* inhibiting effect not be generalized? *All* the general traits which manifest themselves in particular episodes of human behaviour, however *nuancé* may be the descriptions we are inclined to give of those episodes, must, we suppose, have a physical base. So why should the inhibiting effect of such knowledge be confined to certain cases? I think the answer—or the beginnings of the answer—is to be found in first noting the fact that these are also the cases which we are favourably disposed to regarding as 'cases for treatment'. They are the cases in which the traits in question are displayed in a form which, of itself, tends to inhibit ordinary interpersonal attitudes in favour of 'objective' attitudes. That is why I said, of such knowledge of causal dependence, only that it *contributes*, in some cases, to inhibiting personal and moral reactions and attitudes. The matter deserves much fuller treatment; but I have not space for it here.[3]

The second point to be made is this. I gave above a particular example of human behaviour and described it in the ordinary human terms of

[3] See n. 2 above.

intention and motive. I dismissed the idea of being able, even in principle, to give adequate causal explanations of such episodes, so described, in the terms of the exact sciences. But suppose we were content to abandon the practice of describing behaviour in terms of intentional action in favour of describing it solely in terms of bodily movements. The general principles of exact and adequate causal explanation of behaviour, so understood, would no longer seem beyond our grasp; for the mechanisms of bodily movement show no discontinuity with the finer electro-chemical mechanisms of the human frame. The difficulties of explanation in particular cases would not be different in kind, though doubtless different in degree, from those of explaining the movements of the leaf on the stream.

I make this point only for the sake of completeness. What we were to contest was the thesis that knowledge of the causes of behaviour would undermine a certain range of attitudes and feelings. I pointed out that such general knowledge of causes as we actually possess has not in fact produced this effect. To the hypothetical question whether exact or 'adequate' knowledge would not produce it I respond with a distinction. So long as what we understand by 'human behaviour' is intentional action, such knowledge is unattainable. If we were to exclude from the description of human behaviour all reference to belief, desire, and intention, if we were to see it as consisting simply in bodily movement, then such knowledge might indeed be in principle attainable. But this truth is simply irrelevant to the issue before us. To see human behaviour as consisting simply of physical movement would, *of itself,* exclude the attitudes and feelings in question; for it is only in relation to behaviour understood, or experienced, as intentional action that these attitudes and feelings ever arise.

I have left myself little space to discuss Spinoza's positive conception of freedom of mind. The picture he draws of the free and rational man, in all his detachment, magnanimity, and moderation, is, by and large, both coherent and impressive. It is, by and large, a recognizable picture. Yet there is one central thesis which leaves an insistent doubt. Spinoza equates increase of freedom with increase of understanding; and the understanding he means is understanding of the nature of God, i.e. of the workings of Nature, including, pre-eminently, our own workings. The advances that have been made during the last three hundred years in this kind of understanding—in the natural sciences—are quite spectacularly great. It will hardly be thought that they have been matched by comparable advances towards deliverance from the bondage of human passions.

The free and rational man, as so impressively, so coherently pictured by Spinoza, must indeed have a certain large vision of the world and a certain broad and sympathetic understanding of human nature. He must by no means be a fool. But it is not at all clear that he has to be a natural scientist.

13
Sensibility, Understanding, and the Doctrine of Synthesis

Professor Henrich has given us a most illuminating and instructive account of the methodology of the transcendental deduction and of Kant's transcendental strategy in general. He begins with the juridical analogy, which, as he shows, there is conclusive reason to think Kant had in mind. A deduction in the relevant sense aims to justify an acquired title, or claim of right, by tracing it back to *origins*, to origins which are such as to confer legitimacy on it. In application to the *Critique* this is a matter of elucidating crucial *basic facts* by virtue of which our *knowledge-claims* are justified and upon which our possession of knowledge depends. These basic facts relate to *specific cognitive capacities* of which we have, in reflection, an *implicit* awareness or knowledge. The deduction is then said to proceed, not by linear demonstration, but by a variety of argumentative strategies that will systematize and render explicit the functioning of our cognitive capacities and, in doing so, will, it is hoped, exhibit the necessary 'validity of the categories for all objects of experience'.

Given this programme, with its emphasis on crucial basic facts regarding our specific cognitive capacities or faculties, it is obviously important to be clear what exactly those basic facts *are*. Crucial here is the distinction between sensibility and understanding: on the one hand, the (intuitive) faculty of receptivity through which the materials of knowledge are given to us; and, on the other, the (discursive) faculty of thought through which they are conceptualized and through which judgement is possible—both faculties being indispensable to beings like us who lack the power of intellectual intuition. To these must surely be added, as Professor Henrich stresses, the self-consciousness (the 'I think') that can accompany all our cognitive operations, but is not merely an accompaniment or correlate of other thoughts; but rather something pervasively indispensable in the elaboration of the argument that is to lead, it is hoped, to the conclusion that the categories are necessarily valid of objects.

However, in these brief comments, I do not propose to attempt an analysis of the stages of the argument. I wish, rather, to raise what might be called a meta-critical point: a point concerning those 'crucial basic facts' about the dual faculties of sensibility and understanding; specifically about the a priori forms of sensibility and about the forms or functions, and hence the pure concepts, of understanding.

In a well-known sentence at B145–6, Kant writes: 'This peculiarity of our understanding, that it can produce a priori unity of apperception solely by means of the categories, and only by such and so many, is *as little capable of further explanation as why we have just these and no other functions of judgement or why space and time are the only forms of our possible intuition.*'

The clear implication of this passage seems to be that we must take it as a basic *fact* indeed about human cognitive faculties—as something fundamentally *contingent*, given, and inexplicable—that we have just the forms and functions of judgement, and just the (spatial and temporal) forms of sensibility, that we do have. If this is so as regards the forms of judgement, then it will indeed follow that no *further* explanation can be given of why we have just the pure concepts of an object in general, the categories, that we do have; for the latter are precisely held to be derived from the former. Moreover, the inexplicable givenness, or bare contingency, of our possessing just these and no other functions of judgement and forms of intuition will constitute no objection, from the *critical* point of view, to bestowing the title 'a priori' both on the pure concepts and on the spatio-temporal forms of sensibility; for, as conditions of the possibility of empirical knowledge of objects—as virtually defining what can count as objects *for us* and our purposes—they will certainly not be themselves empirical, that is, derived from within experience. Again, it may not *matter* from the critical point of view, that the possibility of synthetic a priori knowledge is seen to rest on a contingent foundation, a human 'peculiarity' (*Eigentümlichkeit*), to use Kant's word; though the fact that what is a priori is represented as having a *contingent* foundation will be found at least worthy of remark (and perhaps, to some, disturbing).

But if we shift our stance, if we stand just a little outside the critical point of view, we may legitimately wonder whether it really *is* quite inexplicable that we have just the functions of judgement (the logical forms) and just the spatio-temporal forms of intuition that we do have. First, as to the logical forms. The fundamental logical operations or forms of judgement recognized in Kant's table are such as are, and must be, recognized in any general logic worthy of the name. By 'the fundamental logical operations' I mean: predication (subject and predicate), generalization (particular and universal forms), sentence-composition (including negation, disjunction, conditionality, etc.). Now it is not a mysterious but an analytic truth that judgement involves concepts, that concepts are such as to be applicable or inapplicable to one or more instances, that judgements or propositions are capable of truth or falsity. From such considerations as these it is not too difficult to show that the possibility of the fundamental logical operations is inherent in the very nature of the judgement or proposition. Wittgenstein expressed the point with characteristic epigrammatic obscurity when he wrote in the *Tractatus*: 'One could say that the sole logical constant was what *all* propositions, *by their very nature*, had in common with one another. But that is the general propositional form.'[1] Of course there are differences between the notational devices and forms recognized in different systems of general logic, notably between the forms listed by Kant and those that we find in modern (standard) classical logic. But in spite of their differences in perspicuity and power, the same fundamental logical operations are recognized in both systems. It does indeed seem pretty clear that Kant himself regarded the truths of logic and the principles of formal inference as analytic. Why, one may ask, did he not also see the forms of logic, the fundamental logical operations, as themselves analytically implicit in the very notion of judgement? Had he done so, he could scarcely have said that it was *beyond explanation* why we had 'just these and no other functions of judgement'. The only answer I can think of to my question—the question why he didn't see it this way—refers to the idea of an intellect that is not discursive at all, but purely intuitive: to the idea of 'intellectual intuition'. But that is really no answer. For a non-discursive, intuitive intellect, which had no need of sensible intuition, which as it were created its own objects of knowledge, would presumably have no need of

---

[1] Ludwig Wittgenstein, *Tractatus Logico-Philosophicus*, trans. D. F. Pears and B. F. McGuinness (London: Routledge and Kegan Paul, 1964), sec. 5.47. I have argued the same point myself in a lengthier and more cumbersome way in 'Logical Form and Logical Constants', in *Logical Form, Predication and Ontology*, ed. Pranab Kumar Sen (Delhi: Macmillan, 1982), pp. 1–17.

judgement either. (I say this tentatively, however, having no more conception than Kant had of what intellectual intuition would be like.)

What now of the doctrine that it is a bare inexplicable fact of human sensibility that we have just the spatial and temporal forms of intuition that we do have? Is it really inexplicable? Does it simply inexplicably *happen* to be the case that the spatial and the temporal are the modes in which *we* are sensibly affected by objects? Well, one very simple explanation, or ground of explanation, would be this: that the objects, including ourselves, *are* spatio-temporal objects, are *in* space and time—where by 'objects' is meant not *just* 'objects of possible knowledge' (though that is also meant) but objects, and ourselves, as they really are or are in themselves. The reason why this would be an adequate explanation is fairly straightforward, granted only that we are indeed creatures whose intellects are discursive and whose intuition is sensible. For such creatures must, in judgement, employ and apply general concepts to the objects of sensible intuition; the very notion of the generality of a concept implies the possibility of numerically distinguishable individual objects falling under one and the same concept; and, once granted that objects are themselves spatio-temporal, then space and time provide the uniquely necessary media for the realization of this possibility in sensible intuition of objects. I say 'uniquely necessary', because, although distinguishable spatio-temporal objects falling under the same general concept could certainly be distinguishable in many other ways, the one way in which they *could not fail* to be distinguishable—the one way in which they are *necessarily* distinguishable—is in respect of their spatial and/or temporal location. (I repeat here an argument I have used elsewhere,[2] but it seems sufficiently important to be worth repeating.)

I have argued that *both* our possession of just the logical functions of judgement (and hence, arguably, just the pure concepts) that we do possess *and* our possession of just the spatio-temporal forms of intuition that we do possess—I have argued that, on certain assumptions, both of these admit of perfectly adequate explanation. Two of these assumptions—*viz.* that our intellect is discursive and our intuition sensible—are admitted, indeed proclaimed, by Kant himself. The third assumption—namely that objects and ourselves are, as they are in themselves, spatio-temporal things—is an

---

[2] In introductory lectures regularly given at Oxford University; see also P. F. Strawson, *Analyse et métaphysique* (Paris: J. Vrin, 1985), p. 66.

assumption that he would, it seems, reject, although the significance of this rejection is not, perhaps, entirely clear.

But there is a more important point to be made, which is this. Nothing in what I have said is, in itself, sufficient to challenge for one moment the status of space and time as a priori forms of intuition. For spatio-temporal intuition of objects, through whatever sensory modalities it may be empirically mediated, appears even more strongly than before as a uniquely fundamental *condition* of any empirical knowledge of objects. Similarly, given the status I have claimed for the logical functions of judgement, then, if the derivation of the categories from the forms of judgement and their ensuing deduction are both sound, it will follow that they, too, have a parallel status to that of the forms of sensible intuition as a priori conditions of empirical knowledge. So nothing in what I have so far said threatens this aspect of Kant's transcendentalism. Equally, and still more obviously, nothing threatens his empirical realism.

What, then, of his version of idealism, the apparently sharp distinction between things in themselves and appearances, the latter alone being objects of empirical knowledge? The question here is one of interpretation. *If*, in accordance with the purely negative concept of the noumenon, the thought of things in themselves is to be understood simply and solely as the thought of the very things of which human knowledge is possible, but the thought of them *in total abstraction* from what have been shown (or at least argued) to be the conditions of the very *possibility* of any such knowledge, then it must surely be concluded that the thought is empty; for the doctrine that we can have no knowledge of things *as they are in themselves* reduces to the tautology that no knowledge of things is possible *except under the conditions under which it is possible*; or: we can know of things only what we can know of them. In that case, though the empirical realism is secure, the 'idealism' in Kant's 'transcendental idealism' would appear as little more than a token name, or as, at most, the acknowledgement that though indeed we can have knowledge of things, there may be more to the nature of those things than what we can know about them—an acknowledgement that most of us would be perfectly happy to make.

However, it must, I think, be admitted that it is far from clear that this is the intended, or at least the consistently intended, interpretation of the distinction between appearance and thing in itself. And if it is not, then we are faced with a host of familiar difficulties (regarding the relations between a super-sensible and a sensible world) which it would be irrelevant now to recall.

In his paper Professor Guyer confronts the question whether Kant's transcendental deduction of the categories is to be understood as 'psychological' in character. There is a sense of that word in which to understand the deduction as 'psychological' would certainly be damaging to its claim to establish the a priori objective validity of the pure concepts of an object in general. Drawing on examples from Hume and J. N. Tetens, Professor Guyer mentions three connected characteristics or arguments or explanations that are psychological in this sense.

First, such explanations or arguments refer or appeal to the actual occurrence at determinable moments of specific mental experiences and mental acts. Second, it is only contingently true that acts of these types occur. And, third, it is only empirically that their occurrences can be established or certified.

Two things are immediately clear. First, any account or argument that did indeed have these characteristics would be quite alien to the aims of the deduction and quite unable to fulfil its purposes. But, second, it is only too easy to read some passages of the deduction (especially in the first-edition version) as if what were being spoken of were actual occurrences of mental acts and processes of reproducing and synthesizing or combining sequential elements of the sensory manifold. Such a reading runs into the obvious difficulty that, on the one hand, it is hard to see how there could be any but *empirical* knowledge of any such occurrences; whereas, on the other, the argument of the deduction seems to require their occurrence to be an antecedent condition of the possibility of any empirical knowledge at all.

Professor Guyer aims to show that the deduction is not psychological in the damaging sense; consequently that the reading above referred to is incorrect and the difficulties inherent in it do not arise. I think he is substantially successful in this aim and I will endeavour, first, to state very summarily what seem to me to be the main points of his argument. First, it has to be admitted that the sensory input that supplies us with all the materials of knowledge comes to us over time, as a series of 'variable and transitory data', a temporal manifold. A mere series of transitory, and *unconnected*, representations or receptions of successive elements of such a manifold would not amount to cognition or knowledge. To achieve the latter, some form of representation is required that *holds together* the successive elements of the manifold. Or, in Professor Guyer's own words, 'there must be some way in which the current representational state of the knower can be interpreted to include representation of its previous representational states'. And this in its turn is possible only if the knower deploys, in his current representational state, concepts that themselves exemplify or incorporate the crucial categories or concepts of an object in general, specifically those of substance and cause; that is, the concepts to be deployed are concepts 'of enduring independent substances whose states stand in rule-governed relations of succession and have determinate effects upon the succession of our states as well'. (This is most clearly spelled out, Professor Guyer suggests, in Kant's subsequent reflections on the Refutation of Idealism.)

However, the line of thought I have so drastically—no doubt too drastically—abbreviated here does, I think, require some interpretation if the shades of Hume and Tetens are to be finally dismissed. It is true, of course, that the sensory input we receive is extended over time and hence that it can in principle be thought of as a series of successive impressions, each with its own intrinsic instantaneous character. But, if the *intrinsic* character of each single successive impression were thought of (on Hume-like lines) as *not* already involving the objective concepts to be argued for, then it would seem that something like a retrospective *act* of reproducing past impressions and *combining* them with a present one by the *imposition* of a unifying objective concept would be called for. But *that* story would be altogether too reminiscent of the dreaded psychological model, with its attendant difficulties, for it to be acceptable to Professor Guyer (or, for that matter, to me). Rather we must insist—and to do so is, incidentally, to be quite faithful to the actual character of our ordinary perceptual experience—we must insist, I say, that at *any instant* in the ongoing stream of 'episodes of sensible affection' (as Professor Guyer calls them) our perceptual experience involves the deployment of concepts of objects of the desired sort; that our representational states *at each moment* are thoroughly permeated by such concepts. The truth that perceptual experience *at any given moment* is to be thus characterized is precisely what is necessary and sufficient to link the actual current perception or representational state to other, not actually current, past, or possible future representational states; to effect, if you like, their necessary combination. Concepts of enduring objects with causal powers have precisely this nature: any actual current perception, or representation, of something as falling under such a concept is essentially linked to other non-actual, non-current perceptions of the same kind. As I have put it elsewhere, non-present perceptions 'are in a sense represented in, alive in, the present perception'. This is why Kant gives such an important role to the faculty of imagination, qualified as 'transcendental'; for imagination, as more commonly understood, is just the faculty of representing the non-actual.[3] And I think, and hope, that much of the same thought is present in Professor Guyer's mind when he writes: 'The synthesis of reproduction cannot take place independently of the synthesis of recognition in a concept because it is only the application of appropriately interpretative concepts to the current representational state of any knower that reproduces the data to be synthesised.'

However, given the present state of research in cognitive psychology, there is something to be added to this. As far as our *conscious* experience is concerned, it is right to insist, as I have done, and as I think Professor Guyer implicitly does, that our successive states of conscious perceptual experience are, throughout, such that they cannot (in general) be accurately characterized without employing concepts of enduring objects with causal powers; and it is true, too, as the deduction is designed to show (or to prepare the ground for showing), that so much is a necessary condition of knowledge arising from perceptual experience. But we have also learned, from the results of studies in physiological psychology, that our *conscious* perceptual experience is causally dependent on neuro-physiological processes of immense complexity, processes of which we are *not* conscious at all while we are enjoying the conscious experience that depends upon them. The studies in question are empirical, as are their results. They relate to particular occurrences and processes in the brain and nervous system, themselves occasioned by impingements on the external organs. Perhaps—though I speak in ignorance—the phrase 'information-processing' is correctly applied to these internal operations. Now, as I earlier remarked, much of the language of Kant's deduction—notably in the theory of the threefold synthesis—does invite and encourage interpretation in terms of particular occurrences of events and processes—of reproduction and combination—that culminate in the application of concepts falling under the categories. May it not be that the Kantian theory of synthesis, interpreted in this style, has at least analogues—and

---

[3] See P. F. Strawson, 'Imagination and Perception', in *Freedom and Resentment* (London: Methuen, 1974), and in *Kant on Pure Reason*, ed. R. C. S. Walker (Oxford: Oxford University Press, 1982).

perfectly respectable analogues—in the empirical theories of the physiological psychologists? If so, and even if (as seems likely) very little can be made out in the way of detailed parallels, the Kantian theory of synthesis, understood in *this* way, could be seen as a brilliantly imaginative anticipation of the results of scientific investigation—indeed of what might, with peculiar, unexpected, and certainly *unintended* appropriateness, be called 'the physiology of inner sense'. I think that Professor Guyer perhaps hints at something of the kind himself when he remarks that the Kantian theory 'may well place constraints on anything that would count as human cognitive psychology'.

If both parts of these comments of mine on Professor Guyer's paper are on roughly the right lines, then a certain inevitable tension in our understanding of Kant's deduction can be satisfactorily resolved. On the one hand we can safely deny that Kant's theory is psychological in that damaging sense that Professor Guyer illustrates by reference to Hume and Tetens. At the same time we can construe those passages in Kant's work that undeniably *suggest* such a reading as pointing, rather, toward developments in what is undoubtedly empirical (and physiological) psychology—developments of which it was impossible to form an accurate or detailed conception at the time at which he wrote. Both views of the matter are perfectly compatible with each other—they can be held simultaneously—and both may be seen as underlining his genius. Neither constrains us to see Kant as conducting an exercise in what I once somewhat rudely called 'the imaginary subject of transcendental psychology' and which, as Professor Guyer rightly remarks, might more correctly be described as 'transcendent' rather than 'transcendental'.

14
Two Conceptions of Philosophy

It is sometimes said, of some philosophers, that they fail to disclose, or are even unaware of, the deep underlying commitments or presuppositions of their work; that a philosopher may be unable, or reluctant, to acknowledge what are, in the strict sense of the word, the *prejudices* which determine the cast and direction of his thought. Of none of our contemporaries could this be said with *less* justice than of Van Quine. The charge, if it is a charge, would, in his case, be singularly ill-aimed or inappropriate; for he has, frequently and explicitly, made clear the aims and methods, the governing principles, of his work. 'Philosophy', he writes, 'or what appeals to me under that head, is continuous with science.'

'Continuous with', not 'identical with'. It is not the philosopher's business to amend, or add to, physical theory: but it is part of his business to address the question of how we come to have the very thought of the objects of physical theory; indeed, of how we come to have the thought of objects at all, of any kind. Since thought is too elusive to be studied except in its linguistic expression, the question about thought of objects becomes a question about verbal *reference* to objects; and we are launched into the philosophy of language, into an enquiry which is at once semantic, epistemological, and, of course—since what we count as objects of reference are what we recognize to exist—ontological.

But the scientific commitment ('Philosophy of science is philosophy enough') places severe restrictions on the nature of this enquiry; and on its outcome. Our ordinary habits of reference embrace many sorts of purported objects that are vague and undefined. For the scientific philosopher, on the other hand, nothing is to be admitted, in serious philosophical theory, which does not satisfy the stringent requirements of exactitude which physical theory imposes. There is a certain theoretical latitude in the interpretation of these requirements. Quine sketches one theoretically available interpretative path which would lead to a dramatically unified ontology. He remarks that bodies, as ordinarily understood, are the primitive objects of reference; but adds that the criteria of individuation and identity of such bodies over time and space are vague and the general category correspondingly so. This vagueness can be dissipated by replacing the ordinary notion of a body with the generalized notion of a physical object conceived of as 'the material content of any portion of space-time, however irregular and discontinuous and heterogeneous'.[1] Physical objects so conceived meet the requirement of a precise criterion of identity: they are identical if and only if coextensive.

Science, of course, requires more than physical objects. Because quantitative laws are its mainstay, it requires abstract objects: classes and numbers. But the resulting appearance of a dualistic ontology can be overcome. If we first reinterpret physical objects as the corresponding place-times, characterized by states; fill out the category of place-times with the empty ones; then drop the space-time regions in favour of the corresponding quadruples of real numbers according to an arbitrarily adopted system of coordinates; and, finally, model the quadruples within pure set theory—*then* we are left with a single abstract ontological domain!

This is an ontological *tour de force* indeed. But science does not oblige us to perform it. Indeed 'empiricist discipline' may make it prudent to forswear it. That discipline requires theoretical sentences to remain answerable to observation sentences; and the latter are most conveniently understood as involving reference to bodies. So the scientific philosopher may, with a good conscience, rest content with a dualistic ontology of both physical and (his chosen) abstract objects.

The chosen abstract objects—classes (including numbers)—are not simply tolerated in the interests of physical science. They independently satisfy the requirements of precision and clarity; for classes have a clear general principle of individuation: they are identical when their members are. There is no such clear principle for other purported abstract entities: properties or attributes, and intensions generally (propositions, senses, meanings). To say, for example, that properties are identical when exemplified by the same objects would be self-defeating: it would be to

---

[1] W. V. Quine, *Theories and Things* (Cambridge, MA: Harvard University Press, 1981), p. 10.

assimilate them to classes, and hence to deny what is held to be their distinctive character. To say that they are identical when they belong to just the same classes would, given the identity-condition for classes, be obviously circular. Quine glances at one further theoretically possible way of finding, or constructing, for attributes, a general identity-condition, which makes no mention of classes. If we were given an *exhaustive* list of predicates which could, in our theory, be appropriately affirmed or denied of attributes or properties, then we could define identity of attributes in terms of it. Attributes would be identical if just *the same predicates* were true or false of them. But Quine makes it clear that he knows, and expects to know, of no such theory and no such list. (He does not explicitly make the point that he could in any case consistently regard such an identity-condition as satisfactory only if he had an independent general identity-condition for predicates; but perhaps the point is implicit in the notion of an 'exhaustive list' of the relevant predicates.)

Of course the difficulty could be overcome if we were allowed the full resources of modal logic: property-identity could then be explained by *necessary* equivalence of predicates. But necessity goes with essences and falls, with them, under the same ban as other intensions. We are locked in a circle of notions which, in Quine's eyes, lack 'the markings of a proper annexe to austere scientific language';[2] they do not measure up to this demanding standard of clarity.

It is important to note that Quine does not absolutely deny the existence of everything not accommodated in his chosen ontology. For example, his materialism is not a denial of the mental, as the latter is commonly understood; rather, it is the claim that the common understanding falls short of the stringent requirements of scientific understanding. So it is by no means true that Quine *equates* experience, in all its 'heady luxuriance' (his own phrase), with triggered nerve-endings and verbal responses; rather he isolates, in complex phenomena, components which he finds, by his own standards of clarity, clearly explicable. The aim is to see what can be done, in the field of philosophy (of thought, language, experience) with materials amenable to impeccably scientific treatment. Those materials, saving the abstract objects, are material. So physicalistic or behaviouristic terms serve

---

[2] Ibid., p. 128.

as scientifically acceptable, and scientifically adequate, surrogates for, or interpretations of, mentality.

I have so far given but a bare outline or sketch of this conception of a strictly scientific philosophy—an outline which can convey little sense of the mastery with which, by Quine, the programme has been carried out. It is needless for me to dwell on the admiration that I and all of us feel for the fertility and power, the elegance and wit, displayed in the elaboration of a system capable of meeting the severe demands of that programme.

Instead I would like to sketch, by way of contrast, an alternative conception of philosophical aims; and to illustrate, by way of a case already alluded to, how this alternative conception allows for a more liberal ontology than that of the critical, scientific philosopher. Let me make it clear that I am not concerned to evaluate the relative merits of these two conceptions. Each has its own worth and its own appeal; and the choice between them is, ultimately, perhaps, a matter of individual temperament. Let me make it clear, too, that the alternative conception I have in mind is not such as to meet the needs of the student who looks for inspirational or edifying writing in philosophy; I agree wholeheartedly with Quine that such a student 'is misguided and probably not a very good student anyway, since intellectual curiosity is not what moves him'.[3]

So what is this alternative conception? Well, the common, as distinct from the scientific, understanding is a complicated affair, embracing an indefinitely large range of ideas or concepts. Within this indefinitely large range it is possible to distinguish a number of fundamental, general, pervasive concepts or types of concept, which together constitute the structural framework, as it were, within which all ordinary detailed thinking goes on. To name a few at random, I have in mind such ideas as those of space and time, object and property, event, mind and body, knowledge and belief, truth, sense and meaning, necessity and possibility, existence, identity, action, intention, causation and explanation. Some of these, and some of the more specific concepts which fall under them, can be understood, or at least interpreted, in ways which satisfy Quine's scientific standards of clarity. Many cannot: they remain, by those standards, vague and ill defined. Yet it is possible, without discarding common understanding, so to exhibit the interrelations and interdependences of all such

---

[3] Ibid., p. 193.

pervasive concepts and concept-types as to make relatively perspicuous the interlocking frameworks of ideas on which we weave our systems of particular belief. The philosophical aim of those who adhere to my alternative conception of philosophy I take to be that of elucidating the character of such concepts as these and their interconnections. I would particularly stress the notion of interconnection. For, as I have suggested, such ideas as these do form an interconnected structure within which we build up our detailed pictures or theories of how things are.

Of course, whatever choice is made between these contrasting conceptions of philosophical aim, there are gains and losses on either side. If the alternative conception is chosen, there is an obvious gain in fidelity to the structure of our common thinking, balanced by an obvious loss in scientific precision, elegance, and economy. But do we not *all* aim at fidelity to the truth? Indeed. But the question is: truth to what? That question is one of allegiance; and Quine makes *his* allegiance honourably clear.

So much for generalities. I remarked earlier that I intended to show, by reference to one particular case, or range of cases, how the alternative conception allows for a more liberal, or, as one might say, a more catholic, ontology than that of the scientifically inspired philosophy. It might seem that the general point is too obvious to be worth making. But the particular case has its own ramifying interest; so I shall develop it.

The case in question is that of attributes or properties. It is obvious that in common speech we frequently treat such items or pseudo-items as objects of reference, quantifying over them or referring to them by name. But the looseness of common speech cannot be allowed, by the scientific philosopher, to be an adequate criterion. Quine, as we have seen, sets a stiffer test for the status of object or entity. It is summarized in the memorable slogan, 'No entity without identity'. The slogan indeed admits of one harmlessly trivial interpretation: *viz.* there exists nothing which is not identical with itself. But this is not how Quine understands it. He takes it to require, of a putative entity, of any apparent candidate for the status of real object, that there should exist some common *general* principle or criterion of identity for *all* things of the *general kind* to which the putative entity belongs. We have already seen how properties in general fail this test. That need not in itself be decisive even if we accept the test; for it seems that subcategories of qualities or properties might pass it, even if the general category does not. But in fact the subcategories fail as well: there is, as far as I can see, no common general principle of identity for virtues or for qualities of character generally; for intellectual qualities; or for qualities, such as colours, of the various sense-modalities. This failure extends, indeed, beyond what we would most naturally call properties or attributes, to other general things or features, though not to all; it extends to personal traits, like ways of walking or manners of speech, to architectural styles, literary styles, even hairstyles. I said that the failure does not extend to all general things; and the limits of failure, the areas of success, are precisely such as to gratify the scientifically inspired philosophy. Of numbers and classes I have already spoken; but it can, in our day, be added, perhaps, with reason, that there exist general principles of identity common to *all* animal species or, again, to *all* chemical substances. The reason is, of course, that in each of these fields there has developed a *science* which supplies a systematic taxonomy, or general principles of classification, which allow us to make sense of talking of general criteria of identity not just for all specimens of this or that kind, but for the general kinds themselves. Natural history gives birth to natural science and so to this possibility. But art history and literary history are unlikely to have any comparable offspring; and it is correspondingly unlikely that there will ever be general criteria of identity for literary or architectural styles.

But the question is, of course, whether we should accept Quine's test for the status of entity or object, i.e. whether we should accept his interpretation of the identity-condition on objects. It is clear that whatever we can count as an entity must satisfy some identity-condition; and a reasonable constraint on any existence-claim is the following: that everything that really exists (and hence qualifies as a genuine object of reference) must be capable, at least in principle, of being *identified* as the thing it is. All *entia* must be *identifiabilia*. Now the properties and other general things, which fail Quine's test, certainly pass this one: they are, in general, things we can identify, or learn to identify, can recognize, or learn to recognize, as the same again in different situations.

Consider, to begin with, such adjectival general terms as 'blue', 'witty', 'cheerful', 'generous', or such relational words as 'loves'. Anyone who has mastered the use of these expressions knows how to apply them to *visibilia*, persons, and pairs. Thereby he knows how to *identify* the corresponding colour, intellectual quality, quality of character, and affective attitude. The criterion of application of the predicate *is* the individual criterion of identity of the *individual* quality or relation. The *sense* of the general term gives the individual essence of the general thing. So there is no need for common *general* criteria of identity for all things of the kind to which the general thing belongs.

Evidently there is here an appeal to a notion—that of the *sense* of a general term—which the scientific philosopher disallows as vague and ill defined. But the notion of the sense of terms is precisely one of those which, on the alternative conception of philosophy, are to be, not discarded, but given their appropriate place in the elucidation of the general structure of our thought.

Not all the general things which fail Quine's test, but satisfy the more liberal identity-condition, are so conveniently associated with general terms. Consider distinctive smells, musical timbres, ways of walking, manners of speaking, or hairstyles. These too are recognizable and identifiable things or features, but in general lack names which give their essence. Such names as they have, when they have any, are derived from association with, for example, particular persons or substances or places or types of object. But the very same things may exist and be identified when divorced from those particular associations.

To this more liberal approach it may be objected that the identities I have been speaking of are fatally lacking in sharpness of definition—that the properties and general features in question are vague and ill defined. And so they are. In the cases where the general thing has a corresponding predicate, as with the properties I first mentioned, the extensions of those predicates have no sharp cut-off points. It is not quite clear where wit ends and (mere) sarcasm begins, where cheerfulness turns into boisterousness, where we no longer have the Transitional style but the true Gothic. But the same thing is true, as he himself remarks, of those material things or particulars which Quine is normally prepared to allow as genuine objects of reference. It is not quite clear when we have left the town or are out of the wood, when the mountain ends and the foothills begin or when the estuary becomes the sea. And there are other aspects of indeterminacy, affecting either or both of general and particular things, which I will not dwell on. The general point is that the identifiability of a thing, whether general or particular, does not require that its boundaries be sharply defined.

A different objection may now be raised. I have contrasted the more liberal condition on objects or entities—that any admissible candidate for this status must be identifiable as the thing it is—with the more exacting condition proposed by Quine—that any such candidate must belong to a kind such that there exists a common general principle or criterion of identity for all things of that kind. The more liberal condition allows for what I have called an individual principle or criterion of identity, supplied, in some cases, by the sense of the name, or of the corresponding predicate, for the item in question; the more stringent condition does not: it requires a general principle. Let us call the objects that satisfy Quine's more stringent condition 'Q-certified objects'. The new objection runs as follows. What I have been representing as identifiable general things which are *not* Q-certified objects are really, at least for the most part, nothing but rather vague principles of discriminating among, or grouping together, independently identifiable things which are Q-certified objects. Thus qualities of intellect or character belong to, or are manifested by, people; architectural styles are exemplified by buildings; hairstyles by heads of hair; and so on. And people, buildings, heads are independently identifiable objects just because, and only because, they are Q-certified objects. For such kinds of spatio-temporal particulars—and indeed for all kinds of identifiable spatio-temporal particulars—there do exist, and must exist, common *general* criteria or principles of identity; since no particular instance of any such kind can be represented as having an *essence* which could effectively serve as an individual principle of identity for that particular. Therefore the non-Q-certified properties or general things of which I have been speaking are, at best, *dependent identifiabilia*; they depend for their identifiability on the independent identifiability of Q-certified objects. And here is a reason for regarding the latter, and only the latter, as genuine objects or entities.

However, this reason, this objection, backfires. For what constitutes our grasp of the *general* criterion of identity for men, or of that for horses, or for planets or storms or buildings or battles—or indeed for any kind of particulars—is precisely our grasp of the general concepts under which they respectively fall or (what comes to the same thing) our grasp of the senses of the general terms for the kinds in question. And these kinds are not themselves Q-certified objects. (As already noted, a minor qualification may now be called for, in the case of biological species; but the emergence of the kind-concepts, man or horse, did not wait for the development of a scientific taxonomy.) So the dependence-argument is reversed. It is the Q-certified objects in question which depend for their identifiability on the identifiability of the non-Q-certified kinds to which they belong. Or, to use old-fashioned and perhaps provocative language: as far as identifiability is concerned, universals are prior to particulars.

I have so far been presenting the case, or part of the case, for rejecting the principle that only Q-certified objects are genuinely objects or entities. The sacrifice of precision which this rejection involves, and which the scientific philosopher will deplore, is no sacrifice from the point of view of the alternative conception of philosophy which I sketched. But there is point in enquiring further into the reasons, apart from the scientific demand for exactitude, which may help to account for the appeal of the rejected principle. I shall suggest that part of its appeal lies in the combined force of two very different kinds of consideration which tend, up to a point, and not accidentally, to reinforce each other.

Interestingly enough, we can, to a certain degree, find both kinds of consideration linked together in Aristotle's doctrine of primary substances. He identified primary substances as a subclass of spatio-temporal particulars, namely those relatively enduring substantial spatio-temporal individuals which exemplified some distinctive principle of organization—such as (in the *Categories*) the individual man or horse. This marries with the simple and humanly natural thought that it is the readily distinguishable material individuals of the world—the bodies—that are the real entities, the original, pre-eminent, undeniable objects. But Aristotle also proposed a formal or logical criterion for primary substances: they were to be irreducibly *subjects* of predication or, as we now say, objects of reference. And this marries with Quine's own notion that entities are just those things which are indispensably among the subjects of predication—or, as he puts it, among the values of the variables of quantification.

Now the substantial organized individuals which Aristotle declared to satisfy his formal criterion, and which, as bodies, Quine described as the primitive objects of reference are, of course, as I have already emphasized, Q-certified objects. They have no *individual* essences by which they must be identified if they are to be identified at all; but must, rather, be identified as the particular instances they are of the general *kind* to which they essentially belong. But they certainly and indispensably figure, in our common discourse, as objects of reference or subjects of predication. So these three characteristics: being among the things we most naturally and primitively regard as real entities or objects; being indispensably, in practice, among the subjects of predication; and being Q-certified objects— these three go strikingly and triumphantly together. And this may partly account for the attractiveness of the thesis that Q-certifiability is a necessary condition of entityhood.

But to explain is not to vindicate. And if we return to Quine's original and basic criterion of that status—*viz*. objects or entities are what figure indispensably among the subjects of predication—we find a very different result. When we take account of the needs of common discourse we find that countless kinds of general things or universals, besides satisfying the identifiability test, satisfy also that basic criterion. There is no prospect of our saying what we need to say about techniques (such as acupuncture or quantification), about social conditions (such as unemployment or war), about dishes (such as rice pudding or hotpot), about games (such as cricket or baseball), and about hosts of other general things, without at many points treating them as subjects of first-order predication. Of course the needs of common discourse are not those of a strictly scientific philosophy, as understood by Quine; but they are precisely the needs which the alternative conception of philosophy must reckon with. On this conception, we should regard our need to treat an identifiable item, of whatever kind, as capable of supporting a pointful predication as a sufficient attestation of its worthiness to do so. This catholicism of entities does not open the gates to non-entities: we know, or learn, how to distinguish between names which really do name *identifiabilia* of some kind from names which only purport, or are mistakenly supposed, to do so.

But, it may be said, are you not now, in defending the real existence of universals at large, in effect defending Platonism? And is not Platonism a discredited myth? I answer: there are no doubt mythological elements in some versions, including perhaps Plato's own, of realism about universals; but there is none in mine. If I am said to be defending Platonism, let it be added that it is a demythologized Platonism. Entities are just the identifiable things, general or particular, which we need in practice to acknowledge as supporting predication.

I said, earlier on, that the issue I am going to discuss—that of properties and universals in general—had a ramifying interest. Let me conclude by mentioning two theses which might reasonably be seen as consequences of, or supplements to, the position I have argued for.

One concerns propositions—or what it is now more fashionable to call propositional contents. They are meant to be understood as distinct from both type- and token-sentences and also, if only because of the indexical elements that most uttered sentences contain, as distinct from the meanings of type-sentences. They are, if they exist at all, abstract objects; and are widely regarded, and for much the same reasons, as falling under the same ban as properties or attributes. But if I am right in defending the reality of properties etc., the main objection to admitting the reality of propositions, so understood, evaporates. In the simplest case in which a general term is predicated of one or more particular, directly identified items, the identity of the proposition is determined by the identities both of the particular individual or individuals referred to and of the property or relation associated with the general term. This contention itself needs elaboration and has several further consequences which I will not pursue now. But it also raises one other question which I shall pursue.

Frege, as we know, distinguishes sharply between *objects*, which are designated, or referred to, or meant, by definite singular terms, and *concepts* which are designated, or referred to, or meant, by predicate-expressions. Concepts, in his view, are not objects: they are, as he says, incomplete or unsaturated and the expressions which stand for them are essentially predicative. We find a partial, though substantially modified, echo of this doctrine in Quine's own doctrine that predicates do not stand for, or refer to, anything at all, but are simply true or false of objects.

But once properties are admitted, we can make a case for revising both views. We can represent the properly predicative expression as a complex expression consisting of the root general term, designating a property, plus a copulative device, the two together yielding a truly predicative expression. The nature of the copulative device may vary, depending on the syntactical category of the general term and on idiosyncratic features of the language employed: if the general term is an adjective or common noun, it may, in English, be the form 'is' or 'is a'; if the general term is itself a verb, it may be the employment of a finite form of the verb; or again, it may simply consist in the device of concatenation with a singular term. Thus the predicate-expression in a complete simple sentence both introduces and copulates a property. The syntactical variation between 'Socrates has courage' where the property is introduced by name and copulated by 'has', and 'Socrates is courageous', when the property is introduced by general term and copulated by 'is', is not more than that—a syntactical variation. We do not have to say that the resultant proposition is a curious compound of concrete and abstract object. We can say, instead, as above, that the identity of the proposition, as purely abstract object, is determined by, or the resultant of, the *identities* of the concrete individual and the abstract object, the property. This has the further consequence that quantification into predicate-position (more precisely, into general-term position) is just as securely objectual as quantification into subject-position.

I realize that these last remarks are heterodox and may seem like a reactionary harking-back to long-exploded and absurd positions. But I have thought it worth trying them out. In any case, they are supplementary to, and not absolutely required by, my main contention concerning the more liberal ontology allowed by a conception of philosophy which is an alternative to that scientifically inspired conception so brilliantly implemented by Quine.

I said, much earlier on, that I am not concerned to evaluate the relative merits of the two conceptions of philosophy. Each has its own validity on its own terms. I added that the choice between them is ultimately, perhaps, a matter of individual temperament; and if I have made my own preference clear, it is no more than that—my own preference. It has been said that the best conceptual scheme, the best system of ideas, is the one that gets us around best. The question is: in what milieu? For one content to lead his life—at least his intellectual life—in the rarefied atmosphere of science, the choice, on this test, will go one way. For one content to lead *his* intellectual life in the muddier atmosphere of the more mundane—of what, in another tradition, has been called 'expérience vécue'—it will go the other way.

15
Review of Paul Grice, *Studies in the Way of Words*

Of the English and American philosophers born in the present century I think I have known all the most gifted. I do not think I have known any who is or was the equal, in certain respects, of Paul Grice. Others have had and will have a more pervasive and more lasting influence. None, however, was so formidable a critic, so skilled at detecting the flaws in another's argument or the fatal weakness in a philosophical position; and none so persistently ingenious in pursuing the implications of a position of his own, in discerning possible objections or difficulties, and in contriving defences or modifications to meet them.

Although critical penetration and elaborative ingenuity are the characteristics which will remain most forcibly present in the minds of those who knew him well, it would be misleading to dwell on these to the neglect of those aspects of Grice's work which constitute a substantial and enduring contribution to philosophical and linguistic theory. Most prominent among these are two. (A) First, there is the attempt to give a reductive analysis of the concept of linguistic meaning in psychological terms—a project originally and brilliantly sketched in the 1957 article 'Meaning' (reproduced as Essay 14 in the present book), and subsequently elaborated in a series of lectures and articles (Essays 5, 6, 7, and 18).[1] (B) Second, there is the development of the theory of conversational implicature, which has rightly won a secure place in linguistic theory, on both of its necessarily connected semantic and pragmatic sides (Essays 1, 2, 3, 4, 15, and 17). In the course of both of these highly original theoretical

---

[1] Paul Grice, *Studies in the way of words* (Cambridge: Harvard University Press, 1989).

ventures, Grice has occasion to draw a variety of distinctions which must be acknowledged by any clear-headed student of language and its uses.

The set of distinctions to be first considered are those drawn in Essay 5 in connection with project (A) above. They are, in Grice's own terminology, the distinctions between (1) the timeless meaning(s) of an utterance-type; (2) the applied timeless meaning of an utterance-type (i.e. with the lexical ambiguities resolved); (3) the occasion-meaning of an utterance-type (i.e. what the utterer meant on a given occasion by the expressions, or devices, belonging to the utterance-type in question); and (4) utterer's occasion-meaning (i.e. roughly the message the utterer intended to convey to his audience). The first three of these four divisions are standardly, though not necessarily, taken to involve reference to linguistic utterance-types. It is far otherwise with the fourth, in respect of which, although such reference must ultimately be involved if the project (A) is to be carried through, the original examples (in Essay 14) involve none at all. For the project is first to show how the concept of utterer's occasion-meaning is wholly explicable in terms of utterer's intention, with no dependence on semantic concepts and no reference to linguistic devices, and second, to explicate or analyse the other three divisions of meaning in terms of the notion of utterer's occasion-meaning (together with other non-semantic concepts).

The project encounters two main difficulties. The first, and less serious, is the difficulty of giving a satisfactory analysis of utterer's occasion-meaning in terms of utterer's intention, i.e. a satisfactory account, in non-semantic terms, of what it is for someone to intend by his act to communicate a specific message to another. Grice's first attempt at such an account (Essay 14) prompted counterexamples which seemed to call for elaboration and complication of the original analysis. The revision prompted further and more complex counterexamples. Regress threatened, and the prospect of a realistic non-regressive solution began to seem poor. It was, above all, Stephen Schiffer (*Meaning*, 1972) who showed a Gricean ingenuity in multiplying difficulties of this order. But Grice contrives ways both of inhibiting the regress and of dealing with other examples of a different kind which call for adjustment to the original analysis.

A more serious problem arises when the greater difficulty is confronted—that of producing a genuinely reductive analysis of full-blown linguistic meaning in non-semantic, psychological (and social) terms. Grice marshals, to considerable effect, the full resources of his subtlety to deal with the admitted fact of the interdependence of language and (at least developed) thought (see pp. 141–3 and 352–9). Yet one suspects that doubt remains even in his own mind. Of our actual working concepts of the semantic on the one hand, and the psychological (and social) on the other, it may well seem preferable to settle for the notion of mutual interconnection and abandon the seductive idea of the reducibility of the former to the latter.[2] But the issue cannot be regarded as finally closed.

Whereas this reductive project (A) has engaged the attention mainly or only of philosophers, the theory of conversational implicature (project B) has captivated linguists as well. Here again the development of the theory has been attended by the drawing of distinctions, all clearly drawn and all essential to a correct understanding of language and its uses. I set them out, as before, in numbered form, but this time in a mixture of Grice's terminology and my own. We are to suppose a certain sentence of a certain language L, uttered on a particular occasion. We can distinguish (1) the literal meaning (or meanings) of what is said, as determined by the syntax and lexicon of L (Grice's 'timeless meaning(s) of the utterance-type'); (2) the same as (1), but with any lexical or referential ambiguities resolved, the latter by reference to the circumstances of utterance; (3) *what is said* in Grice's 'favoured, and maybe in some degree artificial, sense of "said"', which is the same as (2) with the exclusion of the implications conventionally carried by such conjunctions as 'therefore' and 'but', by such exclamations as 'Alas!' etc.; (4) those implications of what is said which are conventionally carried by precisely such expressions; and (5) those further implications of what is said, the specification of which 'falls outside the specification of the conventional meaning of the words used'.[3]

Grice's conversational implicatures fall, of course, within (5) above. It is historically interesting that his introduction of the notion (Essay 1) embodies at one level a criticism of some aspects of those 'Oxford' philosophical methods and practices which elsewhere, as we shall see, he effectively defends. Some practitioners of these methods, he suggests, were overimpressed by the link between the meaning of some expressions and certain conditions of their (normal or appropriate or non-misleading) use, to the extent of misconstruing the nature of that link. In its extreme form, the misconstrual might involve claiming that no account of the

---

[2] As argued, e.g. in Anita Avramides, *Meaning and Mind* (Cambridge, MA: MIT Press, 1989).
[3] p. 118.

meaning of the expressions in question could be correct or complete which did not include a statement of those conditions. Grice's own view, on the contrary, is that, at least in many such cases, meaning on the one hand, and additional conditions of appropriate use on the other, are quite different things; and that the existence of the conditions in question is to be explained by the interaction of meaning, strictly and literally understood, and certain quite general principles of conversational interchange. Given the meaning of an expression, which of course partially determines the strict and literal truth conditions of any assertive utterance embodying it, it may well be that these general principles of discourse will require the fulfilment of some one of a range of extraneous conditions in order to ensure that such an utterance is not in some way pointless or misleading or inappropriate; but however pointless or misleading or inappropriate such an utterance may be in the absence of any such condition, the utterance may nevertheless be strictly and literally *true*.

Hence the generation of conversational implicature and, with it, an improved account, surely valid for many cases, of the link between meaning and use.

Some qualifications are called for. First, I think we need a distinction between what I shall call 'general presumptive' implicature and 'highly context-dependent' implicature. A standard case of the former is that of someone's giving a disjunctive answer ('Either 65 or 67', 'Either in London or in Oxford') to a questioner whose need for information ('How old . . . ?', 'Where . . . ?') would be more satisfactorily met by mention of just one (the correct one) of the disjuncts. On the assumption that the answerer is complying with the principles of cooperative discourse, his use of the disjunctive form implies that he does not know which of the disjuncts is the right answer, though he knows, or has good reason to think, that one of them is right.

Highly context-dependent implicature arises when the speaker intends to be understood as implying something beyond, or even inconsistent with, what he actually says, but relies on his and his hearer's shared knowledge of relevant circumstances to enable the hearer to grasp the implied message. In such a case the implied message could properly be said to be part, or even perhaps the whole, of 'what the speaker meant' by what he said, whereas this phrase would not usually be apt for general presumptive implicature.

This distinction is in fact recognized by Grice, though less explicitly than as formulated above. But a different and more specific comment is in order. The typical subtlety, ingenuity, and resourcefulness which characterize Grice's entire treatment of the topic are nowhere more fully and brilliantly displayed than in his application of the doctrine to two particular, controversial cases. These are the cases of indicative conditionals and definite descriptions. Grice argues that the conventional meaning of an indicative conditional is in each case exhausted by the stipulated meaning of the corresponding material, or Philonian, conditional; and that the literal meaning of a sentence containing a definite description is in every case precisely as represented by the expansion proposed in Russell's famous theory. The principles of discourse which generate conversational implicature are then invoked to explain the appearances which, in the latter case, give rise to the doctrine of presupposition and, in the former, to the view that, at least in its core meaning, 'if' carries a *conventional* implication of a ground-consequent, or quasi-inferential, relation between the antecedent and the consequent of a conditional. It is impossible not to admire the skill, and the fertility of invention, with which Grice conducts the argument on both fronts, more particularly in the case of definite descriptions. It is also impossible not to acknowledge that the more widely received contrary views encounter (not insuperable) difficulties. Moreover, one should acknowledge that in certain clearly marked cases the Russellian expansion of a definite description is clearly correct: e.g. 'The only man who refused to sign was a Quaker'. Yet, these admissions being made, one is left (or I am left) with the sense that what we have here are instances of an idea of the greatest interest and importance being pushed beyond the limits of its just application. About this I may, of course, be wrong. But in any case, Grice's arguments are models: anyone who cares to observe first-class intellectual equipment operating at full stretch, even in a limited area, should study them.

I remarked earlier that in developing the theory of conversational implicature of the general-presumptive variety Grice was partly reacting against certain excesses on the part of some practitioners of the 'Ordinary Language Approach to Philosophy' in post-war Oxford. I have just suggested that the reaction itself may have erred, in two cases, on the side of excess, but it remains important to realize that Grice's general theory of the distinction and interplay between linguistic meaning, strictly understood, on the one hand, and standard purposes and principles of speech, on the other—an interplay which generates characteristic features of the use of certain linguistic expressions—is not a repudiation, but a refinement, of the 'ordinary language' philosophers' approach. Any such philosopher who ignores the Gricean theory thereby throws away the chance of gaining enhanced comprehension and control of his own material.

In Essay 10, under the title 'Postwar Oxford Philosophy' Grice addresses himself to the question of the philosophical relevance of the ordinary use of language. He introduces the notion of 'conceptual analysis'. He draws, clearly and decisively, the essential distinction between the practical grasp of a concept (manifested, above all, in the correct and mostly unhesitating use of the word or words which express it) and the theoretical understanding of it (the ability to state clearly the general principles which underlie or govern that use). He remarks, too, on the evident truth that possession of the first by no means entails possession of the second, any more than mastery of any practice entails knowledge of the theory of that practice. The achievement of such theoretical understanding is the aim of conceptual analysis. Grice contends that conceptual analysis so understood is at least a major part of the task of the philosopher—not analysis of any concepts whatever, but of those which occupy a structurally central or important place in human thought, such as the concepts of knowledge, truth, meaning, existence, cause, justice, etc.

The connection with the ordinary use of language should now be obvious. Most, perhaps all, philosophically central concepts have linguistic correlates in such words as I have just listed or their cognates. Once it is granted that a practical mastery of the corresponding concepts is manifested essentially in the correct, generally accepted use of the related words (and how else could it be?), then it follows immediately that any philosophical theory of such a concept which runs flatly against what, in given situations, would ordinarily be said and accepted as true by competent speakers of the relevant language must itself be false.

This much, I think, with Grice's own qualifications, as lately discussed, we can certainly accept. Two further qualifications, however, are called for. From the first there is no reason that I can see to think that Grice would have dissented, and there is some reason, manifest in the later-written essays in the book, to think that he would not have dissented. It is a point which I have made elsewhere before, but I think it bears repetition. The idea that the clue to theoretical understanding is to be found in the ordinary use, and conditions of use, of the words which express the philosophically problematic concepts has been and remains an extremely fruitful idea. It continues to be an indispensable check on the extravagances of theory. Nevertheless, it has its limitations. Roughly speaking, it takes too much for granted. Full conceptual understanding demands the exposure of structural features of our thought—connections, analogies, and distinctions—which do not readily display themselves on the linguistic surface. More is required to reveal them than accurate observations of ordinary usage; it is because there is no easily prescribed recipe or methodological equipment for doing the necessary work that philosophy will remain what it always has been, a difficult and exacting discipline.

With these remarks I think Grice would have agreed. Where my second qualification is concerned, there is some evidence that at least in respect of one philosophically central concept, he would rather have held fast to the view I shall question. What is at issue are the implications of the notion of 'analysis'. One familiar implication of the name is that of the resolution of something complex into simpler elements or constituents and the exhibition of the ways in which the constituent elements are related, or united, in the complex. Its application to concepts takes the form of the notion that some problematic concept can be reduced to, or wholly explained in terms of, some others which are felt to be more perspicuous. As already indicated, Grice shows a persisting attachment to this reductive conception of analysis in the case of the surely problematic concept of linguistic meaning, the analysis to be framed in terms of non-semantic concepts of a psychological-cum-social order. But it seems at least questionable whether the reductive ideal is ever attainable in the case of any of those concepts which are of central philosophical importance: these latter, including the concept of meaning, tend to remain obstinately irreducible in the sense that they cannot be defined, or completely explained, without remainder or circularity, in terms of other concepts. 'Irreducible' here does not mean 'simple'. Each such concept has a complexity which can be elucidated by tracing its necessary connections with other complex concepts in a system or network of connected concepts, but without hope or expectation of being able to dismantle or reduce the notions thus examined to other and simpler notions. It is for this reason that I have long advocated the replacement of the *reductive* conception or model of analysis by another, which I call the *connective* model. The word 'analysis' will still be in order, since any systematic account of a problem-situation can properly be called an analysis of it, but a certain over-specific or over-narrow conception of analysis will be abandoned.

These last thoughts relate primarily to one particular, though important, area of enquiry. They do not significantly lessen one's sympathy with Grice's general conception of the philosophical enterprise, and they leave wholly untouched one's unbounded admiration for his philosophical practice. In the Retrospective Epilogue which ends this book, he brings its themes together in a most illuminating way. In its concluding section he draws an engaging parallel between Oxford philosophy of the mid-twentieth century and the dialectical practice of what he makes 'so bold as to call that other Oxford which more than two thousand three hundred years earlier achieved not merely fame but veneration as the cradle of our discipline'.[4] Admittedly the composite figure of Austin and Ryle (with Moore in the background) scarcely challenges comparison with that of Aristotle. But a smaller line can be parallel to a greater, and the case for the parallelism is brilliantly persuasive.

[4] p. 378.

16
Knowing From Words

No one disputes that much, probably the greater part, of our knowledge is derived from hearing what others say or reading what others have written. It is also indisputable that much, though not all, of what we thus hear or read we accept without question as true. In brief, a great part of our systems of belief rests upon testimony. The question is whether we are to regard testimony, so understood, as a direct and immediate source of belief based upon it or whether we are to regard belief so based as being, in the last resort, essentially the product of other, more fundamental sources of knowledge, or, in brief again, is testimony, as a source of knowledge (or belief), *reducible* to these other sources?

To make any progress with this question, we must clearly enquire what these other sources might be. What are held, by those inclined to a reductionist answer, to be the *basic* sources of our knowledge of the world about us? Perception, memory, and inference are the traditional candidates. But inference, though naturally destined for a role in any likely reductive account of the contribution which testimony makes, cannot itself be, in the strictest sense, a basic source of knowledge. For inference requires premises; and though, in any given inference, some of its premises may themselves be inferentially derived, the process must, in the last resort, rest on foundations which are not inferential. This fact does not, of course, disqualify inference from playing a part in a reductive theory. It merely indicates that its role must be subordinate to that of the other members of the cast.

What of the other members? How do perception and memory stand in relation to testimony as sources of knowledge? Well, even the most committed anti-reductivist must acknowledge that perception is a necessary condition of the acquisition of knowledge from testimony. We cannot *acquire* beliefs from the written word without looking and seeing; nor from the spoken word without listening and hearing. And a parallel admission is required in the case of memory. For, first, we cannot *retain* knowledge thus acquired without remembering what we have thus learned; and, second, even the acquisition of such knowledge or belief requires that we understand the sentences that we read or hear, and this in its turn invokes a form of memory, *viz.* our retention of our acquired knowledge of the language to which the sentences belong.

It is worth adding a further point. The joint exercise of both memory and perception is not only a *necessary* condition of the possession of *all* knowledge or belief derived from testimony; that joint exercise may be a *sufficient* condition of the possession of *some* knowledge, the acquisition of which is in no way at all dependent on testimony. I use the modal 'may be' because some philosophers (e.g. Davidson) would dispute the thesis that anyone can so much as have beliefs without being an 'interpreter' of the discourse of others. But this seems an implausible contention. The 'wild boy of Aveyron' surely had some beliefs, indeed some knowledge, of the resources of his environment before he was discovered, taken into human society, and given some rudimentary linguistic instruction. (He never progressed far.) So here, if I am right, is one respect in which testimony cannot be on a *perfectly* equal footing with perception and memory as a source of knowledge.

However, the case of such rare individuals, in a state of complete isolation from human and linguistic communities, is of only moderate interest in itself and is, in any case, irrelevant to our present concern. For that concern is precisely with human beings living in a community and equipped with knowledge of the language current in that community. And even though, as previously remarked, the employment of perception and memory is a necessary condition of the acquisition and retention of any knowledge (or belief) which is communicated linguistically, it does not immediately follow that such acquisition of knowledge (or belief) is *reducible* to the exercise of those faculties, supplemented by inference. For no account of such a reduction is remotely plausible, if it is supposed to hold generally; and if it is not supposed to hold generally, the reducibility thesis is abandoned.

The last qualification is important. No one doubts that there are occasions on which, when we are told or read something, we, at least temporarily, and perhaps, permanently, withhold assent to, or belief in, what we are told or read, perhaps because it strikes us as intrinsically implausible, perhaps because of doubts about the reliability (trustworthiness or competence or both) of the speaker or writer in question. If, on such occasions, we finally accept what we are told or read as true, incorporating it in our belief-system, we do so as a result of some further process of assuring ourselves of the reasonableness of accepting what we are offered as genuine information. In such cases understanding and acceptance have genuinely come apart; the transition from the former to the latter is mediated by whatever steps, possibly merely mental steps, are taken in the process of self-assurance; and the testimony cannot, in such cases, be viewed as a direct and immediate source of the belief we arrive at.

However, there are several points to note about this:

(1) In many cases the checking process just alluded to consists in nothing other than seeking confirmation from other sources of testimony: we consult authorities or witnesses and normally accept the testimony of one or another of these, without further question, as clinching the matter. So even when testimony requires checking, it is normally just further testimony which supplies the ultimate check.

It may be objected that this is an inadequate reply to a reductivist point; for our ultimate acceptance of the purported information as genuine may be based on an inference from the *agreement* of diverse authorities to the *reliability* of those sources, an inference itself based on the presumption that truth is the best explanation of the convergence of diversely sourced judgements; or, again, we may have independent *grounds* for regarding one particular source as a fount of truth.

This may indeed be so in some cases; and when it is so, we cannot indeed regard the testimony on which we rely as a direct and unmediated source of knowledge. But it is not always so. There are powerful reasons for holding that it *cannot* always be so. This leads to the next point.

(2) It is clear that just as the purported information we receive from testimony may sometimes be erroneous, so our first-hand judgements of perception and memory may sometimes be erroneous. None of these sources of knowledge or belief is immune from error. Indeed error stemming from any one of these three sources may infect any of the others. But it is also true that the way in which each of us builds up his system of beliefs about the world is governed by certain powerful presumptions. One is the presumption that the beliefs a man acquires from direct first-hand experience of the world will generally be, *within the terms available to him*, substantially accurate. The other is the presumption that the elements of his world-picture or belief-system which are directly derived from testimony will also be, generally, substantially accurate. I call these 'presumptions'. But they are

more than that. They are, rather, conditions of the possibility of the existence and use, in human communities, of the concepts of knowledge, accuracy, truth. The knowledge (or belief) system of each member of the community is a highly complex fabric in which the strands of perception, memory, and testimony are inextricably interwoven in such a way that none could be reduced to the others without unravelling the whole. Of course, perception has a distinctive role in so far as our knowledge (or belief) system has, at any moment, to accommodate those beliefs which, at that moment, current experience may force irresistibly upon us; but—setting aside the fact that it may be precisely an item of communicated information (testimony) that our current experience obliges us, at a given moment, to accept—it is quite generally true that what current experience does thus force upon us in the way of belief is a function of the character of the pre-existent system, i.e. is largely determined by beliefs already possessed, the sources of which will almost always include instruction or testimony.

(3) To reinforce the last point, consider the overwhelming extent to which *what* we in fact perceive, the very nature or character of our perceptual experience itself, is determined by the instruction, the information, we have received from the words of others. To apply (or as some would say, to misapply) a phrase of Wittgenstein's, much, perhaps most, of what we see we could not see *as* what we do see it *as*, without the benefit of such instruction. It is precisely from such instruction that the majority of the concepts which figure in any veridical account of our perceptions derive their origin. I see that the petrol gauge on my car reads zero. *Could* I see *this* if I had not been *told* that what I am looking at is an *instrument* with a certain specific *function*? I hear the clock strike twelve. Could I hear *this* without grasp of the concept of a clock and of the number system? And whence does this grasp derive? If we are to say, as we must, that the knowledge we derive from testimony depends on perception, must we not equally say that the knowledge we derive from perception depends generally on testimony, on verbally transmitted instruction and information? Kant said that intuitions without concepts were blind. In the present context we may modify the dictum and give it a more immediate relevance and resonance by saying: perception without the concepts and attendant information which derive from the spoken or written word is, if not blind, pitifully short-sighted. We need not say that the wild boy of Aveyron knows nothing at all; but we must assert that, however naturally

acute his senses, they tell him, unaided, very little. The word is accessible only through perception; but perception, *our* perception, is powered and driven by the word.

My conclusion has already been foreshadowed. In any community of language-users, perception, memory, and testimony are not only equally *essential* to the construction of the belief-or-knowledge-systems of its members. It is also true that all three are on an equal footing in that there is no possibility of a general reductive analysis of any one of the three in terms of the others, supplemented by inference. The interdependence of all does not entail the reducibility of any. If we (often) know, directly and immediately, what our eyes tell us, then we (often) know, no less directly and immediately, what other people tell us.

17

What Have We Learned from Philosophy in the Twentieth Century?

There is a fairly obvious problem with the question that defines our topic. Is it addressed to us collectively—as a collectivity—or to each of us individually? If the former, the prospect of any reply at all being forthcoming may seem, at least at first, remote. And this for the very same reason as that for which there will be no shortage of replies if the question is taken as addressed to each of us individually. For in that case it amounts to asking, of each of us, which, after a lifetime of the practice of philosophy, do you regard as the most central and important of the views you have come to hold? And, of course, there is no expectation or even likelihood that the most central view or views held by any one of us will be the same as, or even compatible with, those held by all or any of the others.

Yet the prospect of some measure of agreement is not altogether blank. Philosophy differs from most other disciplines in that one of the questions with which its practitioners are professionally concerned is its own nature. Neither is there anything surprising in this since, having no special subject matter of its own, it is free, and perhaps obliged, to enquire into the special nature of *every* discipline. Now here, at this meta-philosophical level, we may at least hope to find some common ground; though at the same time we must, here also, be prepared for large divergences of view.

I might begin by mentioning two semi-practical points that I think we might all agree on—points that I made at the end of an address to my fellow Oxford philosophers on the occasion, eleven years ago, of my formal retirement. They took the form of advice to be transmitted to our young putative successors—in effect our graduate students—and the advice was that they should beware of two quite distinct mistakes: one was the mistake of supposing that only what has been published in the last two or three decades is worth serious attention; the other was the mistake of supposing that any one philosopher, however great, has a valid and exclusive claim to have got things finally right on some substantial matter. And that goes, I now add, equally for Plato, Aristotle, Aquinas, Kant, Hegel, Frege, and Wittgenstein—or anyone else you may feel inclined to add.

But now I must add, to balance that caution against accepting the final authority, on any matter, of any of the great dead philosophers of the past, a countervailing point which will also, I think, command general agreement: *viz.* that the thoughts of some of those great dead thinkers may still have a unique weight and sustenance for us; that the great dead may speak to us more powerfully and suggestively than even the most gifted of our own contemporaries. In this reflection, which many of us will have arrived at through long experience, I echo some remarks made, late in his career, by a former teacher and colleague, Paul Grice, in his replies to the editors of a volume on his work published by the Oxford University Press in 1986.[1] In that same volume, under the same heading, of 'Opinions', he makes two other points in both of which I found echoes of views which philosophical experience has forced upon me. One of these, the more divisive, I will return to later. The other is a view that may well find at least a partial echo in the minds of many others besides myself; perhaps of all of us. This is the opinion, to quote Grice's words, that 'despite its real or apparent division into departments, philosophy is *one* subject, a single discipline'; or, to use my own, that ontology, epistemology, the philosophy of language, and logic (and even, in some central aspects, the philosophy of mind) are indivisible; that clear commitments in any one of these sub-areas are inseparably linked with clear commitments in the others. And I think that philosophers with very different approaches, and even sharply opposed or contrasting views, will often, perhaps regularly, be found to share this conviction of the unity of the discipline. Grice even extends the thesis to include ethics and the philosophy of value in general. In spite of some considerable sympathy, I am more hesitant about going

---

[1] *Philosophical Grounds of Rationality: Intentions, Categories, Ends*, eds Richard Grandy and Richard Warner (Oxford: Claredon Press, 1986).

the whole way with him here, though it is clear from some notable examples, e.g. Kant, that he is by no means alone in this.

Of course agreement must come to an end somewhere; and if that point has not already been reached, it soon will be. Suppose we ask: what in general are we, or should we be, up to in philosophy? What is, or should be, our objective? To establish how we should live, the nature of the good life? To determine the scope and limits of human knowledge? To achieve self-understanding? If *properly* understood, I think the last suggestion is correct. I don't mean that we should turn into psychologists or social scientists, I mean that our essential, if not our only, business is to get a clear view of our most general working *concepts* or types of concept and of their place in our lives. We should aim at general human conceptual self-understanding. I take this to be also Wittgenstein's view of the matter, at least in his later period. But I also think that his almost obsessional anxiety to liberate us from seductive illusions, the myths and fictions of philosophical theory, led to a certain loss of balance in his thinking. It did so in two ways. First, it led him to a distrust of systematic theories in general, and hence to a disregard of the possibility, indeed, to my mind, the truth, that the most general concepts and categories of human thought do form, in their connections and interdependencies, an articulated structure which it is possible to describe without falsification—and thereby to illustrate what I earlier referred to as the mutual involvement of ontology, epistemology, and the philosophy of language, logic, and mind. Second, the same obsession led him to minimize or dismiss, or at least give too little acknowledgement to, some pervasive features of our thought and experience. It is true of these features that they can, in philosophical thinking, lend themselves to gratuitous inflation, to mythologizing, to false imaginary pictures—all of these proper targets of Wittgenstein's hostility and scorn, the 'houses of cards' he took as his mission to destroy. But none of this justifies the failure to give them full acknowledgement as the harmless inescapable features that they are.

So what are they? What do I have in mind? I have in mind two things: the first is the reality of subjective experience in all its richness and complexity or, as one of our most distinguished contemporaries expressed it, in all its 'heady luxuriance'; the other is the inescapable presence in our thought of abstract *intensional objects*. Both are easily misunderstood, prime sources of the generation of 'pictures to hold us captive'. Neither should, for that reason, be denied or downplayed, or made the subject of fruitless attempts to reduce them to, or replace them by, items of a more concrete and more manageable kind.

In an earlier circular the participants in this very event were asked, not, collectively, 'What have *we* learned etc.,' but each, individually, 'What is the most important *philosophical* lesson *you* have learned in the course of your career?' That of course is a difficult and dangerous question. But just at the moment I feel disposed to risk an answer to it. The answer echoes, indeed reproduces something I wrote in my last contribution to the volume forming part of the series which is the occasion for this event. Not that I learned the lesson as late as that. I had already grasped it, in an incomplete and inchoate form, before 1950. But a sense of its importance and its ramifications have steadily grown with me since. It is this: that the fundamental bearers of the properties of truth or falsity, the fundamental subjects of the predicates 'true' or 'false', are not linguistic items, neither sentences nor utterances of sentences. It is not, when we speak or write, the words we then use, but what we then use them to say, that is in question. It is whatever may be believed, doubted, hypothesized, suspected, supposed, affirmed, denied, declared, alleged, and so forth, that is, or may be, true. Any of these words may be followed by a noun-clause of the form 'that p'; and it is precisely the item designated or referred to or introduced by these noun-clauses, as used on this or that occasion, that are the bearers of the properties of truth or falsity. We do not have, in common use, a general word for these items; for in practice we always use a nominalization of one of the verbs in question as the subject of the predicate (e.g. 'your belief', 'his allegation', and so forth) or a noun-phrase such as 'what he has just said' or even the form 'that p' itself. Philosophers have made various attempts to supply this deficiency: Frege's 'thought' is one; Austin groped towards it when he distinguished the 'locutionary' act (in terms of sense and reference) from the 'phatic' on the one hand and the 'illocutionary' on the other; G. E. Moore and others have happily used the term 'proposition' (which, more recently has shown a tendency to be replaced by 'propositional content'); an older term still is 'judgement'. Whatever term we use for an item of this kind—and I am content with old-fashioned 'proposition'—the essential point is that such an item is not to be identified with an inscription or an utterance or a type of inscription or utterance: it is an intensional abstract entity, but nonetheless an item of a kind such as we constantly think of and refer to whenever we think of, or comment on, what someone has said or someone has written, or indeed a thought that has, as we say, just entered our own heads. It is objected that there is no clear general criterion of identity for such items. Never mind; we get on well enough, and communicate well enough, without one. With the admission of propositions (or judgements or thoughts) as abstract intensional entities there goes along of course the admission of others: of senses, of concepts, of properties, and universals in general. It is here, perhaps most obviously, that the risk of inflation comes in: the risk of seductive images, pictures to hold us captive, myths and fantasies such as are often fathered, justly or not, on Plato. But, in order to acknowledge the items in question as the harmless, necessary things they are, regularly recognized in ordinary thought and talk, there is no need to be thus seduced, no need to yield to such temptations.

Earlier, referring to some views expressed by Grice under the heading 'Opinions', I mentioned, first, his emphasis on the value of consulting our great dead predecessors; second, the doctrine of the unity of philosophy across apparent departmental divisions; and I referred to a third view with which I also expressed sympathy, but which, I said, would be found more divisive than the other two. This Grice described as his opposition to 'Minimalism' in philosophy, a heading under which he ranged a number of other 'isms', including 'physicalism' and 'extensionalism'. In my immediately foregoing remarks, stressing first, and briefly, the reality of subjective experience and second, and at greater length, the pervasiveness in our thought of intensional abstract entities, I clearly enlisted myself under the anti-minimalist banner—in opposition to unqualified physicalism in the first case and to extensionalism in the second; and it is there, in particular, that the divisiveness most clearly shows.

In conclusion, though not irrelevantly, I should like to comment on a mildly ironical feature of our subject in the later twentieth century. If anyone is entitled to be called the founder of our subject, it is generally acknowledged to be Plato; and if anyone can be called the father of its modern development, most of us would nominate Descartes. The irony is that to accuse a philosopher of Platonism or Cartesianism is currently felt to be a seriously damaging charge. But if, and in so far as, I have exposed myself to it, I am unrepentant. Of course both these great men were guilty of exaggerations and more or less grave mistakes. But each had a grasp, however uncertain, of features of our thought and experience which it would be a much graver mistake to overlook, to deny, or to minimize.

18
A Category of Particulars

I should say, first, that the central notion of this chapter is by no means new. It has a long history, and has been variously interpreted and exploited at different times by different philosophers, as will become clear later. My own use of it will be to make a relatively unambitious attempt at a modest simplification in the theory of universals and particulars. But it may strike others as a gratuitous complication, with more than a whiff of scholasticism about it.

To begin with a few familiar points. It is generally accepted that ontological categories include that of individual substances, that is, relatively enduring space-occupying items with, at least normally, some internal principle of organization. Such items belong to the more comprehensive ontological category of particulars; and by 'particulars' I understand individual things which have at any time some spatial location. (A minor qualification to that last provision is required in some cases.) Particulars come into, and go out of, existence, can have causal efficacy, and unless they are instantaneous particulars, are generally subject to change.

Of those particulars which are individual substances, it is also generally accepted that any one such falls under some *sortal* concept, a sortal concept being a concept such that no two different individuals falling under the *same* sortal concept can occupy exactly the *same* space at exactly the *same* time. A given substantial individual will normally fall under a number of different sortal concepts at different times—as 'boy', 'lawyer', 'old-age pensioner', and so on. But such different concepts will normally cluster round a certain central sortal concept, with reference to which the others are explained, which applies to the given individual throughout its or his existence—which, indeed, is sometimes said to give the essential nature of the individual in question: in the cases mentioned the concept 'man' or, better, 'human being'. Of any substantial particulars falling under such a sortal concept, central or non-central, I shall say that it is an instance of the universal of which the concept in question is a concept; and I shall, without argument, take universals to be abstract objects, that is, non-spatio-temporal items without causal efficacy, objects sometimes of thought but never, themselves, of sense perception.

Substances are not the only particulars which fall under sortal concepts. The same would generally be allowed to be true of particular events and processes—births, deaths, explosions, parliamentary elections, battles, and so on. Each particular such event is an instance of the appropriate sortal universal.

What I want to argue for—or call attention to—is the existence of another class or category of particulars. 'Argue for' is appropriate because philosophical claims on behalf of this category have sometimes been philosophically derided; 'call attention to' is appropriate because there is evidence that the category in question is already and unreflectively recognized and acknowledged in our ordinary thought and speech.

So what is this category? Its characterization can perhaps be best, that is, most persuasively, approached by referring to a certain subclass of the already acknowledged category of events. Particular members of this sub-class include, for example, particular smiles, blushes, grimaces, sneezes, gestures. Each such event is a *unique* individual particular, with its own spatio-temporal position, a particular instance of its appropriate sortal. Of course the word 'particular' has its own invariably bothering ambiguity here. It may be pointed out, for example, that a particular gesture may be repeated a hundred times, that a daughter may reproduce her mother's smile, but these repeated gestures or shared smiles are not the particulars I am speaking of; indeed they are not particulars at all; they are the rather specific universals—if you like, the general patterns—of which the particulars I *am* speaking of are instances. All the examples of this subclass of particular events that I have so far given have a distinctive feature in common: the identity of each such particular is intimately linked to the identity of a particular, indeed personal, substance. A standard way of specifying the identity of any particular smile or gesture, for example, would consist in specifying the identity of the person in question, and the time at which he smiled that particular smile or made that particular gesture. This standard way is not an invariably available way. A particular gesture, for example, could be identified by the occasion, the time and place, of its being made without any knowledge of who exactly made it; if it was a profoundly offensive gesture, it might subsequently be referred to as the triggering cause of ensuing hostilities between two sects or nations. Nevertheless the peculiarly intimate link between substance and event in any such case is in fact exclusive even if unknown. If a particular smile is smiled at a certain time by John, no one else can smile that very smile, nor can John smile that very smile at another time (though, of course, he or others may smile an exactly similar smile).

All the above has been to emphasize the particularity of particular events. Among the examples I mentioned I choose one which may help to ease the transition to the category of particulars which is my topic. The example I choose is that of a blush—a particular event which is an instance of the event-sortal blushing. It took a relatively short, though noticeable, time-interval. The subject blushed. Her face became red, and remained red for the interval in question. I shall say that *the red* with which *her* face is suffused during that interval is itself a *perceptible particular*: it has a short history during which it is itself subject to change, for it may grow less deep or less brilliant before it fades away completely. It is a particular instance of the property redness; and I shall call all particulars of the same type or category as this one 'property-instances'. It may help to reduce resistance to the particular example I have just given if we notice a feature of the word 'blush'. It is both a verb and a noun. In either capacity it may refer to an event, an event of blushing. But it may also, as a noun, refer to what I have already called a particular instance of redness, to *the* red which suffuses the subject's face. The particular visual appearance of the surface of her skin is the blush which first grows deeper, then grows less deep and fades gradually away. It would seem perverse not to acknowledge the existence of this particular perceptible item—a particular instance of redness—as it comes into existence, undergoes change, and finally disappears.

I remarked at the outset that the general notion I want to promote has nothing new about it. Indeed I myself referred to items of the type in question some forty years ago, describing them as 'particularized qualities'; and others have given them other names. More of that later. First I want to promote the idea a bit further with the help of other examples; and among them I shall unblushingly include some I have already used elsewhere. Here they are: '*Her happiness* shone in her eyes'; '*His hatred* was visible in his whole countenance and demeanour'; 'John loved to gaze on *the brilliant blue of her eyes* and *the crimson of her lips*'. The emphasized items are particulars: they have spatial location—directly and simply in the case of the colour-property-instances; loosely, and derivatively, from the identity and location of their subjects, in the case of particular states of mind like her happiness and his hatred. They all have duration and are subject to change: her happiness, alas, was short-lived; his anger cooled quite rapidly and with it his hatred dwindled; the blue of her eyes dimmed. So they are sharply to be distinguished from the universals—the general properties—of which they are instances. For it does not make sense to say of the universal itself that it dims or is short-lived. One might indeed *say* 'happiness is generally short-lived'; but that would be merely a brachylogy for saying that most particular cases or instances of happiness are of short duration. Further examples of such particulars could be multiplied *au plaisir*. Different particular instances of the same property can be compared with each other. Someone is on record as having remarked that the pride of Wordsworth was equal to that of Lucifer; and few would dispute that the ambitiousness of Caesar or that of Napoleon exceeded those of most, perhaps of all, of their contemporaries. Of course I am ready to admit that for most remarks in which reference is explicitly made to such particulars, equivalent paraphrases could easily be framed which are free of such references. Thus 'Wordsworth was as proud as Lucifer', 'She was not happy for long', and so on. But this, by itself, is a feeble weapon to use against claims made on behalf of a major ontological category, when there are no good independent reasons for disputing those claims and adequate reasons for accepting them.

I have said more than once that there is nothing new about the central idea I am advocating. It figures in the Nyāya analytical stream in classical Indian philosophy. This was brought home to me initially when, in a train in Bengal, I was talking about universals with a young Indian philosopher and remarked that a brown table would be an instance of brownness. He corrected me sharply, maintaining that, not the table but the brownness of the table, was the instance of brownness. Though disinclined at the time to accept this restriction on the use of the expression 'instance', I do now see the point and value of it. The notion of property-instance has also been attributed to Aristotle—I think (though I haven't the scholarship to support this) by some medieval and renaissance scholars, more recently by Bolzano, and, more recently still, by some modern scholars. The correctness of the attribution to Aristotle has been strongly disputed by at least one heavyweight Aristotelian scholar. In any case, however it might be with attributions to Aristotle, Bolzano himself certainly accepted the idea of the items in question, though he called them not, as I have done, 'property-instances' or 'particularized qualities', but rather 'adherences' or 'conditions' or 'individual accidents'. But he was emphatic that each could belong to or be a condition or adherence of only one substance, that none could belong to more than one. (This must be modified, and is by Bolzano modified, to allow for the case of particular *relational* adherences or conditions, which could clearly be of, or belong to, a pair of substances, but, again, not to more than one such pair or trio. For simplicity's sake I shall not further consider the relational case).[1]

Recent twentieth-century advocates of the notion include John Bacon, Keith Campbell, C. B. Martin, Peter Simons, and C. C. Williams. But the *locus classicus* for that century is probably the work of G. F. Stout, in his British Academy lecture of 1923 and his contribution in the same year to the symposium, 'Are the characteristics of particular things universal or particular?', published in the *Proceedings of the Aristotelian Society*. Stout's case, somewhat carelessly stated, was, in the same symposium, rubbished by G. E. Moore—an exercise applauded by Ramsey, who declared that Stout had been 'sufficiently answered'. But I think this was a case of uncharacteristic blindness or conservatism on Moore's part and of a certain lofty indifference on Ramsey's.

As for terminology, I have mentioned a number of variations on 'property-instance', such as my own 'particularized quality', and Bolzano's 'adherence' or 'condition'. There are yet others: for example, 'individual accident (or moment or case)'. Less happy seems to me the phrase 'abstract particular', which to my ear has an oxymoronic ring—though it may just be passable in certain very special cases as that of the equator, which is certainly a spatio-temporal item of a sort, though not sensorily perceptible or causally efficacious or in any relevant way embodied. Least happy of all, to my mind, though it has recently gained quite extensive currency, is the expression 'trope', which has been used to convey either the very idea that is in question or at least one very closely related to it. While acknowledging the currency of this expression, I personally refuse to embrace it in the present connection, since the vocable has a well-established and

---

[1] The source of my reference to Bolzano is an article by Wolfgang Künne, entitled 'Substances and Adherences', which deals with the ontology in Bolzano's 'Athanasia'. Künne's article appears in the first volume of a new series, *Logical Analysis and History of Philosophy*, eds Neuwen and Meixner, Paderborn: Schöningh, 1998.

correct use in application to literature and rhetoric: tropes are nothing other than figures of speech in general, such as metaphor, metonomy, and the like. In the present connection the expression either has no relevant suggestiveness at all or, if it has any, the suggestion it carries is entirely inappropriate.

As I earlier hinted, some of the authors I have mentioned, not content with recording and advocating recognition of the ontological category of property-instances, proceed to make large metaphysical claims on their behalf. They have been described as 'the elements of being' or 'the building blocks of the universe'; such phrases are indicative of attempts to show that things generally or often regarded as belonging to some self-standing major ontological categories can, and should, be seen as reducible to, or constructed out of, these elements. The good Stout himself presents one example of this ambition, aiming to represent every property universal—say, wisdom—as what he slightly mysteriously calls the 'distributive unity' of the members of the class of particular wisdoms such as the wisdom of Socrates. The principle of this unity remains a little opaque, though some relation of more-or-less resemblance must presumably play some part in it. Other more recent writers more simply and straightforwardly identify the universal property with the resemblance class of instances. A different, though comparable, reductive-constructive enterprise is undertaken by some authors who wish to represent individual substances as some sort of quasi-mereological sums of property-instances. All such attempts, whether directed at universals or at substances, seem to me misguided and generative of gratuitous problems, calling for equally gratuitous exercises of ingenuity, but bringing no genuine illumination. For this reason I shall not bother you or myself with a list of exact references for these last remarks.

If we set aside these ambitious metaphysical aims, we are left with two questions: what advantages if any, and what problems if any, come along with acceptance of the ontological category of property-instances? The two questions can be considered together.

In earlier work, among universals applicable to individual substances I distinguished sharply between the sortal universals which such substances, as I said, *instantiate* and the property or quality universals by which, as I then said, they can be *characterized* or which they *exemplify*; and correspondingly, with reference to the bonding of universal and particular, I spoke, in the first case, of an *instantial* tie and in the second, of a *characterizing* or *exemplifying* tie, taking care to emphasize that these expressions were not to be seen as themselves naming relational universals. But given the recognition of the category of property-instances, we see that we need not two different types, but only one type, of bonding between particular and universal, namely that of instantiation. For whenever, as we correctly say, a particular substance X is *characterized* by a universal O, this is no more than to say that X has a particular instance, say Y, that is, a property-instance, of O. So a modest reduction is achieved: X's *exemplifying* or being *characterized* by O is no more than the logical product of X's having Y and Y being an instance of O. The point is elegantly made by Pranab Sen in the first chapter in this volume [i.e. *Universals, Concepts and Qualities*, 2006].

It might now be said: have you not purchased one simplification at the cost of raising a fresh problem? What of the bond (relation?) between Y and X, between the particular property-instance and the particular substance that 'has' it? Well, in ordinary discourse we habitually use a possessive or genitive form: *her* happiness, *his* anger, the deepening redness *of* her cheeks, the wisdom *of* Socrates—or, again, in a non-substantial case, the wisdom *of* so-and-so's decision. Philosophers, generalizing, tend towards more elaborate terminology. Thus, Bolzano, as I have remarked, speaks of 'adherence'. I myself in the work earlier referred to spoke of another non-relational tie, the 'attributive'. Some have been tempted to think that Aristotle's 'being present in' was meant to fulfil just this role. (Aristotle might have made a better job of *The Categories* if he had intended this.) But, whatever the terminology, it is clear that no *relational* universals or instances thereof are called for here. It is the very nature of the substantial individual *both* to be an instance of some sortal universals *and* to exemplify some general properties, that is, to 'have' particular instances of those properties. A substance must necessarily *both* be a something or other *and* be some *way* or other, that is, *have* some property-instance or other.

So am I saying, *inter alia*, that property-universals applicable to particulars are themselves sortal universals just as are the universals of the kinds or sorts to which substantial individuals belong? Yes, I am. It is equally true of sortals of both species that no two different individual instances of a given sortal of either kind can occupy exactly the same space at exactly the same time; though in the case of property universals this might be more lucidly expressed by saying that no two different individual instances of the same property-sortal can be 'of' or 'had by' the same individual substance (or event or process) at exactly the same time. Of course there are some differences. Of some individual-substance sortals it is contingent that their instances do instantiate them. Thus it is contingent that Horatio Nelson is a naval officer; whereas it is essential to his existence and identity that he is a human being. But it is essential to any particular instance of a property that it is an instance of that property. It is contingent, let us say, that Nelson is brave or that Mary is, at some time, happy. Nelson's bravery or Mary's happiness might not have existed. But Nelson's bravery could not be anything but a particular instance of bravery nor Mary's happiness anything but a particular instance of happiness.

Sortals of either variety easily yield criteria of identity and principles of individuation for their instances. Concepts of central substance-sortals, *man* or *horse*, are themselves individuative. The case of properties which may characterize individual substances is a little more complicated: as indicated above, individuation of their particular instances is normally secured by specifying the individual substance in question and the time at which it 'has' the property-instance in question; or, if this is not available, by the (spatio-temporal) *occasion* of their appearance. The case for regarding properties applicable to particulars as sortal universals is complete. What holds for such properties holds also, *mutatis mutandis*, for such relations. The particular instance of the relation of loving is adequately specified in the old Scottish ballad, which, having mentioned the principals in question, goes on, 'And deep and heavy was *the love* that fell the twa' between'. That particular instance of love can't fall or lie between any other couple. I would go so far as to say that the same holds of any universal whatever that has, or may have, application to particulars. Thus the property of being three in number has one particular instance which belongs to, or is of, the members of some particular trio of musicians, and another particular instance which belongs to the members of some particular family of two parents and one child. Some may object to treating *being three in number* as a universal, a property; but I see no reason why.

Now for some other questions. I have asserted that particular instances of the universals I am concerned with are in general and in principle perceptible, possible objects of sense perception; whereas this is not so with the universals themselves, which I declared to be non-spatio-temporal abstract entities, objects of thought perhaps but not of perception. But here, in this negative contention, I run contrary to some other traditions, notably the Nyāya tradition in classical Indian philosophy, to which I have referred with respect; and contrary not only to respectable philosophical traditions, but also, it seems, to the accuracy of common speech; for the names of universals can often figure as the grammatical objects of verbs of perception. Thus we can correctly speak of witnessing brutality, observing courage in action, tasting sweetness or saltiness; or, to repeat my earlier examples while deleting the particularizing possessives before the abstract nouns, we can properly say 'Happiness shone in her eyes' or 'Hatred was visible in his whole countenance'. One may even say 'I have just seen beauty itself' and not be misunderstood. These are all legitimate idioms; but what we really sensibly perceive in all these cases is not the general thing itself, but a particular instance of the general thing, located in a particular substance or action. Given the acknowledged legitimacy of the idioms, this last comment may sound like a merely dogmatic rejection of the claim that the general property is itself perceptible. But perhaps we can at least come close to an accommodation here. For we could not rightly be said to perceive the particular substance or action at all except as somewhat and as somehow, that is, except *as* of some sort and *as* qualified in some way. We see the particular action *as* courageous, we see the particular woman *as* beautiful, we taste the particular mouthful *as* sweet. How much difference does it make whether we say we see the universal in the particular, courage in the action, beauty in the woman, or say that we see *his* courage, *her* beauty? In so far as the answer is 'Very little', the difference between the two positions seems minimal, seems perhaps merely verbal. So a compromise is available. We can accept that locutions which have us saying that we perceive the universal itself in the particular as a legitimate shorthand for the metaphysically more precise and literally correct claim that we perceive the particular instance of the universal and recognize it as what it is, that is, an instance of that universal.

Yet, this concession made, we must of course still maintain the distinction between property-universals and their instances. For we must, as already illustrated, be able to say things about the particular property-instance that it wouldn't make sense to say about the property itself. And again we can think about the property or universal itself in total abstraction from all actual instances; and indeed can think about a universal or property, given that we can form a coherent concept of it, even if it has no instances at all.

But now a final question may be raised. Do I really need that initial unargued assumption that properties, and universals in general, unlike their particular instances, are non-spatio-temporal items without causal efficacy? Couldn't I settle for general concepts instead, equally abstract items indeed, but less generally disputed? I think the answer is 'No'. Property and concept, though closely related, are clean different things. The difference becomes clear if we consider what it is to possess, as we say, or exemplify, a property and what it is to possess, as we also say, or grasp, a concept. It is perfectly possible for someone, or something, to have a property and lack the concept of it; it is equally possible for someone to grasp the concept and lack the property. All substantial things, animate, inanimate, or abstract, have properties; only conscious beings and cultures can be said to possess concepts. In this sense concepts are mind-dependent; but the properties they are concepts of are not—nor mind-independent either in the sense that much of the natural world is. If to exist is to be part of the natural world, then universals do not exist, though their instances, if any, may do. The natural world consists of particulars. Universals, by contrast, are essences, intelligibilia. They exist as such; and as such, are possible objects of coherent thought, objects which may, or may not, have *naturally* existing, and possibly, sensibly perceptible, instances.

19
Paul Grice

I hope I may be forgiven for starting with a short personal reminiscence. During one of my terms as an undergraduate at St. John's I was fortunate enough to have Paul Grice as my tutor. I had never previously encountered such a formidable critic or such a subtle and resourceful thinker. Later, after the war, he and I collaborated for a time in a series of seminars which we gave in the early 1950s. Sometimes we would take it in turn for each to present a paper on his own. Sometimes, and much more arduously, we would engage in joint composition, arguing over each sentence until we reached an agreed version. The publication of our only joint article, 'In Defence of a Dogma', was one delayed result of this demanding exercise; though even then I had to undertake the final writing up myself because of Grice's extreme reluctance to venture into print. This reluctance was so great that it was only after persistent bullying on my part that he brought himself, some years after its composition, to publish his own highly original, ingenious, and justly celebrated first article on Meaning (1957).

During that period of collaboration I formed the opinion—which I have had no occasion to modify since—that no one on the current scene was his equal either in detecting the flaws in others' reasoning, or in the ingenuity and subtlety with which he elaborated views of his own and contrived defences for them. I suspect, sometimes, that it was the strength of his own critical powers, his sense of the vulnerability of philosophical argument in general, that partially accounted, at the time, for his privately expressed doubts about the ability of his own work to survive criticism. After all, if there were always detectable flaws in others' reasoning, why should there not be detectable, though by him undetected, flaws in his own? Hence a certain inhibiting perfectionism; though I think it should be added that when he finally moved to the West Coast of the United States, such inhibitions—as has happened, I believe, to more than one

Englishman—were finally swept away by a warm tide of approbation such as is rarely experienced on these colder shores.

Well, that is enough of that. Now to the work itself. It is, I think, clear that although he has made impressive contributions to a number of other topics, it is his writings both on meaning in general and on the theory of conversational implicature in particular that have deservedly commanded the most attention on the part of philosophers and linguists alike.

Here I should remark, first, that since Grice's thinking was characteristically complex, my own exposition and comments cannot be very simple; and, second, that since he so conspicuously excelled in criticism of others' views, it would be untrue to his spirit if I did not subject his own to criticism; which I shall do.

On meaning in general he began with a heroic two-stage attempt at a classically reductive analysis of the concept of linguistic meaning in psychological terms, specifically in terms of the intentions of speakers to induce certain responses, e.g. beliefs or intentions to act, on the part of their audiences. At the basis of the whole attempt lay the notion of what he called 'utterer's occasion-meaning'. This is roughly the idea of someone—call him the utterer—using some device or other on some particular occasion to get something across, to communicate some message to someone else, the audience. The message in question was what the utterer of the device, whatever it was, *meant* on that occasion by that device. Hence 'utterer's occasion-meaning'. Illustrative examples were given to demonstrate that this notion could be wholly explained in terms of utterer's intention, with no dependence on semantic concepts and no essential reference to linguistic or other conventionally established devices. That was stage one. The next stage, of course, was to explicate the notion of linguistic meaning itself in terms, ultimately, of utterers' occasion-meaning (together with whatever other non-semantic concepts might be called for).

The project encountered difficulties at both stages. Obviously you could intend to get someone, say, to believe a certain proposition, say the proposition that p, and you could succeed in doing so simply by so arranging matters that he would see for himself that p, or by surreptitiously putting in his way conclusive evidence that p. Equally obviously this would not be a case of your meaning, in the required sense, that p. Grice initially suggested that what was required for a case of 'utterer's occasion-meaning that p' was that the utterer should do something, perform some act, not only with the primary intention of getting his audience to believe that p, but with the secondary intention that the audience should come to form this belief *for the reason* that he, the audience, recognized the utterer's primary intention, *viz.* the intention to get him to believe that p. Then, and then only, it was suggested, would the audience appreciate that the utterer *meant* that p by the device he used; only then would he appreciate that the utterer was trying, so to speak, to *tell* him that p. Of course I use the word 'tell' in an extended sense, since the means employed need not be linguistic, and indeed are not in the illustrative examples initially offered.

The trouble at this stage arose from the fact that various ingenious souls were able to devise counterexamples that showed that the conditions initially offered were insufficient. Cases were described in which those conditions were satisfied but in which it could not reasonably be said that someone had intended by his act to convey a message to another, to tell him, say, that p, to mean p. So some elaboration or complication of the original analysis seemed to be called for. But any such revision merely prompted further and more complex counterexamples; and the prospect of a realistic and non-regressive solution began to seem poor.

Of course Grice was the last person to be daunted by complexities. The ingenuity with which difficulties were devised for the original analysis merely prompted him to exercise an equal ingenuity in contriving adjustments designed to circumvent them; and in this exercise, of which I shall not attempt here to record the details, I think he thought to the end that he had pretty well succeeded. For, after all, the central idea, the original notion, did seem to have a lot going for it; enough, certainly, to ensure that, with whatever tinkering was necessary, the central idea could be made to survive.

So, though there were difficulties with this stage of the programme, they did not seem insuperable. The more serious difficulties arose at the second stage—in the attempt to explicate the notion of linguistic meaning in general, hence the full-blown panoply of semantic concepts, in terms of utterer's occasion-meaning (itself explained without reference to such concepts), together with whatever other non-semantic concepts of a socio-psychological kind might be required. In spite of the many subtle manoeuvres he executed around this problem, I do not think Grice regarded himself as having finally solved it. Indeed at one point he refers to his account of the stages by which an artificial system of communication devices, in effect a language, might be thought of as *emerging* from his initially described situations of people meaning something by their acts— he refers to this account as a *myth*, comparable with the political theorist's myth of the social contract: a help, perhaps, to full understanding, but not a substitute for it.

In the course of, or as a preliminary to, these manoeuvres he speaks of three kinds of correspondence one might expect, or even require, between the members of the trio, thought, the world, and language; and aligns himself in principle with some sort of correspondence theory of truth, while declining to develop any such theory himself. I shall come back to this last point later.

Grice's reductive, or quasi-reductive, theory of linguistic meaning in general has engaged mainly the mainly critical attention of philosophers. It is otherwise with the theory of conversational implicature. That has captivated linguists and philosophers alike. Of course everyone has always known that a man may, by saying what he says, imply something additional to, or even at variance with, what he actually says. But it is hardly an exaggeration to say that Grice was the first to attempt a systematic theory of this phenomenon. He introduced the terms of art 'implicate' and 'implicature': on the one hand to do general duty for all the members of a family of terms which include 'imply', 'suggest', 'mean', 'insinuate', and so on; and on the other, perhaps, though he does not say this, to distinguish the concept from that of logical or necessary implication. (It was unnecessary for him to say this, since 'implies' in the *logical* sense does not take a personal subject. It is not the speaker, but what he says, that has *logical* consequences.)

So now to the theory of conversational implicature. As a preliminary, we must first note two connected distinctions which Grice draws. One is a distinction between conventional and non-conventional implicature; the other a distinction between what is said (in a certain favoured sense) and what is implicated, whether conventionally or non-conventionally. To quote an example of Grice's: one who utters a sentence of the form 'p therefore q' *conventionally* implicates that the matter affirmed at q is a consequence of, or follows from, the matter affirmed at p. The implication is carried by the conventional linguistic meaning of 'therefore'. But this implicature is not part of what is *said* in Grice's favoured sense. What is said in that sense (effectively 'both p and q') is not made false by the failure of the implicated consequence-relation to hold. And the point is general: it holds for all implicatures, conventional and non-conventional. The truth value of what is *said*, in Grice's sense, is independent of the truth or falsity of what is implicated.

I take the notion of conventional implicatures, carried for example by such conjunctions as 'therefore', 'so', 'but', 'although', 'because', and other expressions, to be reasonably clear; and I shall for the time being say no more about it. Grice's theory of conversational implicature relates not to these but, as he cautiously puts it, to a certain *subclass* of *non*-conventional implicatures. The caution implied in the use of the term 'subclass' is well-advised. It would be stretching the concept of *conversational* implicature perhaps intolerably to represent it as covering all cases in which a speaker non-conventionally implies something more than, or different from, what he actually says; for to convey the implication to his audience he might be relying on details of his own and his audience's knowledge of a particular situation in a way not provided for by the conditions, whatever they are, which govern conversational implicature. So what finally are those conditions?

Well, there is one central or governing assumption: that rational beings engaged, say, in imparting or exchanging information, may normally be expected to speak in such a way as to forward, rather than impede, the general or particular ends of such conversational exchanges; to contribute positively rather than negatively to those purposes. *Normally* must be stressed here, since obviously there are special circumstances in which any such expectation would be unwarranted. But the *general* principle holds: indeed its holding in *general* might even be thought to be a necessary condition of the very existence of the activity in question. Grice calls it the Cooperative Principle. From it there flow a number of maxims which we will all immediately recognize as such as we *should*, i.e. ideally ought, to observe in conversation: e.g. make your contribution neither less nor more informative than is required; affirm only what you take to be true or have adequate evidence for; be relevant; and avoid faults of expression such as obscurity, ambiguity, prolixity, etc. In the ordinary course of conversation we tend to assume that our interlocutor will be conforming with the Cooperative Principle, hence with the maxims into which it ramifies. So if what he says appears to deviate deliberately in some significant way from such conformity, we shall reasonably take him to be implying by his contribution something more or other than what he actually says, and will normally be able to make out from the conversational context what this implication is.

Here is an example from my recent experience. A and B are discussing the relative intellectual endowments of their colleagues. A remarks to B on the high intelligence of a third colleague, C. B replies: if C were of a more angelic temperament, he wouldn't make some of the pronouncements he does make. Since what is at issue is intelligence, not moral character, the possession or lack of an *angelic* temperament seems quite irrelevant. But B, remembering the familiar adage about fools rushing in etc., immediately cottons on to the implicature, *viz.* that C is not really as bright as all that.

The example I have just given, like many others given by Grice himself, is a particular conversational implicature, specific to the particular context and occasion. More interesting, and more important to the philosophy of meaning in general, are cases of what Grice calls 'generalized conversational implicature'. A standard illustration of this phenomenon is the speaker's use of the disjunctive form, 'A or B', in reply to a question, when the information-seeker's needs would obviously be more fully met had the speaker been in a position to give, and been willing to give, the more specific answer mentioning just one of the alternatives. So, assuming the speaker is conforming to the Cooperative Principle, it follows that he was not in that position, that although he had sufficient grounds for asserting their disjunction, he didn't know which of the two disjoined alternatives was correct. And so, in general, with other less than ideally specific answers like 'Somewhere in the kitchen' or 'In one of the dining room cupboards'. Of course, in all such cases, there might be special circumstances which defeated the implication.

The theoretical importance of the phenomenon of generalized conversational implicature is, Grice argues, considerable. Philosophers, properly concerned with the meanings of expressions, are also properly, and indeed necessarily, concerned with the conditions under which they can be either correctly *or* appropriately used. Grice's distinctive contribution was to insist that one should not confuse the two: a given use may fail the test of 'appropriateness' without necessarily failing the test of 'correctness'. And this will be conspicuously the case if the use of an expression carries a generalized conversational implicature which, by hypothesis, is no part of its conventional meaning. Thus, in the case considered above, while a disjunctive answer, 'either A or B', carries a generalized implication of the speaker's ignorance of which disjunct is the right one, this is no part of the meaning of the disjunctive particle 'or'. What the speaker says may be perfectly true, even if he knows perfectly well that the right, and more informative, answer would be 'A'. Indeed the speaker may correctly and intelligibly go on to say 'A or B; I know perfectly well which it is, but I'm not telling you because I want you to find out for yourself'. Grice finds in this one of the distinctive marks of generalized conversational implicatures: namely, that they can be explicitly cancelled, as in this case. Besides cancelability, Grice mentions another mark, which he calls 'non-detachability'. An implicature is non-detachable if it is not possible to find another way of saying the same thing which simply lacks the implicature. In the disjunctive case, for example, you couldn't detach the implicature by recourse to the clumsier equivalent forms, 'Well, it's not neither A nor B' or 'Of the two possibilities, A and B, one is fulfilled'. These circumlocutions carry just the same implicature as the simple alternation.

So Grice has equipped himself with a potentially very powerful instrument; and he uses it in the case of a number of expressions to demonstrate, or attempt to demonstrate, that features of their normal use which philosophers have been prone to represent as integral to their meanings should rather be seen as generalized conversational implicatures of their use and thus as no part of their conventional meaning. All these attempts are argued, and illustrated, with his customary ingenuity. But not all, it seems to me, are successful. J. L. Austin remarked long ago, apropos of his own discovery of the explicit performative, that anyone who forges a new weapon for the philosopher's armoury may at the same time be fashioning new skids to put under his feet; and inadvertently illustrated the point with the uncharacteristically imprudent remarks he made at one time about the expression 'I know'. So it was, I shall suggest, in at least one important instance, with Grice; although the case was argued, in this instance, with characteristic subtlety and skill.

That for later. In the meantime I want to harvest, from his two exercises on meaning in general and conversational implicature in particular, a series of distinctions which Grice has drawn and which are surely essential to our understanding in the whole area of the theory of meaning as linguistically conveyed. We are to consider an utterance of a complete declarative sentential utterance-type; in drawing the relevant distinctions, I shall not adhere exactly to Grice's presentation, though I shall try to reproduce the sense of what he says.

(1) First, then, we have the literal meaning (or meanings) of the sentential type in question, as determined by the syntax and lexicon of the language used. I use the plural 'meanings' to allow for any of what are customarily called lexical or syntactic ambiguities in the utterance-type in question; though I shall add that in such cases it would be arguably better to say, not that we have an ambiguous sentence, but that we have two different sentences with different meanings. Grice here speaks of the *timeless meanings* of the utterance-type.

(2) So, second, we have the *actual* literal meaning of the utterance-type, *as uttered*, i.e. the literal meaning of the sentence uttered when all the so-called ambiguities are removed. Grice calls this the *applied timeless meaning* of the utterance-type.

(3) Third, if the sentence-type uttered includes any indexical or demonstrative expressions or any proper names, then, even if we know the applied timeless meaning of the words uttered, we still do not know what was said until we also know what, in the context of utterance, is the referential force of all those expressions and names. Then we may be said to know the *literal-cum-referential meaning* of the utterance. Grice does not make a separate mention of this, though he clearly allows for it.

(4) Fourth, Grice here draws a further distinction, to which I have already referred, between what is actually *said*, in his favoured sense, and what, over and above this, is *conventionally* implied by the inclusion in the utterance of certain conjunctions like 'therefore', 'so', 'but', 'although', etc., or certain other expressions like 'Alas' or, in its current mis-usage, 'hopefully'.

(5) Fifthly, then, we have just these conventional implications themselves which, though certainly part of what is meant, form no part of what is said in the favoured sense and have no bearing on the truth value of the latter.

Now so far, with all these distinctions, we have stayed throughout in the area of the conventional meaning of expressions, supplemented only by the determination of reference in the case of indexicals and names.

(6) But sixthly and finally, we come to those further implications of what is said, 'the specification of which falls outside the specification of the conventional meaning of the words used'. This is the area in which the theory of conversational implicature finds play; though, as I earlier

remarked, Grice is wisely cautious enough not to maintain that all nonconventional implications are to be explained in terms of that theory. For one may well imply something by what one says without expecting one's audience's comprehension to be mediated by any tacit assumption on his part that one is observing the maxims dictated by the Cooperative Principle; relying, rather, on no more than our shared knowledge of the details of the situation to which one's remark relates.

A little while back I observed that Grice himself was not immune from the philosophical temptation to push a new and fertile idea beyond the limits of its just application; and I wish now to say something about what seems to me the most signal instance of his doing so with the theory of generalized conversational implicature. He argues that the conventional meaning of an indicative conditional is always the same as that of the stipulated meaning of the material or Philonian conditional of truth-functional logic; that an indicative 'if p, q' is identical in meaning with '$p \supset q$' which is itself equivalent to the simple truth-functional disjunction '$\sim p \vee q$' or to the simple negation of the conjunction 'p & $\sim q$'. Any appearance to the contrary is explained by his theory. It is obvious how the argument, on his principles, will go. Simply to affirm the bare alternative, either not-p is true or q is true, without any indication of which is true, is obviously less informative than a straightforward denial of p or a straightforward assertion of q. So it is ruled out by the maxims flowing from the Cooperative Principle, unless one has some reason for affirming it other than knowledge of the truth value of either of the alternates. But any such reason one might have would precisely be a reason for thinking that the truth of p, if established, would be a ground for taking q to be true as well, i.e. would have the truth of q as a *consequence*. And this is exactly what the ordinary man, in my view correctly, takes the locution 'if p, then q' to *mean*. In Grice's view, of course, what the ordinary man takes to be the meaning of the conjunction is not its meaning at all, but simply a generalized conversational implicature of the use of an expression which really has the same meaning as the truth-functional connective.

It is important to notice the shape of the argument here. What Grice has really demonstrated has itself the form of a conditional: viz. that *if* 'if p, q' really means no more and no less than '$p \supset q$' (or, in other words, if the natural language conditional really is the truth-functional material conditional) then the consequentialist implication of the use of 'if p, q' can be and will correctly be explained as a conversational implicature of its use, and hence no part of its conventional meaning. But to demonstrate, as Grice does, *this* conditional about ordinary conditionals has absolutely no force at all to show that *its* antecedent is true, viz. that the ordinary conditional is indeed really a material conditional. That conclusion would follow only if it were also shown that the consequentialist implication of the ordinary use of 'if' could *not* be explained *in any other way*; that the offered explanation was the only possible one. But that is quite obviously false. For a much simpler explanation is immediately available: viz. that it is precisely a feature of the *conventional* meaning of 'if' that it carries the consequentialist implication—which is just what the ordinary man naively, and correctly, thinks. That is to say, just as 'p, therefore q' or 'p, so q' (as Grice himself proclaims) conventionally implies the holding of a consequentialist relation between the asserted proposition p and the (hence also asserted) proposition q, so 'if p, q' conventionally implies the holding of the consequentialist relation between the unasserted, merely hypothesized, proposition p and the equally unasserted proposition q. Nothing could be plainer.

A footnote here. If we accept what I have just maintained, and at the same time follow Grice in maintaining a strict distinction between what is said in his favoured sense and what is implied, whether conventionally or conversationally, and if we further hold that only what is actually *said* in the favoured sense can be assigned a truth value, then we shall have to deny truth values to ordinary conditionals, since neither clause of the conditional is actually asserted; and some philosophers have adopted this view. In fact we don't in general quite do this in practice, and it is natural that we shouldn't. If we regard the consequentialist implication as clearly correct, we tend to treat the conditional as a whole as true; if we regard the consequentialist implication as clearly incorrect, we may dismiss it as false, saying, by way of denial, 'That wouldn't follow at all', or 'It could perfectly well turn out that p without its being the case that q'. If, as is perhaps more common, we regard the implication as uncertain, we hedge, with such expressions as 'Maybe', 'Quite possibly'; or assign it some degree of probability or reasonableness.

These last remarks are no more than a footnote—not really important for the central issue. But we haven't yet quite finished. I remarked earlier on a feature which Grice declares characteristic of generalized conversational implicatures, viz. their non-detachability. An implication is detachable only if it is possible to find an alternative way of saying what is meant by an utterance, a way which is free of the implication in question. Thus the conversational implicature carried by the use of the material conditional is, in virtue of the maxims flowing from the Cooperative Principle, non-detachable. But what I have represented as conventional implication of the use of the ordinary conditional is equally undetachable. Regarded as an argument for the conclusion that the implication is conversational and not conventional, this is, of course, invalid. It has the form:

All generalized conversational implicatures are non-detachable. The consequentialist implication of 'if p, q' is non-detachable. Therefore the consequential implication is a conversational implication.

—a simple case of one of the commonest logical fallacies.

To conclude this topic, I wish merely to remark on how natural it is that a language should contain a particle with just the conventional force or meaning that I have claimed for 'if'. Consider how often military commanders, business men, politicians, and the rest of us have occasion for what we call contingency planning, i.e. for considering various possibilities of future developments (e.g. moves of the enemy), and working out the consequences that each of them would have or be likely to have, with a view to planning an appropriate response in each case. Just as there is a strong presumption in favour of the existence in a language of a particle with the conventional force of recording our drawing of a consequence from an already accepted truth, so there is an equally strong presumption in favour of the existence in a language of a particle whose conventional force is that of recording our drawing hypothetical consequences from hypothetical premises. Just as 'p, therefore q' or 'p, so q' perform the former function, so 'if p, then q' performs the latter. And indeed no language with which I am acquainted lacks such a particle.

It is interesting to note another case in which Grice's use of the notion of conversational implicature exhibits the same general shape as I detected in the case of his treatment of indicative conditionals. Thus he argues that those features of the use of singular definite descriptions which have encouraged some philosophers, including myself, to hold that failure of reference may result in failure of truth value (or, as Austin once put it, in the utterance being 'void for lack of reference') could, and perhaps should, be explained in a different way, namely the following. First take it that some form of Russell's Theory of Descriptions gives the correct analysis of what is said when a declarative utterance is made which includes a singular definite description in subject position. Then the theory of conversational implicature, together with certain ancillary devices or assumptions, will account for the impression that the success of the reference apparently made by the description is a presupposed condition of the utterance having a truth value. Hence Russell's analysis can be seen as correct. This view of Grice's, more tentatively advanced than his account of conditionals, has not won general acceptance among linguists. Nor should it have. For what he has demonstrated is simply the following conditional: *if* we view a sentence containing a definite description as simply a definitional contraction of an appropriate form of the Russellian expansion, *then* the existential presupposition seemingly carried by such a description can be explained with the aid of the theory of conversational implicature. But of course establishing this conditional has no force at all to show that the view mentioned in its antecedent is correct. In fairness I should stress the tentativeness with which Grice advanced his account. He did not positively align himself with it, but rather, I suspect, regarded it, as we should also, as an interesting exercise. So there is here a marked contrast with his attitude in the case of conditionals.

While I am still in the critical vein, there is one other matter I should like to refer to. Grice himself rightly criticizes an early and ill-considered attempt of my own, long abandoned, to represent one particular use of the word 'true' as the complete account of its semantic function. He himself, as I remarked earlier, says he favours some version of a correspondence theory of truth; and although he explicitly declines to develop such a theory on his own account, it seems clear from his incidental remarks that what he had in mind was something on the general lines of a 'words-to-world' correspondence theory such as we were offered, many years ago, by J. L. Austin. There is much to be said about this idea; but one central point is the following. It is perfectly possible to take the notion of *truth* for granted and to proceed, on this basis, to attempt to construct a general theory of the semantics of a formalized language (cf. Tarski) or even of a natural language (cf. Davidson). The outcome, however, whether the attempt is wholly (Tarski) or only partly (Davidson) successful, is not a theory of truth; it is at best a truth-based theory of semantics. To attempt a generalized theory of *truth* on these lines is vain. Perhaps this is why Austin was tempted apparently to follow an old tradition and elect *facts* as the worldly term of the correspondence relation; for the word 'fact' does promise, and indeed possess, the necessary generality. But it does not serve the intended purpose. A fact is not a worldly item. As Frege neatly put it, a fact is nothing but a true thought.

This is not to say that the notions of correspondence and fact have no part at all to play in the explanation of the notion of truth. They have a plain, indeed platitudinous, part. Truth can be significantly (truly or falsely) predicated of anything that is stated or believed or conjectured etc. I shall, following, with G. E. Moore, another old tradition, call such items propositions or, more fashionably, propositional contents. No one will dispute the validity of all exemplifications of the schema: 'the proposition that p is true if and only if p'. Here is one such exemplification: 'the proposition that the Titanic sank is true if and only if the Titanic sank'. The first clause of this bi-conditional is about a proposition, something stated or believed. The second clause is about what happened in the world; it relates to a historical event and represents a historical fact. There is a clear sense, then, in which the bi-conditional as a whole represents a correspondence between the proposition and the fact, viz. that the same words are used in specifying both.

But now, it may be said, have I not abandoned the contention that facts are not items in the world? Certainly the ship, the Titanic, was a worldly object and its sinking was an event in the world; and the fact, like the proposition, is *about* these particular concrete worldly items. But it does not follow that the fact, any more than the proposition, is itself such an item.

There is an obvious, though obviously fallacious, objection to be considered here. Surely, it may be said, the following two things must be admitted: (1) the sinking of the Titanic is a fact; (2) the sinking of the Titanic is a definite worldly event—it took place in a certain region, the North Atlantic, in a certain year, 1912, on its maiden voyage. Therefore a fact is nothing abstract, like a proposition, but something concrete such as, in this case, a historical occurrence. This simple argument has the distinction of combining formal invalidity (generalization from a single case) with the more sophisticated fallacy of equivocation. The gerundial expressions it exploits are deceptively two-faced; they play a double role. They *can* designate events: the *event of the Titanic's sinking* did indeed take place there and then. They can also designate facts: the *fact* of *the Titanic's sinking in*

1912 on its maiden voyage did not take place anywhere at any time, any more than the *fact*, in its less specific form, of *the Titanic's sinking* or, what is the same thing, the fact *that the Titanic sank*.

I may seem to have drifted away from Grice here, directing my fire more at Austin; but in so far as Grice, in the matter of truth, seemed disposed to follow the latter, the drift has not been far.

Well, that is enough of criticism. I have concentrated so far on my subject's well-known theses in the philosophy of language; but he has of course made major contributions in other areas as well. His exposition and defence of a version of the causal theory of perception, although it has been subjected to some extremely penetrating criticisms of detail, still seems to me in essence incontrovertible; and the use he made, in the course of it, of the distinction between what is true and what is linguistically felicitous or appropriate, still seems to me sound, though inessential to the main contention. Of more general interest and significance—in fact of the greatest interest and significance—are Grice's many reflections, variously distributed in his writings, on the nature and the history of the philosophical enterprise as a whole. In this extended area he is released from the constraints of close detailed argument and illustration, and precision of statement, which he characteristically imposed on himself in more limited discussions; and consequently his writing in the wider area is marked by a freshness, elegance, and even wittiness not much in evidence elsewhere in his work. Examples may be found both in *Studies in the Way of Words* and, more especially, in his own contribution to the volume of essays on his work edited and introduced by Richard Grandy and Richard Warner.

In the section of that contribution which Grice entitles 'Opinions' I would especially like to call to your attention—and indeed, in the strongest possible terms, *commend* to your attention—two particular passages. The first is to be found on pages 64–6 of the Grandy–Warner volume and concerns two aspects of the *unity* of philosophy, the 'latitudinal' and the 'longitudinal' as he calls them. We are all familiar with those departmental-sounding names which reverberate throughout the discipline: ontology, epistemology, philosophy of mind, philosophy of language, ethics, and so on. In speaking of the latitudinal unity of the subject, Grice is not merely making the point that there are cross-connections between these. He wants to insist on a stronger unity than this; that all are but aspects of one single enquiry; or, at its strongest and in his own words, 'that it is not possible to reach full understanding of, or high level proficiency in, any one sub-discipline without corresponding understanding and proficiency in the others'. He disclaims any ability to prove such a thesis; but sketches some suggestions of ways in which it might be supported.

The thesis of the Longitudinal Unity of Philosophy, i.e. of its unity through time, is one with which no Oxford philosopher will have difficulty in agreeing. We all accept that, as Grice puts it, we should 'treat the great but dead philosophers as if they were great but living, as persons who have much to say to us now'—while at the same time we must remain aware of those radical changes in the idioms of speech and climates of thought which, if not fully appreciated, carry risks of misunderstanding.

The other passage to which I particularly invite your attention follows immediately upon these reflection on the unity of philosophy. In it Grice voices his strong opposition to what he calls Minimalism in philosophy: a comprehensive heading under which he groups a cluster of other -isms, giving pride of place among them to the one which bears the name Extensionalism, but including also Nominalism, Positivism, Reductivism, and (in the currently favoured sense of the term) Naturalism—besides several others. What is common to them all is a species of exclusiveness—a denial of legitimacy or, so to speak, of philosophical citizenship to all but a privileged and restricted class of objects or concepts.

Once more disclaiming argument, Grice admits that his 'antipathy to minimalism depends much more on a concern to have a philosophical approach which would have prospects of doing justice to the exuberant wealth and variety of human experience in a manner seemingly beyond the reach of minimalism than on the availability of any argument which would show the theses of minimalism to be mistaken'; and acknowledges that what he has said against it has been 'perhaps a little tinged with rhetoric'. Well, if that is a fault, it not a grievous one; and I, for one, being profoundly in sympathy with him on this matter, would not be inclined to reproach him with it.

Not everyone will be equally tolerant of a certain mischievousness he displays at one point. Thus, speaking of the difficulty of thinking oneself into the thought of a past philosopher he writes: 'Of course, if we are looking at the work of some relatively minor philosophical figure such as, for example, Wollaston or Bosanquet or Wittgenstein, such "introjection" may be neither possible nor worthwhile.' Isn't it preposterous, it will be said, so to classify and couple Wittgenstein? I think it is preposterous; but also explicable. For, as is evident from others of his general remarks, Grice believes that philosophy should aim at generality, at systematic and explanatory theory; whereas Wittgenstein *seems* to eschew in practice, and to repudiate in principle, any such aim. But the difference may be superficial, more apparent than real. Certainly it would be a bolder man than I who would seek to give a systematic general account of Wittgenstein's overarching views and methodology; but it would be a yet bolder who said there were no such things. And if the attempt were made and succeeded, it might emerge that Grice's hostility to minimalism and reductivism found subtly pitched echoes in Wittgenstein's approach. The variety of 'forms of life' may correspond, in a certain fashion, to Grice's variety of human experience. But this is speculation. The mischievousness remains; but perhaps in view of his many counterbalancing virtues, it may be overlooked. Other anglophone philosophers born in the present century have done work of more lasting significance; but, to end as I began on a personal note, though I have known all the most gifted of these philosophers, I have known none *cleverer* than Paul Grice.

20
Why Philosophy?

The question that forms my title is a rather brutally truncated form of the question which was originally proposed to me. That was: 'If you had your time over again, why would you do philosophy?'

You will see at once that this question has a flaw: you can't ask why something did or would happen unless you take it for granted that it did or would. That is to say, the question presupposes an affirmative answer to a prior question, namely: 'If you had your time over again, would you do philosophy?' But this question too has a fault: the terms of the condition are under-specified. Is it to be supposed that I am to consider the question in full awareness of how things have actually turned out in that time? Or am I supposed to assume ignorance of that? Neither supposition guarantees a clear answer. Given the first, the assumption of complete knowledge, one might think on the one hand that since experience has shown that I am reasonably competent and successful in philosophy, I would certainly go for it again; so the answer would be 'Yes'. But, on the other hand, since I have had my public say, in books and articles, on the philosophical questions of greatest interest to me, I would hardly want repeat myself or spend my working life simply on the correction and refinement of what I had already said; so the answer would seem to be 'No'.

Given the other hypothesis, that of ignorance, the answer is equally unclear. Since I came up to the University as a scholar in English literature, it might naturally be supposed, as my then College expected and wished, that I would continue with that noble subject—and end up as a Professor of English rather than of philosophy. On the other hand, I had already felt the pull of philosophical questions and of abstract thought; and given that the year was 1937 and that European civilization seemed threatened, and threatened, moreover, from within Europe itself, I had also felt that I ought to know something more about such serious subjects as Economics and

Politics; all these factors drew me towards PPE, which in fact, and with some reluctance, the College eventually allowed me to do.

So let us put the original question on one side and return to its truncated form—to my title 'Why Philosophy?' This abrupt query is worth considering because of two other questions which are sometimes posed. The first is blunt enough: 'What's the use of it?' The second is, or seems, a bit more sophisticated: *viz.* 'Why is it that, unlike the natural sciences, there seems to be no development, no progress in philosophy? And that its practitioners seem to be in perpetual disagreement, continuing to argue over the same issues that engaged their predecessors centuries ago?. There is, I think, an acceptable answer to this second question. Other disciplines are defined by their distinctive subject matters which delimit the regions among which truths are to be sought and found. They define, as it were, a principle of selection among ascertainable truths. So agreement among experts in special sciences, and in exact scholarship too, may reasonably be hoped for and gradually attained. But philosophy, which takes human thought in general as its field, is not thus conveniently confined, and (I am now quoting myself): 'truth in philosophy, though not to be despaired of, is so complex and many-sided, so multi-faced, that any individual philosopher's work, if it is to have any unity and coherence, must at best emphasize some aspects of the truth to the neglect of others which may strike another philosopher with greater force'. Hence the appearance of endemic disagreement in the subject is something to be expected rather than deplored; and it is no matter for wonder that the individual philosopher's views are more likely than those of the scientist or exact scholar to reflect, in part, his individual taste and temperament.

This point carries with it some riders of which at least one should serve as a caution to any young aspirant philosophers. It is this: that in spite of the charms of discipleship which evidently some, though not I, have felt or feel, it is a mistake to suppose that any philosopher, however great, has a valid and exclusive claim to have got things finally right on some substantial matter. And that goes, I must add, for Plato, Aristotle, Aquinas, Hume, Kant, Hegel, Frege, Wittgenstein—or anyone else you may feel inclined to add. But now, to balance that caution against accepting the final authority, on any matter, of any of the great dead philosophers of the past, I must add a countervailing point which I think few will dispute: *viz.* that those great dead thinkers were, for the most part, a great deal cleverer than any of us; that their thoughts may still have a unique weight and sustenance for us, that they may speak to us more powerfully and suggestively than even the most gifted of our contemporaries.

A less obvious rider of my general characterization of philosophy is that, in spite of its real division into departments, it is one subject, a single unitary discipline. Ontology or metaphysics, epistemology or theory of knowledge, philosophy of language and logic, and even (in some central aspects), the philosophy of mind, are indivisibly intertwined with one another. The more thoroughgoing of us would include ethics in the same parcel—but I am a little more dubious about that.

And now to confront the more brutal question: 'What's the use of it? Of this continuing involved discussion of highly abstract questions which hardly impinge on life as lived at any level?' One may be strongly tempted to reply: like all the *best* things, it is of no use whatever. It is pursued for its own sake alone; and if undertaken for any extraneous purpose, it is false to itself. But, in fact, though that's true in its own way, more can be said than this. The story is told that one aged teacher of the discipline in this University would begin his series of classes by saying: what I am going to teach you will be of no use to you whatever in any of your subsequent careers, whether in the law, the church, the services, administration, or commerce—except perhaps for one thing: it may help you, in discussion of any controversial matter, to tell within a short time if your interlocutor is talking nonsense. Or to put it more conventionally: the reasonably diligent study of philosophy over a period of years, under the guidance of an experienced tutor, will develop in you a *critical* and *sceptical* habit of mind which will be of service to you in assessing whatever you hear or read, not only in its own philosophical domain, but quite generally; and perhaps especially—and perhaps especially today—in the domain of public affairs.

So this is the use of it. Indeed one of my transatlantic pupils was enthusiastic enough to write to me to say, of his philosophical study at Univ: 'It taught me to think'.

Well, enough of that. There are plenty of other questions to ask about the subject. And one surely rather important one I haven't so far even considered. Suppose we ask: What in general are we, or should we be, up to in philosophy? What is, or should be our objective? What are we, or should we be, aiming to discover or establish? Of course, there are different demands and responses here. Some, it appears, yearn for a quite new perspective, a new and revealing vision of human life, the world, and experience; and some thinkers have been only too ready to respond to such a call: for example Nietzsche (with his notion of the 'Übermensch'), Sartre (with 'mauvaise foi' and 'existential choices'), and Heidegger (with something altogether more mysterious and probably more sinister). All of these thinkers have moments of insight; but none of them has acquired, or is likely to acquire, a lasting hold on the minds of those more staid practitioners among whom I find myself and all the other philosophers whom I know—mostly Anglophone.

So to consider some soberer conceptions of what our philosophical objective is or should be. What about these: (1) To establish how we should live, the nature of the good life? There are plenty of classical precedents here (Plato, Aristotle, the Stoics, and the Epicureans, though they all had other concerns as well). (2) To determine the scope and limits of human knowledge? Here too there are plenty of examples (e.g. Locke, Kant, Russell, etc., though again this wasn't their only aim). Or (3) To achieve self-understanding? This last, if properly understood, is the suggestion I favour. I do not mean that we should turn into psychologists or social scientists. I mean that I see our essential business, if not our only business, as that of getting a clear view of our most general working concepts or types of concepts, of their mutual relations and interdependences, and of their place in our lives. We should aim, in a word, at general human conceptual self-understanding.

Now, I take this to be also Wittgenstein's view of the matter, at least in his later period. He also saw that a necessary condition of achieving this result was to liberate ourselves from false understanding; to tear away the veil of seductive illusions or pictures that pervaded much existing philosophical theory, that prevented us from seeing clearly, from getting the clear view that we needed. To this task Wittgenstein devoted much of his formidable powers and did so with the unique effectiveness of genius. But I must also add, as I think, that his almost obsessional anxiety to liberate us from false pictures, from the myths or fictions of much philosophical theorizing led to a certain loss of balance in his thinking. It did so in two ways. First, it led him to distrust systematic theories in general, and hence to a disregard of the possibility, indeed, to my mind, the truth, that the most general categories and concepts of human thought do form, in their connections and interdependences, an articulated structure which it is possible to describe without falsification, and also, incidentally, in such a way as to illustrate what I spoke of earlier as the mutual involvement of ontology, epistemology, and the philosophy of language, logic, and mind.

Second, the same obsession led him to minimize or dismiss, or at least give too little attention to, some pervasive features of our thought and experience. One of these is the reality of subjective experience in all its richness and complexity, or, as one of our most distinguished recent contemporaries expressed it, in all its 'heady luxuriance'. The other is the inescapable presence in our thought of abstract objects or universals, 'intensions' in our jargon, revered by Plato as 'forms' or 'ideas'. Both these features are easily misunderstood in philosophical thinking, lending themselves to gratuitous inflation, such as Plato is perhaps justly held responsible for in the second case (that of universals), or being given an unrealistic scope and priority, such as Descartes and, following him, the British empiricists are, with no less justice, accused of in the first case (that of private, subjective experience).

Both these gross and persistent errors, the source of many false imaginary pictures, were objects of Wittgenstein's formidable hostility and scorn. But none of this justifies the failure to give the features themselves (subjective experience on the one hand, abstract objects on the other) full acknowledgement as the harmless, inescapable features that they are, regularly recognized in our thought and talk.

These last thoughts prompt me to comment on one mildly ironical feature of our discipline in the later twentieth century and probably also in the early twenty-first century. If anyone is entitled to be called the founder of our subject, it is generally acknowledged to be Plato; and if anyone can be called the father of its modern development, most of us would nominate Descartes. The irony is that to accuse a philosopher of Platonism or Cartesianism is currently felt to be a seriously damaging charge. I have already hinted at part of the reason. But if, and in so far as, I have myself here or elsewhere, exposed myself to that charge, I am quite unrepentant. Of course both these great men were guilty of exaggerations, and, in the case of Descartes, of more or less grave mistakes. But each had a grasp, however uncertain, of aspects of our thought and experience which it would be a much graver mistake to overlook, to deny, or to minimize.

To return for a concluding moment to the notion of a clear understanding of our conceptual scheme. Some thinker, who no doubt yearned for something deeper or more exciting and whose name is mercifully forgotten, is on record as having declared 'Clarity is not enough'. Hearing of this, John Austin, a leading light of my epoch, is said to have remarked: 'Clarity is not enough? It will be time to discuss that when we have achieved clarity on some matter.'

21

Intellectual Autobiography

I was born, on 23 November 1919, in one London suburb, Ealing, and was brought up in another, Finchley. I was the second child, with two brothers and one much younger sister. My parents were both school teachers, though my mother gave up teaching on marriage. They had met when studying English literature at Goldsmith's College, London. My mother retained an excellent memory for verse, which I inherited. My father's parents came from Lincolnshire and Yorkshire, my mother's from Hampshire and Gloucestershire. Unlike many English people, I know of no Scottish, Welsh, or Irish ancestry. After my first year's secondary education at the Finchley County School my parents transferred me to the boys-only Christ's College, Finchley (motto: 'Usque proficiens'), where academic standards were higher and where my elder brother, four years my senior, was already being educated. Unlike him, I declined to join the Cadet Corps. I still feel grateful to the French teacher (Miss Jacobi) at the earlier school, who required us to learn the phonetic alphabet and strove to inculcate a correct pronunciation of the language she taught.

At Christ's College I had good teachers and flourished academically. When the time came to choose specialist subjects for what was then called 'Higher Certificate' (modern 'A-Level') I chose English, French, Latin, and History, to the disapproval of my math master who claimed, incorrectly, that mathematics was my best subject. In fact, my best subjects were the literary ones, and especially English, in which an excellent teacher, J. H. Taylor, gave me much encouragement. I developed a liking for grammar and a devotion to English poetry and prose, neither of which has left me. With Mr. Taylor's support I entered for and won an open scholarship in English at St. John's College, Oxford. My Higher Certificate examination results had additionally secured for me a State Scholarship, and an anonymous benefactor had undertaken to supplement my undergraduate income. So I went up to Oxford in October 1937, at the age of 17, with adequate financial provision. This was necessary, since my father's salary, as Headmaster of a poor London school, had been modest, and his early death in 1936—he had suffered bad health ever since the 1914–18 war—had left my mother a widow. So we were rather poor.

Before I joined my college, I had decided to change my course, if possible, from the Honour School of English to that of Philosophy, Politics, and Economics (PPE); and when I arrived in Oxford I succeeded, against some mild resistance, in persuading the Fellows to allow me to do this. My motives for wishing to change were various. One was the perhaps rather priggish thought that since, at that period, the political future and the civilization of Europe seemed threatened, I ought to be better equipped than I was with understanding of politics and economics. More important was the fact that I had already begun to feel the intellectual pull of philosophy. This was partly due to my having read Rousseau's *Du Contrat Social* and been captivated by its combination of passion with what I then mistook for rigour; partly because I had already discovered in myself some capacity for argument and for detecting the flaws, confusions, and inconsistencies in the discourse of others; and partly to reading some popular books on philosophy (notably by the not contemptible C. E. M. Joad) and being taken with the irresistible fascination of the questions, problems, and theories there recorded. It was not that my love of literature had in any way diminished. On the contrary. I had read much, including modern, poetry (particularly T. S. Eliot); and I thought and continue to think of great poetry as the greatest of human achievements. I had contributed poems myself to issues of an anthology of schoolboy verse, called *The Threshold*, published in the 1930s. I am, or was, a competent versifier, and if I had been able to choose my talents, I would have chosen to be a poet. But of course I could not, and am not. So it was rather the assurance, perhaps mistaken, that my enjoyment and appreciation of good writing would not be enhanced—might even be injured—by making a profession or a career of it.

After one preliminary term of eight weeks at Oxford, concluding with a simple examination, for which I read with enjoyment some Tacitus and Pliny, Tocqueville and Corneille, the serious work of the PPE school began. Economics, I found, interested me hardly at all, the historical part of politics much more; philosophy I found congenial and absorbing from the start. Besides the required subjects of moral and 'general' philosophy I chose the only two options then allowed to PPE students specializing in philosophy, *viz.* Logic (broadly understood to include what would now be called Philosophy of Language, and some metaphysical and epistemological questions) and the philosophy of Kant (*The Critique of Pure Reason* and the *Grundlegung*). My principal philosophy tutor throughout was J. D. Mabbott, a very reasonable, courteous, and helpful teacher, whose main interest was in moral and political philosophy and who subsequently became an excellent head of the college. But I also enjoyed one term's tuition by H. P. Grice, the other philosophy tutor at St. John's and one of the cleverest and most ingenious thinkers of our time. Tutorials with him regularly extended long beyond the customary hour, and from him I learned more of the difficulty and possibilities of philosophical argument than from anyone else. His resourcefulness seemed inexhaustible.

By the end of my three undergraduate years in Oxford I knew that, of all the world's possible occupations, the one I most desired was that of a Fellow and Tutor in Philosophy in a college of that University. But the result of my final examination, though it did not greatly surprise me, was a disappointment both to myself and my tutors; so I had no very high hopes of achieving such an ambition. In any case, by then, we were in the summer of 1940. The war was going badly. I was duly called up into the army (the Royal Artillery), and I was sent for basic training to a territorial searchlight battery in Sussex, where, in between learning to drill and to shoot I had an excellent view of the aerial Battle of Britain during the day, and, at night, of the red glow of the Northern sky where London was undergoing bombardment by the Luftwaffe. Fairly soon I was selected for instruction in the mysteries of radar and attended a number of courses, in London and elsewhere, at which I learned a great deal, now forgotten, about electronics. Having no difficulty with examinations in this subject, I was, to the reasonable surprise of senior NCOs, fairly rapidly promoted through the ranks, briefly commanded a small radar station near the Sussex shore, and in 1942 was commissioned in the newly formed corps of the Royal Electrical and Mechanical Engineers.

I eventually attained the rank of captain; but my military career was in no way distinguished. The only part of it in which I took much satisfaction was that of discharging the duty of defending officer at the courts martial of putatively delinquent soldiers, where, though I only once secured an acquittal (of a senior NCO charged with a serious offence of disobedience to orders) I flatter myself I may often have reduced the severity of sentences by the persuasive power of my 'pleas in mitigation'. In 1945, before being posted abroad to the occupying army in Italy, and then Austria, I had the great good fortune of persuading Grace Hall Martin, my girlfriend of some years' standing—whom I had renamed 'Ann'—to marry me: probably the most judicious action of my life.

In the summer of 1946, having unhesitatingly declined the bait of further promotion, I was demobilized. I had served for six years, thinking a little, but not much, about philosophy and devoting most of such private leisure as I had enjoyed to reading the greater French and English novelists. My ambitions, however, for a career as an academic philosopher had not changed. I contemplated returning to Oxford to read for a further degree (a B.Phil. in philosophy); but there were difficulties in the way of that; and my future was in effect decided by the intervention of my former tutor, John Mabbott—in this my guardian angel—who suggested that I apply for the post of Assistant Lecturer in Philosophy at the University College of N. Wales, Bangor, where he himself had taught for a short time before becoming a Fellow of St. John's. It was no doubt largely due to his support that, when I did apply, I was elected on interview. So I set myself to some hard reading in subjects on which I was to lecture—particularly philosophy of logic (for which I read Russell, Moore, Ramsey, C. I. Lewis, and an introductory book by Susan Stebbing) and Kant's moral philosophy. In the course of my year at Bangor I also lectured on the philosophy of Leibniz (studied mainly in the Gerhardt edition) and on ethics in general; and wrote two papers, one an attempt to solve the problem of the 'paradoxes of entailment', the other an attack on ethical intuitionism. The first I submitted to *Mind*, where it appeared, as 'Necessary Propositions and Entailment Statements', my first published article, in 1948. Though it contained the germ of a fruitful idea, it also contained a serious mistake and so failed in its declared aim. The second was much too long and too involved, therefore tedious; so I later recast it in the crisper, dialogue form in which it appeared as 'Ethical Intuitionism' in *Philosophy* 1949 (pp. 1-12 above).

During the same academic year I visited Oxford, where Ann and I shared a flat—she having entered St. Anne's College to read English as an undergraduate—to take the competitive examination for the John Locke Scholarship, as it was then called. My success in winning this had two beneficial results: first, the prize of £80, then worth many times its present value, was extremely welcome to an impoverished couple; second, my papers sufficiently impressed Gilbert Ryle, one of the examiners, for him to recommend me to University College, then in need of a second teacher of philosophy. So, in 1947, I returned to Oxford as, in effect, a philosophy tutor, though bearing the inappropriate title of 'College Lecturer' until, in the following year, I was elected a Fellow. Ann and I were then fortunate enough to be able to leave our North Oxford flat and take up residence in an apartment in the College itself, where we lived until we moved, in 1950, on the birth of our first child, to an elegant College house of the 1840s.

Having thus achieved, at the age of 28, my pre-war ambition, I set seriously to work at the two tasks of tutorial teaching and of thinking my own thoughts. They are not unconnected tasks, for the first is of immense benefit to the second, as the second is to the first. Indeed I think there is no better or more mutually profitable method of philosophical instruction than the one-to-one tutorial exchange. The pupil, who brings and reads to his tutor a weekly essay, prepared on the basis of recommended reading, gains from the attention and criticism of his more experienced listener. The tutor, striving to understand and clarify his pupil's thoughts, will frequently succeed in clarifying his own. This admirable system, like many good things, is under threat.

My colleague, George Paul, and I divided the tutorial teaching between us in a way satisfactory to both. He undertook the teaching of moral and political and ancient philosophy (Plato and Aristotle), while logic and general modern philosophy from Descartes onwards fell to me. The questions which at the time most seriously engaged my attention were questions in the philosophy of logic and the philosophy of language. While still at Bangor, lecturing on these matters, I had become deeply concerned with the matter of singular reference and predication, and their objects—a topic which has remained central in my thought throughout my working life. Now in Oxford I proceeded, beginning in 1948, to supplement my college teaching with a series of University lectures under the title 'Names and Descriptions', in which I referred to and criticized the work of Russell, Moore, Kneale, and some few others. From these I extracted two lectures, given to an American Summer School, in which I concentrated on my critique of Russell's Theory of Descriptions; and the report of these induced Gilbert Ryle, then editor of *Mind*, to say, bluntly, that he wanted them as an article for that journal. Hence 'On Referring' (*Mind*, 1950), which remains, probably, the best known of my writings.

Russell's theory, elegant and ingenious as it is—a 'paradigm of philosophy' according to F. P. Ramsey—seemed to me then, and still does, to misrepresent the true character and function of singular definite descriptive phrases, as, for the most part, we actually use and understand them. It does so by overlooking or neglecting the pragmatic, contextual, and communicative aspects of their use. To the objection that this is to introduce merely pragmatic considerations into what is essentially a semantic question, the answer must be that no serious semantic theory can afford to ignore the points—and their consequences—to which I drew attention. I think my view, with variations, is now generally accepted by linguists, though the issue remains, to some extent, controversial among philosophers. I should add that I had not at the time read Frege and was, regrettably enough, completely ignorant of the work of that great figure; so subsequent references to the 'Frege–Strawson' view of the matter I found, at first, surprising, though in no way disturbing.

I had, after all, jumped straight, with six years military service intervening, from undergraduate to university teacher; so serious gaps in my knowledge were perhaps pardonable. My major influences remained Russell and Moore, whom I viewed, and still view, as the founding fathers of contemporary analytical philosophy. Other influences, of course, were soon to be added: locally Ryle, whose verve and brilliance might excuse, if they sometimes masked, a certain lack of rigour in thought, and Austin, consistently clear, precise, witty, and formidable; more remotely, Wittgenstein, whose Blue and Brown Books began to circulate in pirated copies at the beginning of the 1950s, at once breathtakingly impressive and profoundly enigmatic; and Frege himself, whose articles on Sense and Reference and Concept and Object were made available in English translation by Geach and Black in 1952. Nor should I fail to mention A. J. Ayer, whose *Language, Truth and Logic* I had read, enthralled, in the gardens of St. John's as an undergraduate—even though, by now, I no longer found satisfying his undiluted classical empiricism.

Austin did me the honour of proposing that I should reply to his paper on Truth at the Joint Session of the Mind and Aristotelian Society in 1950. I was already convinced that Ramsey had got the matter essentially right a long time ago, and hence thought that Austin had got it essentially wrong. Though I tried to convey as much in my reply, I also spoiled the effect, and diverted general attention, with a gratuitous flourish of my own, which was itself due in part to Austin's own observation of the 'performatory' function of speech. That little flourish had itself formed the substance of a short article in *Analysis* the year before (apropos of which I remember fatuously announcing to George Paul that I had a new theory of truth; to which he sensibly and characteristically replied: 'Come on now, which of the old ones is it?'). The issue, of course, persists; and, much later, I was able to make my considered position clear and to finalize my critique of Austin in the two articles 'A Problem about Truth: A Reply to Mr. Warnock' (1964) and 'Truth: A Reconsideration of Austin's Views' (1965), both of which were reprinted in *Logico-Linguistic Papers* (1971).

Meanwhile, I had been invited to give regular introductory lectures on logic in the University for the benefit of undergraduates studying for the Preliminary Examination in PPE. This I did, and as a result was further invited by a publisher, again, I think, at Ryle's prompting, to write a book on the subject. It duly appeared as *Introduction to Logical Theory* in 1952 and received the accolade of a lengthy review in *Mind* by Quine, in which he deplored my use of the notion of analyticity but pleased me by his slightly ironical reference to my 'lucid vernacular'. My double concern in the book was to explain the nature of standard elementary logic while at the same time emphasizing the point that, perspicuous, powerful, and elegant as it is, modern formal logic is not an adequate instrument for revealing clearly all the structural features of language as we use it. Rather, it is an idealized abstraction of great power and beauty, an indispensable tool indeed for clarifying much of our thought, but not, as some are tempted to suppose, the unique and sufficient key to the functioning of language and thought in general.

The early 1950s in general were a busy and productive time. For a few years in the first half of the decade Grice and I together held a graduate seminar at which we took it in turn to read papers, some of them (e.g. that which surfaced later as 'In Defence of a Dogma', 1954—see pp. 13-29 above actually produced in collaboration. Among those at different times attending the seminar were a number of senior members, including, on his first visit to Oxford, Quine. At about this time I was charged by Ryle with the task of reviewing Wittgenstein's *Philosophical Investigations* for *Mind*, a task to which I devoted a considerable amount of time and effort, with results (1954) which, though they recorded my sense of the work's genius, also recorded some perplexity, even dissatisfaction, and was accordingly not received with entire approval by the committed disciples. It might not be quite coincidental that Norman Malcolm, as an epigraph to his own review, quoted Lichtenberg: 'Ein Buch ist ein Spiegel. Wenn ein Affe hineinguckt, dann kann freilich kein Apostel heraussehen.'

The birth of my daughter, Julia, in 1950 was followed by the birth of my two sons, Galen (named after his uncle who was named after his) in 1952, and Robert in 1954. Soon after the publication of *Logical Theory* I ceased to give the introductory lectures on formal logic and began instead to think and lecture on the lines which led, ultimately, to *Individuals*. This was a natural development from my already established concern with the operation, fundamental in thought and speech, of reference and predication; an operation fundamental also, as many, from Aristotle to Quine, have thought and stressed, in ontology or metaphysics. So it was natural to address the question of what the most basic or primitive or fundamental objects of reference, or subjects of predication, are. In the first part of *Individuals* I argued that they are—and necessarily are—relatively enduring space-occupying individuals, falling under substance-concepts. Here was an at least partial echo of Aristotle. In the same part I speculated on the theoretical possibility of reproducing the essential structure of our scheme with a greatly attenuated ontology (sounds); sought, perhaps by then unnecessarily, to deliver a *coup de grâce* to Cartesianism and to dispose of the pseudo-problem of other minds; and concluded by examining the brilliantly conceived and finally impossible Leibnizian ontology of monads.

All of this and more I made the topic of one of the seminars I conducted at Duke University, North Carolina, throughout the Fall semester of 1955. This was my first visit to the United States. The other seminar I conducted there was devoted to a series of papers in the philosophy of logic and language: on such topics as reference again, propositions, the constants of logic and their analogues in natural language, necessity, etc. While at Duke, I had the opportunity of visiting and reading papers at a number of other American Universities, on the West and East Coasts and in between. The visit which stays most vividly in my mind, and that for a bizarre reason, is the one I paid to Seattle, Washington State. The paper I read there contained the substance of what became the chapter on Persons in *Individuals*; and one member of my audience stood throughout, with his back turned to me, evidently more willing to hear what I had to say than to contemplate the sight of me saying it.

Another event which occurred, I think, earlier in the 1950s,[1] was an assembly of French and Anglophone philosophers at one of the Colloques

---

[1] Editor's Note: In fact this took place in 1958. See p. 78 above, n. 1.

de Royaumont, which was designed to bring about a meeting of minds between representatives of the continental and analytical traditions. Whether this desirable result was actually achieved remains uncertain. But Austin at least made an impression with his paper, delivered in French, on 'Performatifs'. In a paper entitled 'Analysis, Science and Metaphysics' (pp. 78–90 above) I gave an account of the relations between these three, as I then conceived of them; and this, later published in French in *La Philosophie Analytique* (Cahiers de Royaumont, 1962), appeared later still in English in *The Linguistic Turn* edited by Rorty in 1967. At about this time I wrote my contribution to the Schilpp volume on Carnap, under the title 'Carnap's Views on Constructed Systems versus Natural Languages in Analytical Philosophy'. Completed to a deadline in 1954, it did not appear until the volume was published, nine years later, in 1963.

Philosophical disagreements with Quine—which have in no way impaired a personal friendship of some forty years' standing—surfaced again in 'Propositions, Concepts and Logical Truth' (1957). The disagreements, both then and later, turn on my more than permissive attitude towards a whole range of intensional notions which Quine is unable to countenance; and of which, I then argued, his own account of truths of logic compelled recognition. My next major undertaking was that of getting my lectures on Individuals into shape as a book. This did not take me very long, since the lectures were already pretty complete; but I did rewrite the first chapter and add an introduction about the general character of the enterprise, in which I introduced the term 'descriptive metaphysics'. In the second part of the lectures and of the book I sought both to explain the basic association of two distinctions—the logical or grammatical distinction between subject and predicate (reference and predication) on the one hand and the ontological distinction between spatio-temporal particular and universal on the other—and at the same time to show that and why this association, though fundamental, is not exclusive. Particulars indeed can never be predicated, but universals, and abstract and intensional objects generally, can certainly be objects of reference or subjects of predication; and given the acknowledged connection between being an object of reference and being an entity, we should abandon, if we suffer from them, any natural but ill-founded nominalistic anxieties and recognize such objects in our ontology.

Individuals was published in 1959, and in the same year A. J. Ayer was elected to the Wykeham Chair of Logic, for which I too, encouraged by colleagues, had applied. The result of the election, so far from being a disappointment to me, was a profound relief. I did not yet feel ready for an Oxford Chair, and was perfectly satisfied to continue with undergraduate tutorial teaching. The weekly discussion group for selected dons which Ayer established replaced, in a totally different but equally stimulating style, the Saturday morning meetings over which Austin, before his untimely and much lamented death, had so brilliantly presided. With Austin, proceedings were informal and no standard philosophical issues were tackled head-on; instead, particular specific concepts or concept-groups (words or word-groups), and the conditions of their use, were examined in detail, with results that were always fascinating, and often philosophically suggestive or illuminating. With Ayer, a different member of the group each week would read a paper on a philosophical topic of his choice; then drinks would be served by the host for the term and discussion, usually spirited, never acrimonious, would begin. 'Freddie's group', as it was and is called, survived and survives the death of its founder.

1960 was a full year. I was elected to the British Academy and delivered there a lecture, 'Freedom and Resentment', which is one of my very few ventures into moral philosophy. Another such venture, written about the same time, and published in 1961 (the year of the birth of my younger daughter, Virginia), I entitled 'Social Morality and Individual Ideal'. Between them, these two papers effectively embody all I have thought or have to say in a philosophical area which, important as I recognize it to be, I have never found as intellectually gripping as those to which I have given more attention. The 1961 paper I had previously given as a public lecture in Princeton University, where I had been invited for the Fall semester of 1960. There I conducted a seminar attended by some extremely able graduates and, from time to time, by such teachers as Hempel, Benacerraf, and Vlastos. My subjects were, again, generally in the region of philosophy of logic and language, e.g. singular reference and predication, logical constants and logical form. Colleagues and students were friendly and the standard of discussion was high. While at Princeton I again visited and read papers at a number of other universities.

1960 also saw the publication, in the *Times Literary Supplement*, of a series of articles under the general heading, 'The British Imagination'. I contributed the article on philosophy (pp. 71–7). It was given the title, 'The Post-Linguistic Thaw'—a title not chosen by me and which I deplored. The title was not without point in that, as I indicated in the article, concentration on the actual use of words in ordinary linguistic practice—a philosophical method largely inspired by Austin and cultivated by at least a substantial minority of British, and especially Oxford, philosophers in the post-war period—was already, before 1960, beginning to loosen its grip in favour of more systematic and 'theoretical' approaches. Yet the title metaphor was objectionable in its suggestion of emergence from a period of frozen sterility; whereas in fact the gains and advances in philosophical understanding made in that period were probably as great as any that have been made in a comparably short time in the history of the subject; and the intellectual pleasure and excitement of living through it were correspondingly intense.

In the immediately succeeding years, besides lecturing and writing papers in the philosophy of language—on truth, reference, speech-acts, etc.—I began to lecture on Kant's *Critique of Pure Reason*, a book on which I had regularly tutored those undergraduates, or supervised those graduates, who had chosen to study it, finding it, as most of them did, both baffling and profound. There was a link here, too, with *Individuals*. In that book I had found myself frequently enquiring into the conditions that make possible certain kinds of knowledge and experience that we in fact have, or certain kinds of distinction that we in fact draw; and Kant, in the *Critique*, addresses this kind of question in its most general form, investigating the conditions of the possibility of experience, or empirical knowledge, in general. My lectures on the *Critique*, given in alternate years from 1959 and modified or added to from year to year, finally formed the basis of my book, *The Bounds of Sense*, published in 1966. My endeavour, in that work, was to separate Kant's brilliant and profound account of the structure of necessarily interconnected ideas and concepts which form the limiting framework of all human thought about the world and experience of the world from the overarching theory which he saw as the explanation of the possibility of any such account; and at the same time to explain that explanation and to show why it should be rejected. But I am aware that the last word on what remains the greatest single work of modern Western philosophy has not yet been, and probably never will be, spoken.

This publication naturally did not end my concern with Kant. On the first *Critique*, over the next twenty years, I regularly conducted a graduate seminar which never failed to attract graduate students, many of whom made excellent contributions to it. In an article, 'Imagination and Perception', first published in 1970 and subsequently reprinted, I made some amends for my cavalier treatment of the notion of synthesis in *The Bounds of Sense*. In 1987 I contributed papers to conferences in both Stanford and Stuttgart ('Sensibility, Understanding and the Doctrine of Synthesis' at the former (pp. 157–65 above), 'Kant's New Foundations of Metaphysics' at the latter), the proceedings of which were subsequently published. In 1987 again I contributed a paper on Kant's Paralogisms to a volume in honour of Dieter Henrich on his sixtieth birthday. In 1992 I gave a talk on 'The Problem of Realism and the A Priori in Kant' at a conference in Florence on Kant and Modern Epistemology. More recently I paid tribute to his insight into the nature of aesthetic judgement (in the *European Journal of Philosophy*, 1993).

In 1968 I succeeded Ryle in the Waynflete Chair of Metaphysical Philosophy at Oxford. Before taking up my duties in October of that year I worked hard at preparing a set of introductory lectures on philosophy. My aims were, first, to explain the general nature of the discipline as I conceived and tried to practise it; then to demonstrate the interdependence of ontology, epistemology, and logic; and finally to show how certain central philosophical issues should, in my view, be resolved. I was incidentally concerned both to lay classical empiricism to rest and, in rejecting at least one favoured conception of analysis, to resist the reductive tendency in philosophy in general. I gave the same series of lectures, under the title, 'Analysis and Metaphysics: An Introduction to Philosophy', in almost every succeeding year until my retirement in 1987, keeping the earlier and more general parts substantially unchanged, while varying the choice of particular issues to be treated in more detail in the later parts.

The initial investment of effort in the preparation of these lectures has served me well. Much of a late version I translated into French and delivered as a course at the Collège de France in the spring of 1985; I delivered substantially the same lectures in English, with some variations, as the Immanuel Kant lectures in Munich in the summer of that year; in the Catholic University of America in Washington in September 1987; and as my contribution to the Sino-British Summer School in Philosophy in Beijing in 1988. The French version was published in Paris in 1985 as *Analyse et Métaphysique* and the final English version in Oxford in 1992.

It is customary, though not obligatory, for one newly elected to an Oxford Chair to give an Inaugural Lecture. I was glad of the opportunity to pay tribute to my predecessor, Gilbert Ryle, who, by reason of his energy, his authority, and his vision—besides the brilliance and inventiveness displayed in his own philosophical writing—contributed perhaps more than any other single person to the flowering of the subject in England in the years after the war. I was glad, too, to return in the lecture, 'Meaning and Truth', to my abiding concern with language as an instrument of human communication. Although, in this lecture, I too blithely acquiesced, as John McDowell subsequently pointed out (1980),[2] in an approach suggested by Grice's well-known article on Meaning of 1957, nevertheless the centrality of the notion of fully overt communication-intention to any general understanding of the notion of linguistic meaning remains indisputable. Hence the failure of all inevitably self-frustrating attempts to expel all considerations dismissed as merely 'pragmatic' from the sacred area of semantic theory.

Philosophy of language was indeed a dominant, though not an exclusive, concern in the papers written about this time and in the next few years. Reading Chomsky's *Aspects of the Theory of Syntax* (and attending the John Locke lectures which he gave in the late 1960s) had led me to write 'Grammar and Philosophy', which I gave as the Presidential address to the Aristotelian Society in 1969, and in which I argued that no general explanatory theory of grammar was possible which did not intimately link semantic considerations to syntactic classifications and relations. At the conclusion of this essay I looked forward to the notion of a 'perspicuous grammar' which I developed, though only in a limited fashion, in my next book, *Subject and Predicate in Logic and Grammar* (1974). Though representing a new departure for me insofar as it was explicitly concerned, in its second part, with the theory of grammar, the book also showed its continuity with earlier work in that I began from the basic case of definite singular reference and predication and then proceeded, on this basis, to offer an explanatory account of the grammatical notions of subject and predicate in general. So a central theme of *Individuals*, further developed and exploited in 'The Asymmetry of Subjects and Predicates' (1970), lay at its foundation.

Asked to contribute to a volume of essays on the work of Gilbert Ryle, I chose as my topic the notions of category and category-mistake, which Ryle had frequently invoked and which had long interested me. I showed that the theoretical accounts he had earlier given of these ideas (and later

---

[2] John McDowell, 'Meaning, Communication, and Knowledge', in *Philosophical Subjects*, edited by Z. van Straaten (Oxford: Clarendon Press, 1980).

viewed with distrust) were in fact indefensible and offered a less striking but, as it seemed to me, more plausible alternative ('Categories', 1970). I wrote other articles in a similarly critical vein: thus I argued that Austin, in *How to Do Things with Words*, had failed to give a consistent account of what he called the 'locutionary' aspect of speech-acts (1973); anticipated my later contention that the Tarskian truth-theoretical model favoured by Davidson as a means of elucidating the semantically significant structural features of natural language was not adequate to the task (1974); and argued that the positions available for non-substitutional quantification were more than Quine allowed for, in that they included predicate-position ('Positions for Quantifiers', 1974). I later came to think that I had not fully understood at the time the full implications of this last article; and that a fully developed view would in fact bring me in one respect closer to Quine (all such positions being indeed referential), while in another leaving me equally remote from him (since properties and other intensional entities could properly occupy those positions). This development emerges implicitly in my 'Concept and Property or Predication and Copulation' (1987); but the most general defence of intensional or abstract entities is to be found in my 'Entity and Identity' (1976), 'Universals' (1979), and 'Two Conceptions of Philosophy' in *Perspectives on Quine* (1990, pp. 166-77 above).

In the winter of 1975–6 I made my first visit to India, where I already had friends, including Ramchandra Gandhi, who had written an admirably lucid doctoral thesis under my supervision in Oxford, and Roop Rekha Verma, who had spent a year in Oxford under the auspices of the British Council. While there, I lectured, read papers, and took part in discussions in Delhi, Lucknow, Santiniketan, and Calcutta. In general I was enchanted by this great and various country, by the beauty to be found there, and by the warmth and vivacity of my hosts; and was delighted to repeat my visit, this time accompanied by Ann, in 1979–80.

Issues in the philosophy of language and ontology were not the only ones that occupied me in the 1970s. At a conference in Valencia, Spain, in the spring of 1973, I criticized foundationalist theories of knowledge ('Does Knowledge Have Foundations?', 1974, pp. 100-8 above); at the Joint Session of the Mind and Aristotelian Societies in 1975 I differed sharply from the anti-realist views previously expounded by Dummett and there defended by Wright ('Scruton and Wright on Anti-Realism', 1976, pp. 118-24 above); for volumes in honour of Charles Baylis and Ayer I wrote two papers on the ever-challenging topic of perception ('Causation in Perception', 1975, and 'Perception and its Objects', 1979, pp. 125-145 above); at a high-powered conference held in Jerusalem in 1976 I delivered a paper on the concept of possibility, concentrating on its epistemic use, so frequently overlooked in discussions of modality in general ('May Bes and Might Have Beens', 1979); and on a second visit to Israel in 1977, at a conference commemorating the tercentenary of the death of Spinoza, I spoke on Liberty and Necessity (pp. 146-56 above), complementing the views I had advocated in 'Freedom and Resentment' by adding what I took to be a decisive demonstration that the thesis of determinism, in any form in which it was defensible, had no bearing on the issues of moral judgement and moral responsibility.

In 1977 I received the honour of knighthood; immediately after the investiture in December I departed for Yugoslavia, where I gave lectures in Belgrade, Sarajevo, and Zagreb. I registered a certain difference in atmosphere in the three places. At least in academic circles the intellectual style seemed relatively untrammelled in Belgrade and Zagreb, though the political tone was different. In Sarajevo, where I was only allowed to give one of my two scheduled lectures and had minimal contact with fellow academics, one perhaps time-serving young man in my audience suggested that my lecture revealed an essentially bourgeois outlook. I replied, 'But I *am* bourgeois—an elitist liberal bourgeois'. My interpreter commented, *sotto voce*, 'They envy you'.

In the early 1980s there appeared two collections of critical essays about my work, both of which elicited, and contained, replies by me. One was the book, *Philosophical Subjects* (Oxford, 1980), the other a special number of the Israeli journal, *Philosophia* (1981). Three articles in the first I must particularly mention: the one by John McDowell already referred to; an excellent piece by Gareth Evans, a Fellow of University College and formerly the brightest pupil I ever had there, whose early death can never be too greatly lamented; and that of Hidé Ishiguro, one of the most sensitive and discerning of philosophers. The topics discussed in these collections were as various as those I had myself previously written on. Later in the decade I published two more papers on singular reference, one a contribution to the Library of Living Philosophers volume devoted to the work of Quine ('Reference and its Roots', 1986), the other as summary a statement as I could make of my current views on the question ('Direct Singular Reference: Intended Reference and Actual Reference', 1986). The latter I had already delivered as my contribution to a round table on the subject, at which Quine and Kripke also spoke, at the World Congress in Montreal in 1983. In 1982 I also published two papers, written long before, but hitherto used only in lectures or seminars, one on logical constants, the other on conditionals. The latter ('If and ⊃') had been written many years earlier as a riposte to Grice's ingenious and long unpublished attempt to demonstrate that the meaning of the ordinary conditional was in fact identical to that of the material conditional of standard logic—an application or anticipation of his later elaborated theory of conversational implicature, which, profound and fruitful as it is, is also capable, like most good ideas, of misapplication such as it suffered, I argued, in this case. The other article ('Logical Form and Logical Constants'), which aimed to give a general characterization of the constants of standard logic, I submitted as my contribution to a collection of essays, *Logical Form, Predication and Ontology*, published in India and edited by Pranab Kumar Sen, Professor of Philosophy at Jadavpur University, Calcutta, a leading Indian philosopher and my very good friend.

In the same decade, besides the travels, already mentioned, to France, Germany, Canada, the USA, and China, I made a second visit to Spain, two more to America, spoke for the first time in Switzerland and went for the third time to India. At Valencia, in Spain, I repeated the arguments which formed the substance of the Woodbridge Lectures I gave at Columbia University in 1983 and of the book based on them which was published in 1985 as *Skepticism and Naturalism: Some Varieties*. In that book I had two different, though not unrelated aims. The first chapter was concerned with traditional philosophical scepticisms about, e.g., the external world and induction. In common with Hume and Wittgenstein (and even Heidegger) I argued that the attempt to combat such doubts by rational argument was misguided: for we are dealing here with the presuppositions, the framework, of all human thought and enquiry. In the other chapters my target was different. It was that species of naturalism which tended to discredit, or somehow to reduce to more scientifically acceptable, physicalistic terms, whole regions of ordinary human thought, language, and experience—in particular the regions of moral discourse, of the subjectively mental, and of the intensional. Here my reaction, as well as my target, was different. I did not merely stress the inescapability of the natural or common human standpoint from which we normally take for granted all that is called in question by scientistic naturalism. I also allowed the latter its own validity from its own limited standpoint. Each standpoint could be called a form of naturalism—one with a pronounced bias towards natural science, the other of a more humanistic or, as I called it, 'liberal' variety. But to those—not few—in whom the drive for completely unified philosophical explanation is strong this tolerance may well seem unacceptable.

While in America for the Quine conference at St. Louis (1988) I also read papers elsewhere: at Vassar I distinguished and elaborated different senses or applications of the phrase 'the meaning of what was said'; at Columbia I repeated my views on 'Kant's New Foundations of Metaphysics,' and also critically discussed that philosopher's treatment of the concept of substance; and did the same at Bloomington, Indiana, where I had the pleasure of renewing ties with old friends from Duke, more than thirty years before.

My third visit to India, in the winter of 1987–8, was occasioned by a conference on my work organized at Lucknow by the Indian Council of Philosophical Research. I prepared a paper on my own philosophical development, and there were several seminar meetings at which pertinent points were made. I also gave talks at Calcutta, Delhi, and Hyderabad. Privileged, in the company of Ann and an Indian philosopher from Delhi, to visit many of the great Indian sites in North, South, and Central India which I had not seen before, I was again struck by the inexhaustible variety and great cultural and artistic wealth of the country.

In the autumn of 1987 I retired, under the age limit, from my Chair at Magdalen; but because of the generosity of a former pupil at University College and of the College itself, I have a room there in which I can, and do, continue to work. As already indicated, retirement by no means brought an end to academic travel or to philosophical discussion and composition. My most protracted visit was to the University of Colorado at Boulder in the Fall semester of 1991. There I lectured twice a week to an undergraduate class and conducted a weekly graduate seminar. For the undergraduate class I drew partly on my Oxford lectures, which had already served me well elsewhere, and partly improvised on the basis of other papers of mine. For the first time in my life I had the invaluable help of a 'teaching assistant'—a highly intelligent graduate student who relieved me of much of the burden of grading papers and stood in for me when I was reading papers at other universities, as I did in Seattle, at Yale, and in two states, Wyoming and Wisconsin, which I had never visited before. This was my first experience of undergraduate teaching in the United States, having previously, on semester-long visits, been in contact only with graduate students and faculty members. I found the informality of the proceedings and the enquiring receptiveness of my audience most refreshing, though I was also struck by the surprising difference in level of literary and philosophical sophistication between the undergraduate and graduate students. At the graduate seminar I generally announced in advance which paper of my own was to form the topic of discussion at the next meeting, and then introduced the subject briefly myself; but on the last occasion I read a new paper, entitled 'Individuals', in which I attempted a synthesis of all the matters in the book of that name and subsequent writings, giving special prominence to the union of logic, epistemology, and ontology and to that realist view of universals and of abstract objects in general which I am ready to call a demythologized Platonism. My most abiding memory of Boulder, however, is of the perfection of the climate, the beauty of the mountains, and the courtesy and kindness of the inhabitants.

My most recent journeys, in 1992, were to the Kant conference in Florence in April and, in November, to Kingston, Ontario, where the Queen's University, in celebration of its sesquicentenary, had organized a series of philosophical lectures. My own was entitled 'Philosophy: A Personal View' and substantially followed the line traced in the account of my philosophical development which I had prepared for the 1987 Indian conference on my work. In the course of my career, academic occasions have taken me to all the world's continents except Australasia, to most of the countries of Western Europe, to about half the States of the Union, to Argentina, and to Mexico. These extensive travels, as others of my profession will agree, are among the uncovenanted benefits of an abiding passion for philosophy.

It remains to say something about my methods of work, the influences I am most aware of, my relations with other philosophers and, perhaps, my general conception of philosophy. I certainly did not initially approach the subject with any large general plan of campaign; and I have never achieved, or aimed at, any such comprehensive, integrated system as the great metaphysicians, e.g. Kant and Spinoza, have constructed. Rather I have been moved—often, as Moore reported, provoked by philosophical views that have struck me as preposterous or obviously false or one-sided—by the wish to understand better some particular concept or range of concepts, or the views of some particular philosophers; or by the rare exciting occurrence of one of those moments of what at least at the time seems like a blinding flash of insight into connections of which one had been previously but imperfectly, if at all, aware. Such moments as these are not altogether pleasant: mingled with exhilaration is a slightly disagreeable, even physical, sense of agitation or discomfort, only to be alleviated as the exhilaration also subsides into a cooler and more laborious consideration of how it is to be controlled and the truth, if there is one, conveyed. Such experiences are infrequent indeed. More often, it is a matter of arriving, without excessive excitement, at a reasonably clear idea of the general line one intends to follow and the setting about the task of organizing it, and working out the detail, in readily comprehensible and tolerably harmonious prose. Excitement or not, the working out sometimes requires a good deal of hard and continuous thinking, which can keep one awake for hours. But this too I have found to be infrequent. Usually, when the general line is reasonably clear, the writing, though it calls for care, follows without much strain or is even attended with pleasure.

I have, of course, found philosophical discussion with others, in small groups, enjoyable and stimulating, even sometimes amusing. But except for a brief period in the early 1950s, when Grice and I collaborated in a seminar, I have found it best, indeed necessary, to think and work independently. In this, as in other ways, philosophy differs from natural science, where teamwork is apparently a quite regular thing. Austin, it is true, was attracted by this model, by the *idea* of cooperative endeavour; but what he actually *did* was as essentially individual as Ryle rightly held that all fruitful philosophical enterprise must be. Why this is so I tried to explain in a few lines in the preface to *Skepticism and Naturalism*. What, perhaps surprisingly, I have in the past found most helpful in the way of discussion is the one-to-one tutorial exchange with undergraduates—when one finds oneself obliged to clarify one's own half-formed thoughts in order to make things clear to one's pupil. Seeking a way past, or through, his or her mistakes and confusions, one may find a path past, or through, one's own.

Many philosophers in the past—among them some of the greatest—have seen themselves as starting afresh, as setting out on a new path which they conceive to be the only sure one; and thus as freeing themselves, and us, from fundamental mistakes or misconceptions which have hitherto impeded the discovery of the true way. It is unlikely that any of us, in the second half of the twentieth century, will be buoyed up by any such glad, confident assurance—or, if you prefer, will be the victim of any such vainglorious delusion. Philosophers today tend to be more soberly and modestly aware of the greatness of the achievements of their illustrious predecessors and of the possibility of learning from them. Yet I think it is evident that there is a notable selectiveness in these appreciative responses. It is in no way surprising that this should be so; that each philosopher should respond most positively to those of his predecessors whose work is most in harmony with his own intellectual bent. And this in its turn will imply a certain further selectiveness within the domain of the favoured predecessor's teaching.

So at least I have found it to be. Thus in the case of Wittgenstein, an acknowledged philosophical genius—perhaps the only one in our century—it must be that I am influenced by, for I profoundly share, the view that our essential, if not our only, business is to get a clear view of our concepts and their place in our lives. Such a clearing of the view, freeing it from the seductive illusions of whose fascination he was himself so vividly aware, Wittgenstein in his later work did more than anyone to promote. Yet, at the same time, the very strength of his resistance to the myths and fictions of theory seemed to me to lead to a certain loss of balance in two ways. First, the most general concepts and categories of the human conceptual scheme do form, in their connections and interdependences, an articulated structure which it is possible to describe without falsification; and this possibility Wittgenstein's distrust of systematic theorizing in general seems to lead him to dismiss. Second, at the root of some of the false pictures which earned his particular animus there sometimes lie harmless, commonplace elements of truth which receive in him too little acknowledgement.

The cases of Aristotle and Kant—the two whom I see, without qualification, as the very greatest of our predecessors—are quite different. Neither shrank from systematic theory. If I found, in Kant in particular, much to discard, I also found much to embrace, as answering, with modification, to my own natural prejudices or half-formed ideas, which is why I am presumptuous enough to enrol them both under the banner of 'descriptive metaphysics'.

Finally, a few personal observations. I have no religious beliefs. When asked whether I believe in God, I am obliged to answer 'No'; I have difficulty with the concept. But I am sometimes tempted to add that I believe in grace—a quality which eludes precise description, but is sometimes manifested in the words and actions of human beings. My political views are centrist: I am conservative in my tastes, liberal in my sentiments (principles?). I am of a conciliatory temper—which sometimes extends, in philosophy, into an attempt to reconcile views which appear to be sharply opposed to each other. I am very little, perhaps too little, prone to anger.

I have sometimes criticized the views of other philosophers, dead or living. Such adverse criticism is a form of compliment. It is only the very best with whom it is worth while to differ. My own philosophical views I am prepared to defend, or modify, when required; but their neglect or rejection leaves me relatively indifferent. I enjoy applause, but have no expectation of, or wish for, disciples.

All in all, I count myself extremely lucky. Above all, I am fortunate in my friends and my family; friends whom I made as an undergraduate and to whom I am still close, and others, of many nationalities, whom I have come to know since; a family of wife and four children, all variously gifted and all, to my mind, invariably charming. Philosophy, friends, and family apart, my life has been enriched by the enjoyment of literature, landscape, architecture, and the company of clever and beautiful women. So far every decade has been better than the one before, though I recognize that, in the nature of things, this cannot continue indefinitely.

22
A Bit of Intellectual Autobiography

Most of what I have to say under the heading of intellectual autobiography has already appeared in the Library of Living Philosophers volume published in 1998.[1] But perhaps I can add something bearing mainly, though not exclusively, on my attitude to the work of Kant.

Instead of coming at this directly, I would like to begin by recalling Kant-related episodes in the lives of two other English philosophers of this century. In a well-known passage in his autobiography[2] R. G. Collingwood relates that at the age of 8 he read Kant's *Groundwork of the Metaphysics of Morals*, presumably in an English translation. He did not, he says, understand it; but he knew at once that *this was for him*; that the climate of this kind of thinking was to be *his* climate, the air of philosophical thought the air *he* must breathe; as he did (though not exclusively, since he was also an eminent historian).

The other episode concerns a younger philosopher; namely, A. J. Ayer. His biographer[3] reports that while sailing to Africa in 1943 to undertake a special-operations exercise Ayer undertook to reread Kant's *Critique of Pure Reason*, and, in the early stages of sunstroke, underwent a remarkable epiphany during which he understood for the first time the full force of Kant's argument. Unfortunately, once he had recovered from his fever he was unable to regain the insight.

---

[1] L. E. Hahn (ed.), *The Library of Living Philosophers*, XXVI, *The Philosophy of P. F. Strawson* (Chicago, IL: Open Court, 1998).

[2] R. G. Collingwood, *An Autobiography* (Oxford: Oxford University Press, 1938).

[3] B. Rogers, *A. J. Ayer* (London: Chatto and Windus, 1999).

Sympathetic though one may find both these Kant-inspired experiences, I cannot myself report any close parallel to either. Nevertheless, Kant, or more exactly Kant's first *Critique*, does have a distinctive place in my own intellectual history, such as it is, in a way I will try to make clear. For some years after my first academic appointment just after the war the questions I was mainly concerned with fell in the general area of philosophy of language and logic: questions about reference, truth, entailment, the constants of formal logic and their natural-language counterparts, analyticity, etc. Wrestling with these problems, one had, of course, to wrestle with the work of those philosophers whose views on the questions concerned were at the time, and sometimes still are, influential or even dominant—most notably Russell, Quine, and Austin. Indeed, it was sometimes precisely the views that one or another of these had expressed that fired my concern with the question. Nevertheless, closely as one might study the relevant passages in the writings of the philosopher concerned, it was precisely and only because of their relevance to the question at issue that those passages demanded and received such close attention. It was not because those passages were, or seemed to be, an integral part of some wider system of thought associated specifically with the name of that philosopher, perhaps because initiated by him.

And this is where the difference with my relation to Kant or, to be more exact, to Kant's *Critique of Pure Reason* comes in. It was that complete work itself, rather than any of the many particular issues with which it deals, that became the focus of my concern. Indeed, it is the only work, and Kant the only author of such a work, of which, and of whom, I can say this. The reasons for it are, of course, largely internal to the work itself; but also, I must confess, partly historical—to do, in fact, with the structure of the PPE school in Oxford before the war. Anyone reading for that school at that time who wanted to specialize in philosophy was offered no *choice* of philosophical special subjects; there were just two on offer, and no more: Logic and Kant, the latter to be studied in just two works, the first *Critique* and the *Groundwork*. The *Groundwork*, though like Collingwood I found it deeply impressive, conceived its subject, as I thought then and still think, altogether too narrowly, whereas in the *Critique of Pure Reason* I found a depth, a range, a boldness, and a power unlike anything I had previously encountered. So I struggled with parts of it as an undergraduate, and later as a college tutor teaching those few pupils intrepid enough to take it on, until finally, having been subtly and in part consciously influenced by it in my own independent thinking about metaphysics and epistemology (in *Individuals*[4]), I decided I must try to get to grips with the work as a whole. So I began to give a regular series of lectures on it, a series that ultimately issued in the publication of *The Bounds of Sense*.[5]

In that book I tried to preserve and present systematically what I took to be the major insights of Kant's work, while detaching them from those parts of the total doctrine that, if they had any substantial import at all, I took to be at best false, at worst mysterious to the point of being barely comprehensible. My book was, you might say, a somewhat ahistorical attempt to recruit Kant to the ranks of the analytical metaphysicians, while discarding those metaphysical elements that refused any such absorption. My position on all this I have subsequently sought to elaborate or clarify a little, particularly in the first two of the four Kantian studies included at the end of the collection *Entity and Identity*.[6] Of course I am not foolish enough to suppose that I have got all or any of these things quite right; and I am sure that there are plenty of philosophers willing to show me where I have gone wrong. But I can take some comfort in the thought that, when I have erred, I have done so in the company of most, if not all, of those who have been brave enough to undertake the interpretation and criticism of Kant's critical philosophy.

I shall not here and now undertake anything by way of further elaboration, modification, or defence of the views advanced in my book or the subsequent articles. Instead I should like to consider briefly a recent and, I think, novel attempt to elucidate and defend a central Kantian thesis: the thesis, namely, that we are and must remain ignorant of the nature of things as they are in themselves. I refer to a book published in 1997 by Rae Langton, which is called *Kantian Humility*[7] and which is certainly a most interesting, impressive, and scholarly exercise in Kantian interpretation. Early on in the work she refers, effectively by way of comparison and contrast with her own, to another philosopher's solution of the problem posed by the Kantian doctrine of our necessary ignorance of things as they are in themselves. The view in question is Professor Allison's, and, as she rightly remarks, his solution is both elegant and ingenious. It also has what

---

[4] P. F. Strawson, *Individuals* (London: Methuen, 1959).
[5] P. F. Strawson, *The Bounds of Sense* (London: Methuen, 1966).
[6] P. F. Strawson, *Entity and Identity* (Oxford: Oxford University Press, 1997).
[7] R. Langton, *Kantian Humility* (Oxford: Oxford University Press, 1997).

in her view are distinctive merits. It preserves the objective reality of the natural world as studied by the physical sciences; and it disposes completely of the picture of two distinct realms of being: the one the realm of supersensible things in themselves, the other the realm of phenomena, however conceived. But also—and this is where her approval ends—it completely draws the sting of the doctrine of necessary ignorance, rendering it harmless, anodyne, even trivial. For it does not have the consequence that there must be anything real at all of which we are *necessarily* ignorant, though of course there may be much of which we are and may remain *contingently* ignorant.

And this is where Professor Langton jibs. For in her view it is an essential part of Kant's doctrine that there really is something substantial of which we are necessarily ignorant and of which our necessary ignorance is a source of necessarily vain, but humanly natural, regret. Things in themselves affect our sensibility and thereby make knowledge possible; but they affect us in virtue of their extrinsic, relational, causal properties, which are essentially *forces* constituting the natural world, phenomenal substance, the subject matter of physical science. But these forces, phenomenal substances with which we are acquainted and of which we can have knowledge, though real enough are but extrinsic, relational properties of things in themselves; and as subjects of these relational properties—substances in the pure sense—things in themselves must also have *intrinsic* properties; and these intrinsic properties are necessarily unknown to us, since it is only the matter-constituting forces of which we can become sensibly aware. So, though we have knowledge of their *relational* properties that constitute nature, of things as they are *in themselves* or intrinsically we remain necessarily ignorant.

Of course these few sentences of mine are only a sketch—possibly, though I hope not, a travesty—of what is a very subtly and carefully worked-out position. It is a position, moreover, that Professor Langton skilfully supports with an impressive array of references, not only to the *Critique* itself and Kant's other writings, but also, and often in a critical vein, to the work of his philosophical predecessors, most notably Leibniz; and to that of many commentators.

At the end of her book Professor Langton acknowledges one primafacie difficulty for her position. This is Kant's clear and repeated assertion of the ideality of space, its subjective source; for this may seem to bring into question her firm belief that the objective reality of the material world, the subject matter of the physical sciences, is an integral part of the critical doctrine. It may seem to threaten us (and Kant) with commitment to a kind of phenomenalistic, or even to the Berkeleian, idealism that Kant himself emphatically repudiates. Professor Langton is convinced that the threat is only apparent, and considers briefly a number of ways of circumventing it. The solution that she finds most satisfactory consists in drawing a distinction: the dynamical forces that constitute bodies are genuinely objective properties, but relational not intrinsic properties, of things as they are in themselves; space, though its source is subjective and hence spatial relations are ideal, is simply the *form* in which we have intuitive awareness of real dynamical relations; *spatial* relations are ideal, but they make *experience* of real dynamical relations possible.

Professor Langton is aware that more work would need to be done on this solution. She says: 'the connection Kant sees between dynamical and spatial relations must be regarded as unfinished business.'[8] But she seems to have no doubt that a solution on these lines must be correct.

It seems to me, however, that there is another and quite different difficulty for Professor Langton's interpretation, a difficulty of which she takes no account at all. This difficulty relates not to the objects of outer sense, of which space is the form, but to the contents of inner sense, of which time is the form: in other words, the contents of empirical self-consciousness, which Kant, somewhat like Hume, represents as a succession of constantly changing subjective states, a flux (his own word) of thoughts, perceptions, feelings. How are these to be accommodated in Professor Langton's scheme of interpretation? They are certainly not *intrinsic* properties of any *thing* (presumably, in this case, a self) as it is in itself. They are firmly declared, like the objects of outer sense, to be appearances. But again they cannot have the reality of those real, but extrinsic, relational, causal, dynamic properties of things in themselves that constitute the objects of outer sense, the subject matter of the physical sciences. Yet they cannot just be left in the air, as it were; they must be found a place in the scheme of things, since without them no experience, and hence no knowledge of the objective world, the subject matter of the physical sciences, would be possible at all. They are indeed recognized by Kant as a fit subject for what he called empirical (as opposed to rational)

[8] Ibid., 217.

psychology and picturesquely describes as a kind of physiology of inner sense.

If Professor Langton is to find a place for them, then, it looks as if she must find besides those real but extrinsic dynamic properties of things in themselves that constitute bodies some analogous real but extrinsic properties of things in themselves that are capable of constituting minds or, perhaps better, empirical consciousness. No such account is forthcoming, however; and, even if it were, she would face a problem parallel to that apparently created for the objective reality of bodies by the ideality of space; for time also, the form of inner sense, is declared to be ideal.

For these reasons, though not for these alone, I am unconvinced by Professor Langton's work, interesting, impressive, and scholarly as it is. Yet I recommend it for these, its own, certainly intrinsic, properties.

After that critical interlude, perhaps I should say a little more to justify the title of this chapter. It might reasonably be thought that in order to do that I should at least say, first, whether any other philosopher has had an influence upon me at all comparable with that of Kant, and, second, whether any particular view I have come to hold seems to me of outstanding importance.

For reasons I have already made clear, no single other philosopher and no single work of any other philosopher has had in my philosophical history the position that Kant and the first *Critique* have had. But I can mention other more diffuse influences. First, then: Russell and Moore, the founding fathers, at least as far as England is concerned, of analytical philosophy in our period. Their influence related to the questions and problems they discussed rather than the answers and solutions they gave. Second: the brightest lights that shone on the Oxford philosophical scene in the 1950s—those of Ryle, Austin, and Grice—though here too it was more a matter of style of thought than any particular doctrines to which I responded. And, finally, I must mention Wittgenstein; for, if I share anyone's conception of what our general philosophical aim or objective should be, it is, if I have understood him correctly, that of Wittgenstein, at least in his later period. That is, our essential, if not our only, business is to get a clear view of our most general working concepts or types of concept and of their place in our lives. We should, in short, be aiming at general human conceptual self-understanding.

Wittgenstein saw that a necessary condition of achieving this was to liberate ourselves from false understanding; to tear away the veil of simple seductive illusions or pictures that pervaded or constituted much existing philosophical theory and that prevented us from seeing clearly, from getting the clear view we needed. To this task Wittgenstein devoted much of his formidable powers and did so with the unique effectiveness of genius. But I must add, as I think, that his almost obsessive anxiety to liberate us from false pictures, from the myths and fictions of philosophical theory, led to a certain loss of balance in his thinking. It did so in two ways. First, it led to a distrust of systematic theorizing in general—and hence to a disregard of the possibility, indeed, to my mind, the fact, that the most general concepts and categories of human thought do form in their connections and interdependencies an articulated structure that it is possible to describe without falsification. Indeed, what I tried to show in my work on Kant is that the first *Critique* contains, besides much else that is more questionable, the general outline of many essential features of just such a description.

Second, this same anxiety to liberate us from false theory led Wittgenstein, as I think, to minimize or dismiss, or at least give too little acknowledgement to, some pervasive features of our experience and of our ordinary non-philosophical thought. It is true of these features that they can, in philosophical thinking, lend themselves to gratuitous inflation, to mythologizing, to false imaginary pictures—all of these proper targets of Wittgenstein's hostility and scorn, the 'houses of cards' it was part of his mission to destroy. But that is no reason for failing to acknowledge them fully as the harmless, inescapable features that they are.

So what are these features? I have in mind two things: the first is the reality of subjective experience in all its richness and complexity or, as one of our most distinguished contemporaries expressed it, in all its 'heady luxuriance'—the phrase is Quine's; the other is the inescapable presence in our thought of abstract intensional objects. Both, as I remarked just now, are easily misunderstood, prime sources of the generation of 'pictures to hold us captive'. But neither should for that reason be downplayed or denied the character it actually has in our experience or our thought.

Another thing I suggested I should do in order to justify my chapter title is to answer the question whether there is any particular view that I have come to hold that I regard as of outstanding importance. Well, there is such a view: it is by no means new and I do not think I am alone in holding it. It is not exciting: it is even, I think, a truism. But it has been overshadowed and regarded with suspicion in recent times. It is not a view that

I myself have come to merely recently. Indeed, I had already grasped it in an incomplete and inchoate form before 1950. But a sense of its importance and ramifications has steadily grown with me since. It is this: that the fundamental bearers of the properties of truth or falsity, the fundamental subjects of the predicates 'true' and 'false', are not linguistic items, neither sentences nor utterances of sentences. It is not, when we speak or write, the words we then use, but what we use them to say, that is in question. It is whatever may be believed, doubted, hypothesized, suspected, supposed, affirmed, stated, denied, declared, alleged, etc., that is or may be true. Any of these verbs may be followed by a noun clause of the form 'that p', and it is precisely the items designated or referred to by these noun clauses, as used on this or that occasion, that are the bearers of the properties of truth or falsity.

We do not have, in common use, a general word for these items. We do not have such a word because we do not in practice need it; in practice, we always use a nominalization of one of the verbs in question as the subject of the predicate (for example, 'your belief', 'his allegation', 'that statement', etc.) or a noun phrase such as 'what she has just said' or even the form 'that p' itself. Philosophers have, at various times, made various attempts to supply this deficiency. Frege's 'thought' is one; Austin groped towards it when he distinguished the 'locutionary' act (in terms of sense and reference) from the 'phatic' on the one hand and the 'illocutionary' on the other;[9] G. E. Moore and others have happily used the term 'proposition', which, more recently, has shown a tendency to be replaced by 'propositional content' or merely 'content'; an older term still is 'judgement'. Whatever term we use for items of this kind—and I perhaps date myself by being content with old-fashioned 'proposition'—the essential point is that such an item is not to be identified with an inscription or an utterance or a type of inscription or utterance; it is an abstract, intensional entity, but nonetheless an item of a kind such as we constantly think of and refer to whenever we think of, or comment on, what someone has said or written (in the declarative mode) or indeed on a thought that has, as we say, just entered our own heads.

---

[9] J. L. Austin, *How to Do Things with Words*, ed. J. O. Urmson (Oxford: Oxford University Press, 1962).

It is objected that there is no clear general criterion of identity for such items. Never mind: we get on well enough, and communicate well enough, without one. With the admission of propositions or judgements or thoughts as abstract intensional entities there goes along of course the admission of others: of senses, of concepts, of properties and universals in general. It is here, most obviously, that the risk of inflation comes in: the risk of seductive images, pictures to hold us captive, myths and fantasies that are often fathered, justly or not, on Plato. But in order to acknowledge the items in question as the harmless necessary things they are, regularly recognized in ordinary thought and talk, there is no need to be thus seduced, no need to be taken captive by such pictures.

So I have spoken up for subjective experience on the one hand (the contents of inner sense, as Kant would say) and for abstract intensional entities on the other. And this prompts me to remark, in conclusion, on one mildly ironical feature of our subject in the early twenty-first century. If anyone is entitled to be called the founder of our subject, it is generally acknowledged to be Plato; and if anyone could be called the father of its modern development, most of us would nominate Descartes. The irony is that to accuse a philosopher of Platonism or Cartesianism is currently felt to be a seriously damaging charge. But if, and in so far as, I have exposed myself to it, I am unrepentant. Of course both these great men were guilty of exaggerations and more or less grave mistakes. But each had a grasp, however uncertain, of features of our thought and experience that it would be a much graver mistake to overlook, to deny, or to minimize.

Index of Names

A
Aquinas 192, 223
Anscombe, G. E. M. 76
Aristotle 49, 50, 73, 174, 185, 192, 199, 202, 223, 225, 231, 234, 246
Austin, J. L. 32, 73, 75, 77, 108, 111, 185, 194, 212, 216–217, 219, 226, 232–233, 235, 236–237, 240, 245, 249, 253, 255
Avramides, A. 180
Ayer, A. J. 30, 75, 77, 91, 125–132, 134, 136, 138, 141, 144, 232, 235–236, 240, 248

B
Bacon, J. 200
Baylis, C. 240
Benacerraf, P. 236
Bennett, J. 91–99
Berkeley, G. 91
Bolzano, B. 199, 200, 202
Bosanquet, B. 220
Bradley, F. H. 47
Broad, C. D. 8, 10

C
Campbell, H. 200
Carnap, R. 32, 78, 81–82, 235
Williams, C. C. 200
Chomsky, N. 239
Collingwood, R. G. 248, 249
Cook Wilson, J. 40, 48
Corneille, P. 228

D
Davidson, D. 149, 187, 217, 240
Descartes, R. 93, 195, 226, 231, 256
Dummett, M. A. E. 240

E
Evans, G. 241
Epicureans 225

F
Findlay, J. N. 75
Frege, G. 32, 40, 43–44, 64, 76, 176, 192, 194, 218, 223, 232, 255

G
Geach, P. T. 41, 232
Gandhi, R. 240
Grandy, R. 192, 219
Grice. H. P. v, vi, 178–185, 192, 195, 206–221, 229, 233, 239, 242, 245, 253
Guyer, P. 162–165

H
Hampshire, S. N. 75, 227
Hardie, W. F. R. 12
Hart, H. L. A. 76
Hegel, G. W. F. 192, 223
Heidegger, M. 225, 242
Hempel, C. G. 236
Henrich, D. 157, 238
Honoré. A. 76
Hume, D. 72, 91, 133, 162, 163, 165, 223, 242, 252

I
Ishiguro, H. 241

J
Joad, C. E. M. 228
Johnson, W. E. 43

K
Kant, I. 91–99, 138, 140, 147, 157–165, 189, 192–193, 223, 225, 229, 230, 237–238, 243–244, 246, 248–254, 256
Kenny, A. vi
Kneale, W. 231
Kripke, S. 242
Künne, W. 200

L

Langton, R. 250–253
Leibniz, G. 91, 230, 251
Lewis, C. I. 230
Lichtenberg, G. 233
Locke, J. 91, 93, 125, 132, 168, 225, 230, 239

M

Mabbott, J. D. 229, 230
Mackie, J. L. 122, 125, 132–136, 138, 139, 141–143
Malcolm, N. 233
Martin, C. B. 200
McDowell, J. 239, 241
Moore, G. E. 1, 3, 30–31, 112, 185, 194, 200, 218, 230–232, 244, 253, 255

O

Øvergaard, S. 78

P

Pascal, B. 22
Paul, G. A. 30, 231, 233
Pears, D. F. 30
Plato, 42, 49, 52, 112, 175, 192, 195, 223, 225–226, 231, 244, 256
Pliny 228

Q

Quine, W. V. O. 13–29, 32, 91, 166–177, 233–235, 240–243, 249, 254
Quinton, A. M. 91

R

Ramsey, F. P. 43–44, 47, 53, 121, 200, 230, 232
Raphael, D. D. 2
Rogers, B. 248
Rorty, R. 78, 235
Ross, W. D. 8, 10
Rousseau, J.-J. 228

Russell, B. 32, 43, 52, 182, 217, 225, 230–231, 249
Ryle, G. 32, 73, 76, 77, 91, 185, 230–233, 238–239, 245, 253

S

Sartre, J.-P. 225
Schiffer, S. 179
Scruton, R. V. 118–124, 240
Searle, J. R. 67
Sen, P. K. 202, 242
Simons, P. 200
Spinoza, B. de 146–156, 241, 244
Stebbing, L. S. 230
Stevenson, C. L. 7
Stoics 225
Stout, G. F. 200
Strawson, P. F. 76, 78, 118, 160, 164, 232
Strawson, G. J. 148

T

Tacitus 228
Tarski, A. 217, 240
Tetens, J. N. 162–163, 165
Tocqueville, A. de 228

V

Verma, R. R. 240
Vlastos, G. 236

W

Warner, R. 192, 219
Warnock, G. J. 75, 77, 91, 233
Wiggins, D. vi
Wisdom, J. 11, 12, 73, 77
Wittgenstein, L. 30, 32, 73, 76, 79, 91, 108, 116, 159, 189, 192–193, 220–221, 223, 225–226, 233, 242, 246, 253–254
Wollaston, W. 220
Wright, C. 118–124

The manufacturer's authorised representative in the EU for product safety is Oxford University Press España S.A. of el Parque Empresarial San Fernando de Henares, Avenida de Castilla, 2 – 28830 Madrid (www.oup.es/en or product. safety@oup.com). OUP España S.A. also acts as importer into Spain of products made by the manufacturer.

www.ingramcontent.com/pod-product-compliance
Ingram Content Group UK Ltd.
Pitfield, Milton Keynes, MK11 3LW, UK
UKHW022214230426

12048UKWH00016BA/838